A CERTAIN VOICE

A
CERTAIN
VOICE

by
AUDREY RUSSELL

Ross Anderson Publications

Published in 1984 by
Ross Anderson Publications
22 Higher Dunscar
Egerton
Bolton
BL7 9TE

British Library Cataloguing in Publication Data

Russell, Audrey
  A certain voice.
  1. Russell, Audrey 2. Journalists—
  Great Britain—Biography
  I. Title
  791.44′092′4   PN5123.R/

ISBN 0–86360–017–4

Photoset in Times Roman by
Northern Phototypesetting Co, Bolton
and printed in Great Britain by
Billings of Worcester

Contents

List of Illustrations

To
David Green

CHAPTER ONE

Overture Beginners Please

I was six years old when I was taken to see *Mother Goose* at the Queen's Theatre, Dublin, by an uncle home on leave from France during the First World War. From the day I went to that pantomime I didn't want to be a child any more – but it never entered the heads of my Anglo-Irish parents that this unique occasion was to affect me so profoundly, indeed for almost a life-time.

I was fascinated by the shape of the building we were in, the first theatre I'd ever seen. Such a novel idea! Rows of tip-up seats upholstered in red velvet; lavish gilding of balustrades, marking the front rows of dress circle, balcony and what I soon learnt to call 'The gods'; the heavy plush stage curtains framed by a huge gilded arch – I was spellbound as they swished up and down during the performance. Uncle Dudley explained that the arch was known as a proscenium arch and that we were sitting in the very best seats of a stage box. This vaguely reminded me of a showy gift casket of Cadbury's chocolates called 'King George V Assortment' with an imitation crown on the front.

When the curtain went up revealing Mother Goose (who turned out to be a man), she was swinging perilously from a balloon, rocked by thunder and lightning, so realistic that at first I was terrified. So, apparently, was Mother Goose. Happily, the darkened stage soon disappeared. The brightly lit scenes that followed were splendid and I began enjoying every moment, no longer wishing for my mother or my nurse Nana to be with us to hold my hand. In fact I was already tremulously longing to be part of this exciting realm of fantasy. In one fell swoop, I was stage struck.

All round, my first visit to a theatre was unpopular. Nana, to whom I was devoted, was not at all pleased. She reported that I kept her awake with nightmares and screams for the rest of the week. Even my mother, young and broadminded, took Father's side: like most of his generation, he considered that childhood should be carefully preserved for as long as possible. They both said, 'Far too young to go' . . . Uncle Dudley did not agree.

The reason for Mother's absence from the theatre was that there was plenty going on at home just then. We had moved to a new modern house in a residential area known as Ailesbury Road, Co. Dublin, the other side of town from where I was born. We were still settling in.

My mother disliked the old house, finding it depressing and old fashioned. It was known as Sandford Ranelagh, and had been in the family since the late eighteenth century. I am afraid she also disliked a tyrant of a housekeeper who had looked after Father during his long years as a bachelor and whom she felt obliged to continue to employ, after a lifetime service with the family.

It was said that my father, John Russell, and his father before him were born in the same room as I was – and all on the same date, 29 June. I do not know the significance of this repetition of anniversaries – I only know I never had a birthday I could call my own.

The new red brick house we now lived in was not far from the showgrounds of the Royal Dublin Society. It was situated in a built-up area, but with a fine garden attached. My father's life-style made it seem like a country house. Visitors came for weekends and always during the Horse Show week. The seasons were marked by a succession of 'Game bags' set out in the hall after a few days' shooting (or fishing) somewhere in Kildare. I often watched Father standing proudly beside rows of pheasants, grouse, partridge, snipe and woodcock. It was quite an event for him to await the arrival of a bowler-hatted fishmonger, respectful and very professional, well able to deal financially with 'Misthur Russell, Sir'. Father liked to play the country gentleman and this was the only business transaction he undertook. He could always find plenty to do: he played golf; there were gun dogs to look after; there was much charity work; and he was director of a woollen mill at Lucan, the family firm.

My parents struck a clever compromise. Left to himself, Father would have opted to live in the depths of the country, whilst Mother would have been miserable away from the city. She was more than twenty years younger than he, full of vitality, charm and elegance and with very much the same sense of humour as her only brother (who took me to the pantomime), who was to become known to posterity as Fruity Metcalfe, both friend and Equerry to the King whom history will remember as His Royal Highness the Duke of Windsor.

As a young cavalry officer, Fruity Metcalfe served in India, first with the 3rd Bengal Cavalry and later with 3rd Skinners Horse. He fought with distinction in France and Mesopotamia in the First World War and followed this service by taking part in the Waziriston Campaign of 1919–21. His war record had been noted by Lord Willingdon, then Viceroy, who appointed him as ADC. When the Royal Tour of India was being planned in 1921, Uncle Dudley (as I still called him) was invited to attend the young Prince as one of a select team of experts on various aspects of life in India. As it turned out what was to have been a temporary assignment was the beginning of a lifelong friendship with the Prince.

Many years later, giving his impressions of the new members of his staff, the Prince, then Duke of Windsor, wrote succinctly in his own book *The King's Story*: 'Among the ADCs was a gay, handsome Irishman, Captain Edward Dudley Metcalfe, of the 3rd Skinners Horse. A bold, accomplished horseman, he had a sympathetic and understanding nature: during the tour a bond of friendship grew up between us, and on my invitation "Fruity" Metcalfe left India with me to join my permanent staff as equerry. Three years later he married Lady Alexandra Curzon, the youngest daughter of the former Viceroy.'

When on leave he invariably returned home to Dublin to stay with us and from an early age I was conscious of the heightening excitement in the house as soon as he arrived. There seemed to be much more laughter, more parties and more unexpected expeditions at short notice – sometimes even weekend visits to London.

Uncle Dudley was very fond of children. He took notice of me and I, of course, became his slave. When I was barely four years old he gave me a box of matches and carefully demonstrated how they should be struck. His cautionary words still ring in my ears: '*Downwards* away from the face. Match heads in India break off easily and can burn your face.' Every match the box contained was gleefully struck in the garden that afternoon under his rapt supervision. It wasn't quite as irresponsible as it might now

The author's parents

seem, but predictably this incident sparked further parental disapproval and once more I heard the familiar cry, 'She is *far* too young.' Nevertheless I have struck matches downwards ever since.

Was I always to remain 'Far too young'? I wondered. In fact my visit to the pantomime inspired one question that haunted me for years: 'When will I be grown up?' At twelve? At fourteen? Fifteen perhaps? I dared not voice my impatience; I guessed it wasn't the done thing to hanker after a career in the theatre, but this is what I wanted. The theatre beckoned to me so strongly that I would have taken any job at all as an entry to get backstage: selling programmes, then perhaps painting scenery, managing the coloured lights – anything. It was a conviction I held so strongly that it took the Second World War to break it down. Before long my family recognised my passion for the theatre, but perhaps wisely considered it no more than a passing phase even though I thought of nothing else. Father was much amused when I used theatrical terms and would often tell the story of how on one occasion in church I looked up to the gallery and whispered, 'Who is the little boy in the dress circle?'

Father, although his parents were Quakers, was a regular parishioner of the Protestant Low Church of Ireland, as was Mother. When I grew older I was occasionally taken to a Quaker meeting by Father. I confess I found the sometimes long silences embarrassing and felt equally self-conscious if the Spirit moved Father to speak.

Sundays apart, I saw little of my parents in those early days. They were heavily immersed in the social whirl, going to dinner parties and giving dinner parties back. Dinner parties at home frequently ended with music and in my small night nursery at the top of the house I would be woken by the sound of my father singing, his pure tenor voice penetrating even the silence of the uppermost floors. Yet in spite of the laughter and polite muffled applause the sentiments of his songs seemed very melancholy – 'The Last Rose of Summer', 'Pale Hands I loved', 'Mother Machree' . . . as an only child, I felt remote and completely apart from that adult world: an unhappy sensation which often brought me to the point of tears.

Nor did my parents miss many of the race meetings held in and around Dublin. I often asked to go with them, but a child at a race meeting was unthinkable . . . almost as unthinkable as putting their daughter on the stage. None the less, the names of Irish race courses fascinated me: Leopardstown, Fairyhouse, The Curragh, Phoenix Park. Perhaps in my child's mind I confused these names with creatures I had seen in Dublin Zoo, to which I was often taken as a treat. They presented the same kind of magic.

I did win formal consent, however, to visit the annual pantomime with Nana. Even her attitude to her charge's extraordinary interest softened and one year later she made me a Dick Whittington costume with a pheasant's feather in the cap. I was enchanted and for the first time longed to be a principal boy.

Looking back with grown-up eyes, I realise that some of the social life of the period in Dublin was a prelude to the antics of the Bright Young Things of the thirties. Once I was intrigued to see a shabby barrel organ delivered at the back door of our house. It had been hired by Father for a fancy dress occasion to be held on roller skates at a skating rink in town. Of course I clamoured to try and play the organ, but was disillusioned to discover that the handle did not keep time to the tune being played. It had to be turned at top speed to get any sound out of it at all.

For this occasion Mother went to the party as a gypsy – which with her blonde hair and soignée dress was quite unsuitable. Father forgot about fancy dress and went as

The author as a child

himself, merely grumbling all the time that the organ grinder wouldn't hire out the monkey too. No doubt some charity or other benefited considerably from that event. Father was chairman of innumerable committees and during the First World War was treasurer of the British Red Cross in Dublin. He was too old to get into the Army.

Known as a 'country gentleman', Father loved Ireland but was also immensely proud of the family allegiance to the Crown. A Union Jack would be hoisted in the front garden on the anniversary of his birthday and of course of mine. A few shots were fired at the flag on two occasions, presumably by members of Sinn Fein. When we left Ireland in 1925, the tattered flag was kept as an heirloom for years. We eventually lost it in the Blitz when some of Mother's furniture went up in flames at a London furniture store.

In the early twenties the political situation set many Protestant families to consider the momentous decision of leaving Ireland for good. It was something to be thought about slowly, but even the possibility of it was to affect my life at once.

Plans for me to attend the Junior School of Mother's old school (Queen Alexandra's College) in Dublin were scrapped and I was in for a succession of governesses; so many that I cannot now put names to them all. I will never know why none of them stayed for long.

I think I should have started lessons much earlier than I did. Nana had taught me to read and showed me how to do pothooks but that was all. Life was to become a saga of partings, some most welcome, others sad. The most dreadful of these departures occurred after deep devotion on both sides when Nana had to go home to Cork to look after her ailing mother. I was told she would return to me, but as Nana wept when we said goodbye, I knew it was for ever.

Among the stream of governesses who then came to look after me was Mademoiselle Alma Capirola. It was decided that my general education could be dropped in order that I should concentrate on learning French. Mademoiselle was a natural, if relentless teacher, who insisted from the start that I should learn a certain number of new words a day – from one to at least twenty words in the first weeks. I learnt the first word in French as we went for a walk to search for conkers. These were not *marrons* as I had supposed from tasting the left-over *marrons glacés* at home but *Châtaignes*. I grew very fond of Mademoiselle and that word became a kind of password between us. We would greet and call each other with it and would even say 'good night' with a sing-song lilt of triumph . . . *châtaigne*. She was the best teacher I ever had.

As her name suggests, Mademoiselle Capirola was part Italian and it was planned that we should switch to that language as soon as I became really proficient in French. Alas, this was never to be and some twenty years were to elapse before Mother revealed the sad truth. Mademoiselle had suddenly become restless and depressed. Eventually she gave notice that she wished to leave Ireland to work in England. I felt both sad and hurt. Mother wrote glowing testimonials to the many people who applied through an agency for her services. Mademoiselle chose a family with a good address in London and left looking ill and tearful. No sooner had she assumed her new post than her employer discovered that she was pregnant! Mother received letters penned in fury accusing her of falsehood and deception. Deeply distressed, she begged Mademoiselle to return to us. She declined. None the less, my Father discovered that her lover was a member of his club and made certain financial arrangements for her before she disappeared back to Italy. I never saw her again. This tragedy precipitated my parents' idea to dispense with governesses and to send me to a boarding school in England. I dreaded the very thought: I knew I was backward in lessons and with so many changes I could hardly have been anything else.

I realise now that there was something insidious that affected my progress, created partly by the strict discipline imposed on me from an early age. When I was given a bicycle I was allowed to ride it in the garden, but in no circumstances was I to venture out on the road. One day the temptation was too great. I had seen a pencil box in a shop window at Ballsbridge and wanted to buy it. It was exhilarating to be out in the street bowling along on a brand new bike, but near the entrance to the showgrounds there were people running across the street in all directions. There was also a stationary tram. Then I saw a man sprawled on the pavement. I stopped with one foot on the kerb and watched a dark red substance trickling towards the gutter. It was a huge gobbet of blood. A crowd was silently watching and suddenly I realised the man could be dead.

Cold and frightened I turned round and pedalled for home as fast as I could. I wheeled the bike up the drive slowly as if admiring the flowers. Father was very late for lunch – over three quarters of an hour. I felt giddy and sick waiting, then I heard his voice in the hall telling Mother that something dreadful had happened. A friend of his (and member of his club), a Mr Alan Bell, had been shot at point blank range. As we sat in the dining room he went into further detail: 'He was dragged from the tram and put up against the showground wall.' I remember thinking, 'that's wrong, he was by the kerb.' At that point I passed out. When I came to I was already in bed and the doctor had been sent for. I recall nothing of my recovery and, though I cried hysterically, I never told anyone of the horror I'd seen – I was too scared to reveal my disobedience.

The outcome of this incident was the decision that I was highly strung and over-sensitive. All adventure story books were gradually banished (I was reading R. L. Stevenson's *The Master of Ballantrae* at the time). At the age of twelve I found myself cocooned against reality, and my reading matter back to the level of *Bluebell in Fairyland*. This ill-contrived solicitude and care was touching, but looking back I believe it inhibited the process of growing up.

With the further upheaval of being sent to an English boarding school already on the horizon, I had the strange fancy of writing a long letter to myself. I felt that the experience of school life might be so desperate that my plans to escape to the world of the theatre might well be wiped from my mind. My instructions to myself were fairly sensible for someone without any experience:

1. To subscribe to all theatrical weeklies. (These were mainly of interest to out-of-work actors, actresses and landladies. They stressed the need for specialisation, for example 'Wanted: attractive Midlands Clog Dancer: blonde hunchback required, point work and tap an advantage.' I didn't seem to qualify for anything.)
2. To write to Gladys Cooper (I heard she owned her own theatre).
3. ESSENTIAL READING. A long list of books – mostly the works of Shakespeare but including one by the only person who was later to help and encourage me. The book was called *Speech Training* and its author was Elsie Fogerty.

There were several other instructions which I do not now remember. Eventually I addressed the letter to myself, marked it SECRET and slipped it into the drawer of a small desk. Almost inevitably it got lost in the family move. When the time came I do remember writing to Gladys Cooper, but there was no reply.

My early sheltered years in Ireland were as full of unimportant trivialities as are most childhoods. Yet I see now that a pattern of life was already evolving, to be repeated over and over again to this day. There is never a long careful apprenticeship for me in anything. 'Short-cut training' is all I ever get; in other words I have always had to 'learn on the job'.

Coincidences abound for most people and I have noticed that any that come my way are generally beneficial and helpful. For instance, when I was brought to London in about 1925, George Stubbs, the famous horse painter, was really the only British artist whose work I knew and cared about. (On his last visit to Dublin Uncle Dudley left behind his copy of Stubbs's *Anatomy of the Horse*, which I commandeered.) The night before I went to the dreaded boarding school we stayed in the annexe of a small hotel in the West End of London. It was a Georgian house in Somerset Street, W1. I immediately spotted a blue plaque over the door; 'George Stubbs Lived Here'. To this day I can recall how elated I felt on seeing it. It was an immediate association, one link with a new and totally strange world. It made going to school seem less awful.

The shabby house in which we stayed no longer exists. It has long since been demolished to make way for an extension of Selfridges. To the management's credit, however, they have made handsome, if incongruous, amends to Stubbs – as anyone who happens to purchase a wig there will know. *Two* larger than life-size bronze reliefs of the famous horse Hambledonian (frequently painted by Stubbs) adorn the marble walls of the Hair Piece and Wig Department, to commemorate the fact that George Stubbs lived in a house on the site from 1763 to his death in 1806. I was thrilled to have stayed a night there.

We left early next day for my destination, a private boarding school for girls at Harrow on the Hill called Southlands. It had been recommended to my father by a club friend with three daughters already installed as pupils. 'They are very good at games.' My heart sank. 'Oh the girls will look after you dear.' I knew what that could mean, remembering shared picnics when once they made me eat a sandwich standing up in a bed of nettles for a quarter of an hour, as our mothers gossiped merrily together on the other side of the hedge.

By then I was prepared for almost anything strange and unexpected. In the event I found the school was old-fashioned, genteel and rather dull and uncomfortable. For one thing, there were not nearly enough lavatories for over 100 girls.

I was not a success at school, at either work or games. In the classroom I was way behind most girls of my own age and, as the teams for hockey and lacrosse included two potential internationals, the high standard made it impossible for me to do more than hand round slices of lemon at half-time.

I was quite good at history and literature and adored the drama classes, playing Romeo in an end-of-term production of *Scenes from Shakespeare*. My parents were disturbed that I was not Juliet. Altogether, I must have been a great disappointment to them. After about a year and a half, it was decided that I was doing no good there; to my delight I was allowed to leave and was sent at once to France – as if it were a last hope. They kept saying, 'At least she speaks French.'

Mademoiselle Marie Corniquet was the principal of a small finishing school for twenty pupils at the Villa Saint Georges at Neuilly in Paris. She also owned a lovely rambling old house just outside Rouen named the Château des Ventes. I was deposited there first of all as Mademoiselle decided that I was too young to be 'finished'. I was put in the charge of a Miss Benson, who was recuperating from 'flu and looking after a girl, younger than myself, whose parents were in India. We were both newcomers, but it seemed that Miss Benson and her pupil were already great friends and I was able happily to explore the house and grounds on my own. It was shabby but romantic and I took to it at once. I found an attic that had been used as a studio – someone had even left paints and brushes untidily behind, and Miss Benson said I could have them all.

It was then that I discovered the absorbing interest of painting in oils – with everything to hand: paints, brushes, palette, turps, linseed oil and even two canvases already prepared for work. It was all much more fun than school lessons on how to draw an acanthus leaf. At once I felt more grown up and independent: there was no school uniform to be worn, no team games, no gymnasium, no going for walks in a 'crocodile two by two' and, at first, practically no lessons.

The pupils being 'finished' in Paris took it in turns to visit us at weekends, filling the house with the sound of slamming doors and schoolgirl gossip . . . Did I know (by the way) that Miss Benson was madly in love with the chaplain of the English Church at Neuilly, and that Monsieur Merigot (whom I had not yet seen) was undoubtedly Tata Marie's true love? Mademoiselle Corniquet was affectionately called 'Tata' by her orphan niece who lived with us, and somehow our principal became known as Tata to her pupils too.

Tata Marie Corniquet nearly always appeared at the Château at weekends, creating something of the atmosphere of a country house-party, which I suspect was part of our social training. She was kind and friendly, telling me of the wonderful picture galleries and museums and theatres I would be able to visit when I got to Paris. These conversations nearly always ended in a reverent tone of voice: 'Although you are not taking piano, *il faut faire la connaissance du Professeur Merigot. C'est l'élève de Massenet vous savez.*' Monsieur Merigot was a frail, very elderly music master with thinning white hair and braying singing voice with which he even accompanied scales! He dined with us at least once a week and we were always assured of a delicious meal that evening.

I was soon promoted to Paris (chiefly because of the difficulties of teaching staff being required in two places). I attended lectures on French history, architecture and art and current affairs in the mornings, and joined the others on afternoon outings to the Louvre and other galleries, with frequent visits in the evening to the Opéra and Comédie Française. I revelled in every moment. I had found the world I wanted.

We all spent much time discussing the future and what we wanted to do when we left the Villa. My best friend, Elena, from the Argentine, was to be given a London season, with presentation at court. Elena also had fantasies about the theatre, but married soon after returning home. By contrast, another English girl knew exactly that she would be going straight into the family business – a huge chain of newsagents. She confided in me that she expected to be serving behind one of her father's counters in a few weeks' time. I think I envied her the most.

I enjoyed every moment at the Villa. I had learnt a little more about the theatre and opera, and my love of art and architecture was to be with me for good. But such a superficial education does not promote real specialisation, nor indeed qualifications. Of my future there was still nothing but a large question mark.

CHAPTER TWO

An Attendant Lady

No! I am not Prince Hamlet, nor was meant to be;
Am an attendant lord, one that will do
To swell a progress, start a scene or two ...

T. S. Eliot, 'Love Song of J. Alfred Prufrock'.

When I came back to London from school in France, I found my parents already settled in a spacious mansion flat on the fourth floor without a lift. I was surprised at the neighbourhood they had chosen, for so many of their London friends had South Kensington and Knightsbridge written all over them. Mortimer Mansions was in Mortimer Street, W1, a street that still serves the tailoring and dressmaking trades with all the accessories they could possibly need. Wholesale buttons, braids, beads, buckram, ribbons and ready-made embroideries and lace collars filled the shop windows from the end of elegant Wigmore Street all the way to the Middlesex Hospital and straight on to Tottenham Court Road. At first I feared that the move from Dublin to London must have greatly reduced my Father's income. It did, but later I was astonished, amused and rather touched to learn that this choice of district was all for *my* good. A gossipy friend of Mother's explained the reason. Mother said, 'When Audrey gets back and meets some young men, all she'll want is to go to the theatre. Now, I don't like the idea of her taking long taxi rides very late at night after a show or a dance at her age – but it's no distance from Soho or Shaftesbury Avenue to Mortimer Street.'

I soon began to enjoy the social life of dinner parties and country weekends and being made a fuss of by a few eligible young men – especially the ones who took me to the theatre. I fell in love a few times and then I met Brent, a serious able young barrister, at one of those foolish evening parties that lingered on in the thirties when a gathering of Bright Young Things clamoured to play an idiotic competition. They would set out in and around London in small groups in search of 'treasure' – utterly worthless treasure, taken from a list of objects that had to be collected to win the prize. It might be a Victorian whale-bone corset with laces, a set of false teeth, an autograph of the driver of the Flying Scotsman just before leaving King's Cross, or a fake certificate claiming that a dizzy blonde had persuaded an overworked lift attendant to take her up and down from the top floor of the Ritz twenty times. The worst of this buffoonery was to creep into a ladies' cloakroom at the Berkeley Hotel when the attendants weren't looking and create a wicked chaos by changing the tickets on the evening coats. I refused to join one of these search parties and slid away unnoticed to sit by the fire in the now empty drawing room.

I was quickly joined by a tall presentable young man saying, 'I can't bear this sort of thing either; I said I wouldn't take part and now they say I must be the judge.' He sat down and we spent the evening together waiting for the end of this pointless escapade. We were surprised to discover that we were enjoying the evening very much. When the time came, he made a very good judge, amusing, outspoken and very fair.

We lunched together every day for a week and then he proposed marriage. I was thrilled – and so were my parents. He was eminently suitable, even to the point of being heir to a baronetcy.

I found he was not interested in the theatre very much. It didn't seem to matter at first, while we went through the formality of meeting each other's family and friends and discovering our likes and dislikes. We were very busy with the formalities, but the likes and dislikes did not seem to be very much the same. The beginning of the end came when one day he said crossly, 'It seems you only come to life when talking about the stage.' I feared the worst for us both, knowing by then that it would be out of the question for Brent's wife to have any connection with the theatre and sensing that both pairs of parents in the background would be delighted to agree.

But something of Mother Goose was still in my make-up. We began to quarrel, to be hurtful to each other, and eventually we were in and out of *The Times* in six months. It was the first time I was truly in love and inevitably I was miserable for ages. We met again at the beginning of the war and stopped to talk. He had joined the Army and had married someone else. It was a stilted little conversation, and bitter too. 'You wouldn't have been married long to me. I have a foreboding that I will be found face down in the mud.' Tragically, that is what happened. When under Wavell's command he was killed in Burma in 1941.

In an effort to pull myself together I resolved to get some training for the stage, and without discussing it with the family I applied for an audition at the Royal Albert Hall, where the famous Elsie Fogerty was Principal of the Central School of Speech and Drama. To my amazement and relief I passed the tests and was interviewed by the great lady. Her first comment was, 'Well, you are very tall but you are not a gawk.' I was handed a prospectus with details of various courses and fees and told to discuss it all with my parents.

I went home in triumph at my one and only success. The family had been sympathetic and kind over the broken engagement and had even showed some tolerance of what they believed were my crazy ideas. Surely they could not say no again. But yet another ugly row ensued and I was told to write to 'that woman' and myself say 'no'.

I walked all the way to the Albert Hall next morning and, after a long wait to see Miss Fogerty, told my story with many apologies. There was quite a long silence when I finished, then in a quiet voice Miss Fogerty said, 'Why not come part-time, say three days a week? (Pause.) There will be no fees.' It was the most inspiring thing that had happened. I accepted with alacrity. I was given a time-table of classes and advised not to tell anyone in or out of the school of the arrangement.

I attended classes on mime, verse speaking and the spoken word, and took part in short scenes from famous plays held in the school's private theatre. The stage was built over one of the great square canopied porches in front of the main entrance doors of the Royal Albert Hall.

The space was taken up mostly by the stage, with the minimum of room for an audience, which was reassuring for a total beginner. Personally, I felt more professional working in front of two rows of senior members of staff, including the great 'Fogue' herself, than if we had had to face the unprofessional criticism of friends or family.

I even had a shot at Rosalind in *As You Like It* – a small scene, and I would have loved it but for a certain aspect of theatre conditions that I had not met before. An aspect not for the fastidious. Shortage of costumes worn by a team of Rosalinds that afternoon meant that quick changes were imperative between the scenes. The Rosalind who preceded me was even more nervous than I. The damp garment I was to wear reeked with the odour of perspiration and it nearly finished me – and almost wrecked my brief performance. It was my first lesson on the shabby grubbiness backstage of theatres in general. I grew to accept it, even the rats I encountered in the corridors in certain theatres on tour and the smell of fish left behind by an animal trainer who had presented a performing seal act the week before.

It was three or four months before it leaked out that I was at the Central School three days a week. My mother seemed fairly resigned to the situation by then and even offered to see me appearing as Britannia (of all characters) in a pageant to be held at the November Festival of Remembrance. Not without cause my mother was embarrassed at meeting the Principal; there was the question of fees that could or should have been paid and my appearance as Britannia did not please her either. (It's very hard not to look comic in that helmet.) The evening ended with an unpleasant encounter with Miss Fogerty, for Mother almost hinted that I had been kidnapped by the Central School! All the generous help and guidance came to an abrupt end; I had to leave, and 'Fogue' never forgave me, even though when I met her again I was proud to say I had persevered and was working at the Aldwych Theatre. She just turned her head away.

I was soon to find out that the London theatre was like Disraeli's Two Nations of Rich and Poor – perhaps better described these days as an 'Upstairs Downstairs situation'. With only six months training and no theatrical influence at all, I chose the Downstairs door. I became a theatre dogsbody on the stage management side. I began by preparing stage meals in a repertory company and quickly fell in with the tradition that gingerbread can be served as beef, bananas can be made to look like potatoes and whisky is (nearly) always cold tea. I understudied small parts, I washed up the stage meals and I walked on. Back in London I won the Poetry Society's Gold Medal for speaking verse, and an enormous Silver Cup from the same organisation for speaking verse in foreign languages, two years running. I even dared to produce several plays by unknown authors at an enterprising company run by actors in a minuscule playhouse in Knightsbridge called the Torch Theatre.

Unemployment among actors and actresses was as daunting then as now, but I discovered that it was possible to get dogsbody work if you were prepared to do it for almost nothing. This I was able to afford to do as my parents pressed me to go on living at home. By then they had decided that nothing could be done with such a reluctant débutante.

By an extraordinary bit of good luck I came in contact with a famous man of the theatre backstage, business manager and playwright, Charles Landstone. He gave me my first job, with a weekly salary of £4.10*s*., as Assistant Stage Manager in Rodney Ackland's play *After October*. It opened at the Arts Theatre, transferring for a successful long run at the Criterion and later at the Aldwych. He was strong and wise, a small man with dark Jewish features, always dressed rather unprepossessingly in suits too big for him. The thing I remember most about his appearance was the way in which he walked. He hardly ever stood still. He would walk up and down his office during any discussion or argument of importance – when out in the street one did not see him walking briskly to get from one place to another, his walk was part of his method of meditation, his way of making up his mind.

He was full of golden rules, most of them sensible. 'Never try to find out what another artist is being paid – it can make you unhappy and envious.' He was the most dependable and knowledgeable person I ever met in the theatre and most stage people would agree that the catch phrase for any problem in the company was 'Go and ask Charles.'

The first leading lady that I ever met was a very special one indeed. She was to play a harassed poverty-stricken widow who had got no further than understudying in her own theatre career and was now coping with unpaid bills, housework and lodgers in Rodney Ackland's play. This part did not give much scope for an actress of her calibre, but as a true artist she gave it all it required and the notices were very good indeed. Mary Clare was already famous as the leading lady in Noël Coward's jingoistic epic at Drury Lane – *Cavalcade*. Although this mammoth production had first been presented over eight years earlier, everyone associated her with her tremendous performance as Mrs Marryot, the mother of a quintessential English family whose fortunes are followed alongside the national history of the first 30 years of the twentieth century. Mary Clare never lost the aura that had surrounded her in *Cavalcade*.

Perhaps this helped to make her the absolute prototype of a leading lady. She called everybody 'Darling' and arrived unfailingly in good time to rest before the performance. She was a big star and she knew it. She had just the right amount of 'temperament' and touchiness to make everyone slightly nervous of her reaction to anything that was said. I sometimes thought her performance offstage was as contrived and subtle as any part she played on it. But the prototype ended there. She never, as others sometimes do, exploited the stage management with boring errands to the Lost Property Office or the dry cleaners. To me she was friendly and extremely kind. Above all she was a brilliant professional. My first lesson on how to cope with a long run was learnt from her, watching night after night the precision of her performance which hardly varied by a hair's-breadth, yet which rarely lost its spontaneity.

Mary Clare's name was a great draw. It was her performance that gave us full houses in the difficult year of 1936, the year of the scandal of the King and Mrs Simpson, who were the talk of the town. Every avenue was explored for settlement. Mr Baldwin, the Prime Minister, was in the process of cabling the Dominions for their views as to whether Mrs Simpson should get a divorce, marry the King and come to the throne; or the marriage should be morganatic, with Mrs Simpson *not* coming to the throne; or King Edward VIII should abdicate in favour of his brother, the Duke of York. In this day and age it seems extraordinary that anything but the last should have been considered for an instant.

The Prince of Wales and Mrs Simpson first met some time early in 1931. For some years they remained 'acquaintance-friends' and when they became part of each other's private life the British press tactfully did not break silence for a long time.

My uncle Fruity Metcalfe was the Prince's closest man friend and they had been inseparable for years – on duty at home and abroad as well as in the social life of London, which gradually included some of the smart set of New York. Before Wallis came on the scene, there were frequent weekend country parties: not all at Fort Belvedere. One week it would be the Prince's favourite home, the Fort, the next the Metcalfes' residence at Epsom close to the golf course at Walton Heath (I sometimes stayed there midweek). They were happy years. As the relationship developed, it was easy to see that Mrs Simpsom was ostracising her lover's old friends, ignoring them and dropping them from 'her set'. She tried to bring her world into his life and surrounded him with *her* friends. It was a first glimpse of her great influence over the King. Fruity had been promised more than once that he would be given a place in the Royal Household when the Prince succeeded to the throne, and now that this situation had arrived it must have been hurtful to be overlooked.

Several loyal devotees on the Palace staff resigned from their posts feeling ignored and unwanted. It was said at the time that the heir-presumptive was the most deeply affected, nervous and depressed. He certainly had cause to be so. There can rarely have been such a family 'low ebb', especially a Royal one.

In spite of everything, I always feel thankful that the time did come again when Fruity, the faithful friend, was unexpectedly able to be a wise and helpful supporter of the Duke of Windsor by visiting him during the long stay at Schloss Enzefeld in Austria while waiting for Mrs Simpson's divorce to become absolute. When the Duke realised that his brothers in London would not be attending the wedding in France and therefore would not be his 'supporters', the title assumed by Royalty when looking after the bridegroom, Lord Mountbatten offered to take their place, but the Duke preferred to pay the compliment to Fruity whom he described as his 'real best friend'.

Lady Frances Donaldson, in her brilliant biography *Edward VIII* published in 1974, has included some of the letters Fruity wrote home to his wife, Lady Alexandra, in London. The author remarks that 'Metcalfe was a gifted letter-writer, acute and observant, always telling us exactly what we want to know.' She adds modestly: 'In a series of letters from Enzefeld and later from Cannes and in the war from Paris, we get closer to [the Duke of Windsor] than at any other time . . .'

I knew little of what was going on in Royal circles during the Abdication crisis. About halfway through the run of *After October* Charles Landstone decided that I had gained enough experience to be left in charge of the stage during the entire performance. I was thrilled at this small promotion and engrossed in the job. My Uncle Fruity was home in London but was busy with endless private consultations. However one day I saw him in the Strand and ran to meet him. He looked very serious and tragic. He just said: 'It's all over, it's Abdication.'

He was in a mood of distress and did not want to talk about it. Not that he ever said much to me about the private life or personality of the Prince of Wales, especially not in times of crisis. I think that he believed that any gossip I heard about the King or Mrs Simpson would be fascinating for my friends to hear.

Our conversation was brief, for both of us had plenty to do. Fruity said: 'You must get tired listening to the same play every night.' I longed to contradict him as I had decided that a long run is neither exacting nor as boring as it may sound. I enjoyed the disciplined feel of a well-run theatre. Stage hands, stage staff, from the master carpenter to the wardrobe mistress, do everything in the same way at every performance, almost to the second. You could set a watch by the time a dresser brings down a dress suit for a quick change on the side of the stage, or goes out every night to fetch a port and lemon for one of the cast. It would be hard to imagine a break in the strict routine, but not impossible.

The unique event that shattered the nation took place on 11 December, 1936, when King Edward VIII, speaking for the first time as His Royal Highness Prince Edward, made his farewell speech after signing the instrument of Abdication. The BBC broadcast was relayed to most London theatres and cinemas and I was put in charge of the timing for stopping the play at the the Aldwych and lowering the curtain. We hoped we could bring the curtain down with dignity at the end of Act 2, Scene 1. It was a

'Fruity' Metcalfe (*Bertram Park*)

nervous performance that night; everyone was inclined to gabble their lines but unfortunately they didn't beat the clock and the curtain had to be lowered in the middle of a sentence. Almost at once the deep amplified voice of Sir John Reith filled the theatre. 'This is Windsor Castle – His Royal Highness Prince Edward . . .' I watched the packed audience through a slit in the curtain.

The weary, flat Mayfair-cockney accent we knew so well began tentatively. 'At long last I am able to say a few words of my own . . .', finishing with a courageous note of attempted cheerfulness when he cried 'God save the King', which invested the entire broadcast with an added pathos.

The audience was hushed and still, as if a death had been announced. Then with quiet resignation a number of people began to leave and the cast on stage prepared to tackle the near impossible task of bringing the play back to life. It was an eerie experience. By the end of the performance, there were not more than 50 or 60 people in the audience to rise for the first National Anthem at the Aldwych for the new King.

When *After October* finished its creditable long run of nearly a year, I dreaded facing my first experience of 'resting' – in other words, being out of work. The thirties was a flourishing era in the commercial London theatre with a galaxy of well-made, if conventional, plays specially written as vehicles for famous stars such as Marie Tempest, Yvonne Arnaud and Gladys Cooper. Thrillers including *Night Must Fall*, with the author Emlyn Williams in the lead, were among the most successful. Musicals were still called musical comedies and the average price of seats, including tax, was 1/9 to 10/6.

However, I had discovered an interesting theatre club called the Group Theatre, founded by the dancer, Rupert Doone, in 1932. During the run of *After October* I had seen two of his Sunday night productions at the Westminster Theatre – Auden and Isherwood's *The Dog Beneath the Skin* and a revival of *Sweeney Agonistes* by T. S. Eliot. I was impressed and exhilarated by the originality of both.

If anyone had told me that I was to become the stage manager of this avant-garde theatre I would have been incredulous. But it happened. John Moody, a member of the Group, invited me to meet Rupert as they were desperate for a stage manager who would be content to *be* a stage manager. Everyone else wanted to act or write plays themselves. I was asked to stage manage the next Sunday show at the Westminster Theatre, a new play by Louis MacNeice, *Out of the Picture*. I was to receive the flat rate, like everyone else, of £2 a week once rehearsals began. 'I think', said Rupert pensively, 'we can call you Stage Director.' Promotion indeed! The year was 1937.

Rupert Doone's career as a dancer and choreographer in the twenties was meteoric. His most spectacular appointment was when he was engaged as *premier danseur* by Diaghilev for the Ballet Russe in 1929. Unfortunately, this engagement was tragically short. Diaghilev died in the same year and the whole company was dispersed.

Luckily, Rupert had wider ambitions than the dance. He went on to study acting and the production of plays at the Cambridge Festival Theatre and within a year (1932) the Group Theatre was founded with Rupert as its driving force and inspiration.

Rupert was deeply interested in poetry and saw the possibilities of drama that included the spoken word and the singing voice, combined with all the arts of musician, painter, stage and costume designer as well as dancer and actor. He called it Total Theatre. The names of the original members make impressive reading today. The list included Henry Moore and Herbert Murrell (both before my time), W. H. Auden, Christopher Isherwood, Stephen Spender, Louis MacNeice, John Piper, Robert

Medley, Brian Easdaile and Benjamin Britten. Rupert's Group Theatre gave them the outlet they were looking for: poetry and politics in a setting of modern art.

Poetic drama became a symbol of the thirties. The main aim was to be entertaining and high-spirited on serious subjects. Public figures were satirised and so was everyday life. This attracted the interest of young audiences. As Stephen Spender has written, 'The Group Theatre tried to banish that sense of piety which still commands people to pay bored homage to the "holy Muse".' This was a theatre of writers, artists and musicians. The actors were a team of brilliant interpreters, without thought of self or the star system, performing in poetic drama as if it might be a strip cartoon or a light-hearted revue.

My first play with the Group was typical of this. MacNeice's plot centred round an unsuccessful artist in love with the only painting he had ever completed. Nearly every aspect of life in the late thirties was satirised: the cult of psychoanalysis by people who didn't need it; the dawn of foreign travel for the middle classes, made possible by packaged cruises to the Mediterranean; and, above all, wireless in the home (still a novelty), to be treated by the Group as a series of dialogues between a radio announcer, who did all the voices himself, and a listener-in at home twiddling the knobs. The situations were full of hilarious nonsense, shot with a perceptive truth that holds to this day. This extract is from Act 1 Scene 2:*

Listener-in   I only take what you can give.
Radio Announcer I only give what you want.
Listener-in   You who supply the meaning.
Radio Announcer You who supply the matter.
Listener-In   Is it an important matter?
Radio Announcer Is it an attractive meaning?
Listener-In   Come to me, crystallise out of the air.
Radio Announcer Hypocrite Auditeur, mon semblable, mon frère . . .

It was not until I re-read the play recently that I realised how great in 1937 was the apprehension and fear of the coming war:

> Summer is a-comen in, a packet of sunflower seed to plant along the Wall, a packet of Sweet William.
> What else, my dear? The Children like it you know,
> To have some flowers of their own.
> They like a little garden to look after –
>   (*echo off*: After, After –)
> And what comes after that?
> Flowers in the sky, Rockets and flares.
> Things are not what they were, the time is past
> For growing in a quiet plot,
> For sleeping in an easy bed.
>
> What do you see in the future dim?
> I look ahead and what do I see?
> I see a pageant, a Lord Mayor's procession,
> The Aldermen and the Flunkeys, the Carnival giants,
> The Tableaux on lorries, the flags and the coaches
> And every single one of the people who make up that procession
> Carries a white stick to show that he is blind.

*© The Estate of Louis MacNeice.

The Group was fortunate in being able to afford to rent an office with a big rehearsal room at No. 9, Great Newport Street (now in the hands of a turf accountant), almost next door to the Arts Theatre Club. Only those stage managers who have struggled to reserve rehearsal rooms by the hour in a beer-smelling room over a pub, only to find that it is double-booked by the Charing Cross Buffaloes for a reunion, can truly appreciate the luxury of having your own premises.

The Great Newport Street room was L-shaped; one end formed the office containing Rupert's desk, piled with papers, scripts, unanswered letters and several copies of *Spotlight*. The rest was a sizeable open space, lined with a few cupboards and about twenty attractive modern stacking chairs, used for play-readings and private 'club' performances done in the round. It is incredible that all this was paid for by membership subscriptions and the price of tickets, but the Group Theatre had by then acquired a reputation, and with its association of so many up-and-coming young names had caught on in a big way. When we were working at Great Newport Street I got to know some of these already famous people. Robert Medley, who designed the sets of most of the productions, together with Rupert Doone, were to become very dear friends.

I suppose I am now among the few people who can claim to remember W. H. Auden with a pale, youthful, unlined face. He was frequently at Great Newport Street, generally to be seen monopolising the warmth of the single gas fire as he straddled in front of it, expressing his views before a meeting. He was tall and strongly built, and appeared very self-confident and aloof. (I am told this was due to an intense shyness that was a basic part of his character.) And there was indeed every reason for self-confidence, for he had reached his early mature style in the thirties and was already recognised as the master of any poetic rhythm he chose to work in. Two of his most beautiful lyrical single poems were written within a few months of each other in 1937. Now both extensively 'anthologised', the first was:

> Lay your sleeping head my love
> Human on my faithless arm.

The other was a poem of fifteen quatrains on love and time, with fresh original images:

> I'll love you till the ocean
> Is folded and hung up to dry
> And the seven stars go squawking
> Like geese about the sky . . .

That stage managers are generally ignored by the eminent unless there is a complaint to be registered is more or less a general rule. But listening to conversations was to be aware of a genius in our midst whose flow of language made it possible to produce 'difficult' metaphysical poems, light verse for cabaret songs, witty rhyming couplets near to doggerel and savage satire that could go as far as declaring that another famous poet 'kept tears like dirty postcards in a drawer'. Here was a man involved, like his contemporaries, in public events, ever aware of the details of modern social conditions.

Benjamin Britten had the kind of shyness that made him sidle rather than stump into a room – generally late but politely apologetic. He was 24 in 1937 but had retained the extreme slimness of early youth, giving a look of frailty that was misleading, for his facial characteristics belonged to a maturer, more cynical age. He already had the crooked smile and the slanting drooping eyelid.

Britten was always firm and positive in getting what he wanted for any performance to which he was contributing. He demanded a harmonium for the hymn to be sung in *Out of the Picture*. With a very tight budget, Rupert understandably said no. I had been told to look into the idea but harmoniums were expensive to buy and impossible to hire. Benjamin persisted, backed up by Brian Easdaile. The meeting ended on a quiet sulky note.

Weeks later, when we were all moving our paraphernalia into the scene dock of the Westminster Theatre, I saw a splendid sight approaching along Buckingham Palace Road. Brian Easdaile was pushing a coster's barrow with a Victorian harmonium being held steady on top by Benjamin Britten. Their faces were hot but triumphant; they had picked it up for a fiver in that market known as The Cut, and had wheeled it all the way from Waterloo.

I continued as Stage Director to the Group Theatre for several more productions, including a translation of Jean Cocteau's classic one-act play for one actress, *La Voix Humaine*, with the late Beatrix Lehman. It was produced by Bertolde Viertel, the stage and film director who had been working in Germany. As a matter of policy, the Group management frequently welcomed refugee artists escaping to Britain from the Nazis. I enjoyed every moment of working closely with the two of them, but am not sure that this was entirely reciprocal. I had found that after only a few rehearsals I knew the lines of the play by heart and would prompt Miss Lehman without looking at the book. I soon discovered that this was maddening to the artist who had so much more to think about than mere lines; so then I acted a great business of turning over the pages, before prompting at all.

My final excursion in the theatre before the outbreak of war was unexpectedly exciting and gave me the opportunity of seeing something of lavish productions on a very grand scale. It was the no-expense-spared theatrical empire of Mr Gilbert Miller, as well known and theatrically powerful on one side of the Atlantic as on the other. In London, he was the owner, with Prince Littler, of the beautiful St James's Theatre* in King Street. He also held a long lease on the Lyric Theatre in Shaftesbury Avenue, and it was said that he actually owned the freehold of the Lyric stage.

Audacity, says Cocteau somewhere, is the art of knowing how to go too far. I heard that Miller was in London in connection with a new production and I wrote a careful letter, enclosing a flattering photograph of myself, asking for an audition. I felt it was time to start moving *up*stairs. To my astonishment, I pulled off an interview with the great man himself.

Gilbert Miller was talking on the telephone when I was shown into his office on the first floor over the stage door of the St James's. He waved me to a chair and continued to give instructions about having a hard tennis court in the garden of his country house in Sussex (Drumgewick Manor). I remember nothing of his office or his desk, but was aware of a portly, red-faced man, obviously full of energy and authority, concentrating on what he wanted as a tennis court. The conversation went on for several minutes, which was a strain on my composure. When he put down the receiver, my interview was brief and to the point. He looked hard at me and said: 'What do you *want* out of the theatre, I mean *really* want?' The long wait had made me lightheaded, and I found myself telling him the truth. 'Eventually, I would like to own a theatre and run it and

---

* Since demolished, in spite of a spirited series of 'demos' led by Vivien Leigh in an attempt to save it from the property speculators.

produce plays.' To his credit he didn't smile patronisingly but said, 'What are you doing now?' When I told him I had been a stage manager, but felt that I'd now like to make an appearance on the stage, preferably in one of his productions, he just said, 'Stage manager? I don't believe it,' and rang a bell. Almost immediately his senior stage director, Lewis Allen, came in and we were introduced. 'Lewis, I ask you, they've kept this girl *backstage*. Find her something at the Lyric.' The interview was over.

Lewis looked at me doubtfully and I followed him out of the office. It wasn't going to be easy, he said, there wasn't much I was suited for. Would I walk on and understudy? I agreed and he then made a telephone call to Monty Berman's, the theatrical costumier. 'Go straight round and get measured.'

I had no idea what play was about to go into rehearsal, nor indeed that it held a fictional presage of my future association with royal broadcasting. The play to be presented by Gilbert Miller, with settings and costumes by Rex Whistler, was *Victoria Regina* by Lawrence Housman. Pamela Stanley was to repeat her performance as Queen Victoria which she gave when the play was first produced modestly on a small scale at a club theatre, The Gate, in 1935. The Lord Chamberlain licensed the play for public performance in 1936, some said at the instigation of Edward VIII, who overruled the notion that a direct ancestor of the Monarch (his great grandmother) should not be represented on the stage. It seemed a sensible exception to an old rule. Queen Victoria had reigned for such a long time. She came to the throne 99 years before, in 1837.

After the responsibilities of stage managing, it was a rest cure to appear in *Victoria Regina*. It was also *fun* – fun to be expected to look as attractive as possible each evening.

My two brief appearances were conveniently spaced out in Act 2 Scene 2 (1846, as a lady-in-waiting), and the last scene in Act 3 (as Princess May of Teck in 1897). Once assured every evening that the two players whom I understudied had arrived at the theatre in good health, I did not have a care in the world. I read a lot, and went visiting round the dressing rooms of friends, spending gossipy half-hours and sometimes flirtatious evenings with handsome young men, described as an afterthought in the programme as Royal Guests, Footmen, Courtiers and Officials. It was stimulating to be associated with a great theatrical success and to be in the ambiance of Rex Whistler's décor and costumes – this was surely one of the most stylish and beautiful productions of his distinguished career as stage designer. The production was a copy of the New York version of the play, although it was claimed that Rex did the whole thing from memory for the original designs were lost – or may even have been destroyed. Rex never thought the Lord Chamberlain would license the play for London. Against all regulations, I often crept down on to the stage to hide in the wings to watch the scene changes. There were nine in all, most of them achieved in under one minute.

The atmosphere front of house was almost as glamorous as the scenes on stage. Those were the days when audiences in the stalls, without exception, wore full evening dress. It was quite a sight to look out beyond the floats at the rows of stiff white shirt fronts and shimmering, sequinned evening dresses as we stood for curtain calls at the end. Many members of the Royal Family came to see *Victoria Regina*. One evening I waited at the Shaftesbury Avenue entrance to see Princess Marina and the Duke of Kent arrive, then dashed back full-tilt to dress and make up just in time for my entrance. For some youthful reason this felt rather daring.

I hardly ever came in contact with Gilbert Miller during the run of *Victoria Regina*.

The author (standing, second from R) in "Victoria Regina" at the Lyric Theatre, London in 1938, with Pamela Stanley as Queen Victoria (*Stage Photo Co*)

There was one occasion, however, during a dress-call shortly before the first night, when Rex Whistler inspected every detail of costumes and uniforms and royal liveries as the entire cast was paraded before him. He stood stage centre, with a tea-trolley beside him loaded with accessories – jewellery, ribbons, flowers, Orders and decorations. As he added a rose here and a medal there, it became a Rex Whistler Investiture. I was feeling uncomfortable as my wig was too tight, which had the strange effect of turning my ears a bright scarlet. Miller, as always, was sitting in the stalls watching every detail with concentration. Suddenly, his jovial voice called out: 'I don't like Miss Russell's ears – cut 'em off.' It was typical of him. He was a great impresario, but I believe he liked, sometimes, to *play* the great impresario making outrageous demands on his henchmen, who certainly took no chances and literally ran to do his bidding. This was not surprising; he was known to be given to small impulsive rages, to be abrupt and stern if things didn't go exactly his way. He had charm, money and an interesting intellectual and cultural background. The theatre was what he loved, but he was very knowledgeable about art and possessed a fine collection of rare works in his New York apartment. It has been said that during a fire scare there, Miller's voice could be heard through the smoke calling to his wife: 'Leave the jewellery, Kitty, take the Renoir and the Goya.'

Mrs Miller had inherited a fortune from her father, Jules Bache, the international banker. Miller liked to assert that *his* money all came out of the theatre. 'I have a facility for making hits out of plays I was advised *not* to produce – *Victoria Regina* was one of them.' It became a great money-maker. On the night of the 150th performance, Miller gave a champagne party on stage in celebration. The red carpet, rich draperies of velvet, and gilded pillars and pilasters of the Buckingham Palace set created an imposing background to the occasion. It was supposed to represent the actual room in the Palace that leads to the balcony facing the Mall. Years later I was to discover it wasn't at all like the real thing. Reality was not nearly 'palatial' enough for the climax of the play, which took place on Jubilee Day just after the frail old Queen had returned from a state drive and had appeared on the balcony to the delight of the massive crowds outside. (Sound effects off.) True or false, it was a set of great splendour, giving a feeling of magnitude in the height and depth of the perspective, just right for that moment in the play and just right too for a party.

In the event, it was an odd, awkward, vaguely embarrassing occasion. First of all a rope was strung across the stage to prevent the stage staff from mingling with the principals and other important guests. I and several other people ducked under the rope to join the master carpenter and the wardrobe mistress, Mr and Mrs Boxall, very distinguished in their own *métiers* in the London theatre.

There was further embarrassment to come. The author, Lawrence Housman, was to make the speech of the evening. I should add that the date was early in June 1938, about eight months after the Coronation of King George VI and Queen Elizabeth. Mr Housman, the brother of A. E. Housman, the poet, launched out with extravagant thanks to Mr Miller, and indeed to us all. He then explained in some detail how the play had come to be granted a licence by the Lord Chamberlain, stressing that it was entirely due to the assistance given by the former King Edward VIII, who insisted that the present regulation must be overruled. 'I give you the Toast,' said Mr Housman with enthusiasm. 'To the King across the water.'

There was a definite sudden hush. I was facing Miss Mabel Terry Lewis, *grande dame* of the Terry family – and of the theatre. She looked stunned. Allan Aynsworth looked down at his shoes in silence. People half-raised their glasses, there were a few nervous laughs and the Toast just petered out. After a few minutes the party was resumed almost as if nothing had happened. There was still plenty of champagne.

I cannot remember if Mr and Mrs Miller left early or were not present at all. It was quite likely that they were in Paris or New York for they belonged to what has been described as the '*crêpes Suzette* set', going the rounds of endless smart entertainment. It was known that they had entertained the Windsors as guests of honour at their annual New Year's Eve party in New York. Mrs Miller was a friend of the Duchess; she even faintly resembled her in looks and dressed rather like her. They lived in a world of stylish luxury, and Gilbert Miller was prepared to give much the same standard in the details of his productions; for example, all the stationery used in *Victoria Regina* was die-stamped for Buckingham Palace and Balmoral in appropriate sizes and colours, naturally including full mourning to very thin black edging for the demise of distant relatives of the Queen.

Shortly after the end of the run I was re-engaged with a better contract for the next major production, again at the Lyric. The play, which was running to packed houses in the Henry Miller Theatre in New York, was *The Women* by Clare Booth, with a cast of 40 women. A new company of American stars was engaged to come to London and when the play opened there were only three English girls in the cast, Joan Greenwood, as a child, Winifred Hindle, who played the English governess, and myself.

Once again I was to walk-on and understudy (and perhaps play a small part?), but — and here was the rub — Gilbert Miller, remembering that I had had stage management experience, decreed that I was also to be the assistant stage manager. He liked claiming that he had a remarkable memory. It became my job to sit in the stalls at rehearsals two rows behind Mr Miller as he directed the artists move by move, paragraph by paragraph. When the cast was nearly word perfect, not wishing to disturb the flow of dialogue, he made copious notes that at intervals were handed back to me to decipher and then type out for him to use at the end of the act.

Someone would take my place in the stalls as I raced upstairs to an office typewriter. Miller could never read his own handwriting and very often neither could I. I watched the rehearsals intently and formed my own opinions as if *I* were producing; when the notes were quite unintelligible, I would insert my own suggestions. This was quite a success. He never noticed and sometimes prefaced the remarks with: 'Now here's a good point, I think I meant to make it yesterday . . .' I began to feel that I might make a success in the theatre after all.

The Women was an immense production. The 40 members of the cast had more changes of clothes, jewellery, and furs than there were changes of scene. These amounted to twelve sets, including a fully operational bathroom. Fortunately this exercise was simplified by the use of a revolve that never stuck once.

Keeping the company happy was rather more difficult. On the surface many of the Americans were conscious of status, demanding all sorts of little privileges for the sake of establishing rank. They often seemed alarmingly tough, but I came to believe that was merely a silly façade. Nearly all the younger ones were very homesick — homesick for boy friends, lovers and even Mummies.

The production received rave notices from the London critics. Alan Dent went as far as saying the play was 'shocking, scathing, searing, sizzling and almost unbelievably witty'. The first night was on 20 April, 1939, a bare four and a half months before the outbreak of war. It is a curious reminder of the faith that the majority of people must still have had in the Munich Agreement that was signed on 29 September, 1938. Even the very alert and well informed Miller management was prepared to go forward with such a costly venture as *The Women.*

Not everyone was optimistic: towards the end of the run of *Victoria Regina*, Pamela Stanley (the leading lady) set an example by volunteering to train for Civil Defence. (She drove an ambulance in the London Blitz.) I and several others in the cast attended lectures and training sessions. I volunteered for the London Fire Brigade, later known as the London Auxiliary Fire Service, partly in the hope that theatres would not close for long; as every theatre has a duty fireman on the staff, I foolishly thought they might employ a firewoman instead.

Our visiting American cast naturally did not, at that stage, share our forebodings. When rehearsals were over for the day they clamoured for information about shopping and sightseeing. Their ebullience was exhausting. With such a dichotomy of mood in the company, it was a period of dark confusion and emotions for some of us, and of anxieties of many kinds – particularly for me and my family. After a long illness my father died suddenly less than two weeks before the first night.

As war seemed imminent, his death at that moment made my mother feel utterly vulnerable and bereft. With her strength of character and common sense, she would not hear of my breaking my contract and giving up *The Women* to help her with the clearing up of our home. She bravely came to the first night, buying a seat in the upper circle all on her own without telling me. She explained: 'It would never do to be *seen*. I am glad I went, you looked very nice.' I walked on as a model in the fitting room scene, wearing a rather daring low-cut scarlet dress.

Six days after the first night Neville Chamberlain announced the introduction of compulsory military training, with registration for men of the right age on 3 June, and a possible call-up on 1 July. The play continued before packed houses. The Fire Brigade issued a peaked cap and navy blue uniform to me with a red embroidered badge on the left side – 'AFS London' (Auxiliary Fire Service). This had to be worn during training sessions. I always changed my clothes at the fire station in Maidá Vale, as the new women's uniform was then such a rarity that it made me feel very self-conscious.

In general life was disorientated. I felt closer to reality in the theatre than when I was being questioned by an embarrassed fireman instructor who had never before been faced by a classful of young women. At that early stage we learned to call the fire engines 'appliances', also that fire alarms were situated 440 yards apart in the London area. There were many details stressed about hoses. It was considered essential to teach us that in order to create a very long hose "the male coupling has to be inserted in the female coupling in order to allow the water at high pressure to flow through." The inverted commas were a signal for a LAUGH. I also got to know that a DP appliance (dual purpose) is essentially a life-saving appliance, carrying a 50-foot escape ladder and 40 gallons of water in the first aid tank. It is always the first appliance to leave the station when the bells go down. To this day, I recall that fact whenever I hear the bells in a London street. It may seem that this information had little bearing on what firewomen would actually be doing during the war but training had to begin somewhere, and it was essential to know the jargon. I'm glad I joined early: it was a fairly cold, calm, methodical preparation for the storm that was about to break.

As tensions mounted, one or two of the cast contemplated breaking their contracts to go back to the States, but between endless discussions and enquiries about passages home they were overtaken by events and Friday 1 September was upon us. On that day

Poland was invaded by Hitler's armies and air forces at dawn. That afternoon the debating chamber of the House of Commons was crowded to hear the latest news. It was a brief sitting; no developments were announced.

Next day, Saturday, the first evacuation of children from London began. It seemed the most unnerving thing of a momentous week. I am told the atmosphere of suspense in the House of Commons was almost intolerable. It was the first time for a great many years that the House had a sitting on a Saturday. We made hollow jokes about the inviolability of the British weekend.

That day Gilbert Miller gave instructions that we were to play the matinée and evening performances. With the exception of *The Dancing Years* at Drury Lane, I believe ours was the last play to be performed in the West End before the outbreak. Lewis Allen, the general director, had been out of town that week, and Peter Mather, the stage manager, had already been called up, so I found myself virtually in charge.

The evening performance was unforgettable. Blackout conditions already prevailed in a makeshift way. Electric light bulbs in passages and corridors had been replaced by livid dark blue lights, making everyone look dead. The atmosphere in the theatre was extraordinary – only twenty people paid to see the play, and some of the artists went through the pass door to sit in the stalls with the audience. Most of those who finished their performances early on in the first act simply dashed off to try to catch already overcrowded trains and buses. When I rang down the final curtain, the principal artists took their calls as usual and got a rapturous 'mini' reception. It was touching and dignified. This did not last long. What seemed like a stampede to get away broke out backstage and front. The stage hands simply fled. Not even the master carpenter nor the chief electrician could stop them. I fancy many vanished earlier – nothing was stacked, tidied or set for next day. It was understandable.

The last scene in *The Women* was described in the programme as 'The Ladies' Powder Room at the Casino Roof, Midnight'. It was midnight all right. We soon discovered that, to save time, many of the artists had stripped off their expensive furs and jewellery instead of handing them over to the wardrobe mistress, Mrs Boxall, to put in the theatre safe. Everything was left lying around the set as people had bolted home. There was a definite air of panic, far more than I ever felt when things really began to happen. The three of us, the Boxalls and I, did our best to tidy up and salvage what we could for the strong-room. Mink coats, fox stoles, chinchilla, squirrel, expensive antique jewellery, as well as modern French paste necklaces and bracelets, were everywhere, even on the floor of the stage. The Boxalls had a last train to catch to Harrow but refused to leave until the night watchman arrived. I was thankful to see him lighting his pipe as he appeared in the doorway.

My feelings at that moment were probably rather melodramatic. I decided to take my typewriter and the prompt copy of the play home for I almost believed that the Lyric would be bombed that very night. By then I was alone on the stage looking at the attractive set I had so greatly admired. By the single naked pilot lamp, for the first time, I was seeing it as so much flimsy, shabby canvas and wood. I knew something had finished forever. At that moment a violent thunderstorm broke over London. I walked through the deluge to 77 Gloucester Place, the small private hotel where I had been living since my father's death. I was soaked and very tired, as well as frightened by the ominous thunderstorm.

I was still full of sleep at about ten o'clock next morning when my mother arrived from the country, very alert and definite about everything. She announced that she wasn't going to stay there alone.

Chamberlain's broadcast was at a quarter past eleven. The hall of the hotel was crammed with people from the street waiting to hear it. I remember we sat on the stairs and heard his plaintive, beaten voice informing us that we were already at war with Germany, as the British ultimatum had expired. The Prime Minister had scarcely finished speaking when, to use the words of Churchill in his war memoirs, 'a strange, prolonged wailing noise, afterwards to become familiar, broke upon the ear.' The Churchill reaction, it should be noted, was to go with Mrs Churchill to the flat rooftop of his house 'to see what was going on'.*

We were not so enterprising. I gathered up gas-masks and my fire service tin hat, and we made for a small brick shelter down the street that had just been completed a week ago and where one of the bricklayers had invited me to lay a brick with my name on it for luck. It was the first time in my life that I could feel my heart pounding. I was really frightened. After about ten minutes of almost complete silence in the crowded shelter, the all clear sounded; we emerged feeling relieved, and rather sheepish.

I went to see if there were any letters. There was a buff envelope in the pigeon-hole. The slip of paper it contained was a call-up notice: Russell.A. Dl. 113 to report to 'A' District, Manchester Square, 13 September, 1939.

---

* *The Gathering Storm*, Vol. 1, p. 319.

CHAPTER THREE

Theatre Postscript

My call-up notice to report for duty on 13 September seemed to make National Service a cast-iron certainty. A further memo arrived advising me to bring a change of underwear, a knife, fork and spoon and a bed roll. We took this last to mean a sleeping bag, by then quite unobtainable in the London stores. My resourceful mother found two heavy pink woollen blankets and sewed them together by hand, making a sort of bag. We strapped this up into a sausage shape and I set off on the day with a suitcase, tin hat, gas-mask and a cumbersome pink bundle. At 'A' District, Manchester Square, 1 Chiltern Street, I was told I had been transferred to Station 72 in Shaftesbury Avenue, almost opposite the Palace Theatre. It was easy to locate as the street was swarming with firemen recruits, busily filling sandbags and building them up in layers against the basement windows of the station. It was a noisy scene, with a lot of laughter and whistling which could have been a nervous reaction to knowing that the future was unlikely to be anything but unpleasant.

In the main hall there was a long straggling queue of young women in brightly coloured summer dresses; they were already weary and fairly silent, as they had come some hours before full of good intent and anxious to sign on to join the AFS. I dumped my belongings in a corner and searched for someone to report to for duty. Although I was in uniform, I was told to join the queue. Eventually, when I was able to present my call-up paper, there was further delay as two women officers disappeared to confer on what to do with me. To my utter amazement, they returned to say I was not required at the moment. 'Look,' said one of them, 'now we've got all this lot to train,' as if that was a good reason. I pressed to know when I should return only to be told 'certainly not in the foreseeable future'. It was too good to be true to be reprieved (temporarily no doubt) from that scene of bedlam. I gave them my address, and to celebrate found a taxi to take me home.

My delight was mixed with a certain frustration after all the months of training and preparation – to say nothing of my mother's bruised and scratched fingers from her gallant efforts at sewing and binding four layers of blankets by hand, to send me off fully equipped for the war. This was my first, but not my last, experience of the happy British way of muddling through. Now, with hindsight, I can be grateful to Providence that things happened as they did, for Station 72 was later bombed with severe loss of life in the Blitz. It was at least five months before the fire service required my services.

All London theatres were still closed, but I discovered that another management – Linnit and Dunfee – had taken over the whole Gilbert Miller production of *The Women*, and with an almost entirely new cast were planning a tour of number one cities and towns all over England and Scotland.

'Not required in the foreseeable future' seemed a fair let-out, so once again I found myself stage managing with more authority and playing several small parts. It was the first blackout tour of the war, and moving the scenery out on Saturday nights was like a military manoeuvre. Each time the scene dock doors were opened, a whistle was blown as a signal for all lights to be extinguished. Sets and furniture and props were loaded on lorries act by act in total darkness. The routine was repeated, in reverse, with another signal for doors to be closed and lights turned on. This was an exhausting business, sometimes not finishing until after two in the morning.

Most of us kept wishing we were more closely associated with the war effort; and, after some discussion, the company as a whole volunteered to give an extra matinée (free) whenever we were playing in a city where troops were stationed in some numbers. The management agreed to pay the theatre expenses.

This turned out to be a surprising experience. With a mixed audience, mostly of civilians, the play was as successful as in London – some felt it went better in the provinces than in the West End. Unfortunately, an all-male audience of servicemen neither appreciated the wit, nor really enjoyed the very funny scenes. The cast was inclined to write the men off as out of touch with sophisticated comedy. I am more inclined to think it was another example of the old theory that men *en masse* don't want women to be funny. Sexy, sentimental, *nude* if possible, yes; funny, no. Maybe the title of the play could have been misleading. Eventually it was decided to abandon the project. As we were already committed to three matinées a week, we did this with great relief.

I thoroughly enjoyed playing many different small parts during the tour. (By then I knew the play in its entirety.) My favourite was that of Second Saleslady in a brief dialogue that offered a marvellous opportunity to get a huge laugh. To some performers a great laugh in a packed theatre is as good as a glass of champagne. I am one of them, and looked forward to trying different ways of achieving this every evening for about a fortnight. The situation was two salesladies tidying up after a rich customer had seen innumerable model dresses without buying a thing.

> *First Saleslady* Gee, I wish I worked in a men's store ... what can a man try on?
> *Second Saleslady* (me) Ever see a man try on hats? What they go through, you'd think a head was something peculiar.

Unfortunately this line preceded one of the entrances of the leading lady and she seemed to fear that the roar of mirth from the audience spoiled the calculated effect of her entrance. I was no longer allowed to play it, and was replaced by someone who couldn't get a laugh at all. Sad.

The tour was a hard grind of some sixteen weeks, opening at Streatham, then on to Manchester, Liverpool, Birmingham, Leeds, Southport, Bradford, Nottingham, Newcastle, Glasgow, Edinburgh, Aberdeen, Oxford, Bournemouth, Southsea and Brighton, ending neatly with a fortnight at the Strand Theatre in London, where business was poor. London was in a different frame of mind. The phoney or, as I prefer to call it, the twilight war, as well as my stage career, was coming to an end.

CHAPTER FOUR

Neighbourliness of Danger

Do you remember those mornings after the Blitzes
When the living picked themselves up and went on living,
Living, not on the past, but with an exhilaration
Of purpose — a new neighbourliness of danger?

Cecil Day Lewis

Back in London there was endless talk of invasion. Many of my married friends with young children had managed to rent cottages and houses in the home counties, often sharing with other families; though indeed as the raids on London had not yet started I often felt that the city might be preferable to live in. The prospect of German soldiers tramping across the fields or even walking up the garden path of one's cottage was horrifying and unthinkable. A very dear friend of mine, Eileen Shields, whose husband was a doctor at St George's Hospital and tied to London, took her two babies to live somewhere near Horley in Surrey. She refused to worry about loneliness or fear. 'No problem. When the invasion starts, I shall put out a placard: "Goulash served — piping hot".' I think we got by with courageous if feeble jokes like this.

At that time my grandparents were living in Eastbourne. I went down to see them with the firm intention of packing everything up and moving them somewhere inland. They were hurt and even angry, taking it that I was persuading them to be cowardly. My grandfather was descended from the Yorkshire family of Metcalfe, said to be one of the last families to fight a private war in England.

I should explain that their pet names for each other were the same. They called each other Bosie. 'Bosie, let the child say what she wants to say.' 'Don't be so silly, Bosie, I know what I'm talking about.' 'Be quiet, Bosie.' It made discussion rather difficult.

'We must face the music,' said Grandpa, already in his eighties. They were both very put out. It was useless to point out that they might be in the way of our defence forces if an invasion came. I returned to London alone.

Within a few weeks Eastbourne, a prosperous watering place, was declared a restricted area, up to ten miles inland. The hotels on the front were closed and I made a second journey, packed up and took my two elderly evacuees to an hotel at Ilfracombe, a place they said 'they always wished to visit'. I never saw poor Grannie again. She died in her sleep about eighteen months later, and Grandpa came to live with us.

By then my mother had gone to live in Reigate. The Reigate cottage had been found for us by Eileen who, with me, felt strongly that somehow my mother must be persuaded to leave London before things got worse. The cottage was in the grounds of an hotel in Reigate, which meant she was not entirely alone. This seemed an ideal solution. We were not to know then that the cottage was situated immediately below one of the routes the German bombers would be taking on their way to London, and that Mother and many others with relatives working in the capital would have the anxiety of knowing where the enemy were going and what might happen. I should add that Mother never mentioned this torture to me beyond sometimes saying lightly: 'It was quite noisy last night.'

Some months after she settled in we managed to persuade Nana to join us in Reigate. She had retired to live alone in Richmond. So, more or less, we were all together till the end of the war.

Although the Fire Service gave no indication at all that my services were required, I decided that I must report for duty somewhere on my return to London. I could not face going back to the very unwelcoming station in Shaftesbury Avenue, but I unearthed my uniform, put it on and walked up Baker Street where several shops and offices seemed to have been taken over by the NFS. I asked a young girl in uniform where the officer-in-charge could be found. She looked suspiciously and said, 'What is your business?' Maybe she believed the Hairy Nun story was true. It should be remembered at that time there were several variations of the Hairy Nun story going around, i.e. German parachutists landing dressed as nuns. It was difficult to explain my situation, it seemed so odd. Maybe my uniform looked too new to be real. Eventually she directed me to 49 Baker Street and I met the officer-in-charge on the doorstep. Her name was Flanagan. I need hardly say she was Irish-born, very pleasant, and she invited me back into her office and listened to my story sympathetically. Then with the minimum of fuss she just said: 'We are shorthanded – when can you start? The hours are 48 hours *on*, 24 hours *off*, 2 hours off for meals.'

In this simple unbureaucratic fashion I became a small part of 'A' District Superintendent Station, 1 Chiltern Street, Manchester Square. Owing to my family commitments already described I began as a part-timer, working first in the watchroom on exercises, helping to collate the entries for the Daily Occurrence Book in which every movement of the firemen on duty and their appliances was recorded minute by minute. It was, I suppose, a primitive version of the black box on board a modern airliner. Entries in the Occurrence Book, a huge ledger which called for accuracy and experience, were meticulously kept up at the height of the Blitz, even when hectic incidents were piling up on all sides. I was also given a trial on the PBX telephone exchange and this was nearly my downfall – for some inexplicable reason instruction on how to cope with a busy switchboard was missing from my training, and I stupidly did not want to admit it. I was gently relegated to making endless cups of tea all night and to washing up greasy plates, generally in cold water.

I was not the only auxiliary to be a hazard to the efficiency of the internal telephone. It became necessary to pressgang a number of professionals. Many of these were transferred from the London Telephone Exchange. They were the equivalent of the Brigade of Guards (on the telephone!), highly disciplined and calm, with the special telephone voice of the period. It was a joy to watch them at work. Equally efficient, but much more informal, were the volunteers from bookmakers' offices: young clerks, familiar with taking bets at high speed, holding their jobs down because they so rarely made a mistake.

One beautiful cloudless day in early September 1940, when I was off duty, a friend asked me to have a picnic with her at Kenwood. It has always been one of my favourite open spaces in London, high on its hill between Hampstead and Highgate, with 74 acres of park and woodland surrounding the eighteenth-century Adam house left to the nation by Lord Iveagh in 1928. Kenwood is a great English house that is the product of not one but several generations of artists and architects. The gardens had been landscaped in the eighteenth century to 'set off the view,' which in those days meant St Paul's, Greenwich and the shipping on the Thames.

We spent a peaceful happy day and the war seemed far away – until suddenly we noticed a huge column of black smoke in the distance to the east, stiff and straight as a factory chimney. Within minutes another rose into the air and then another and another. We soon realised the huge fires were marking out the course of the River Thames. It was about 5 p.m. The Germans flew up the river and in from the south, creating sudden havoc. We were too far away to hear any noise at all but we had an eerie panoramic view and the peace and quiet of that historic spot emphasised the implications and the horror. We quickly tidied up our picnic and I drove straight back to the Fire Station. Already our crews and fire-fighting equipment were down at the docks. West Ham Power Station, Becton Gas Works, Woolwich Arsenal, the docks at Millwall, Limehouse and Rotherhithe were all hit. Perhaps the worst casualties of all were in the Surrey Commercial Docks, the main timber importing docks in London, consisting of 250 acres of stacked resinous wood from the Baltic: timber soon to be a roaring sea of flame.

There appeared to be a lull at about 6, but at 8.10, guided by the flames as darkness fell, a fresh wave of bombers swept overhead (estimated at 600 aircraft); they were stoking up fires, renewing the firemen's first experience of fire fighting under aerial bombardment: the Blitz had begun.

The single advantage of that first raid was that we had plenty of water available from the dock basins, but it was more than 24 hours before the tired crews could return to their stations. Later it was officially announced that somehow every fire was in hand, and damped down by midday on 8 September. Later still it was recorded that 90 per cent of the auxiliary firemen who went into action on 7 September had never seen or fought a fire before.

From that date onwards, night after night throughout September and October a raiding force dropped bombs on London. Sometimes the aircraft numbered as many as 400, making more than one journey a night. By 3 November there was a lull and it became the turn of the provinces. On 14 November Coventry was the first provincial city to bear the brunt of the enemy's fury. Raids on London, both day and night, continued sporadically with the last heavy attack when the House of Commons and much else besides was destroyed on 10–11 May, 1941.

One of the surprises of war work for me was that night duty was not nearly as awful as it was made out to be. Everyone would tell you that it affects the digestion, that you can't sleep in the daytime, and that you can never see your friends. I always tried to plump for a late shift. Sleep was nearly impossible during an air raid anyway, and it was pleasant to have a good breakfast in the morning before going to bed. For some reason these topsy-turvy conditions had almost sedative properties. I found I slept well after breakfast and often did not wake up until late afternoon, fresh and ready to go out to an early dinner and dance somewhere in the West End. A rather seedy night club called the 'Night Light' in a basement near Leicester Square was very popular with ARP workers waiting to go on duty. Going out to dance became a kind of ritual as if to prove to ourselves that we could behave quite normally in the very abnormal conditions that prevailed for everyone. I didn't enjoy it very much after the first few times. The place was generally hot, crowded and smelly; it was lit economically by real nightlights until the stock of them was exhausted and we then shuffled around the small dance floor space in the unromantic glare of a single unshaded electric bulb. Even when the sirens had already sounded and guns were grumbling away like a hungry zoo I longed for the air and the walk back to the station.

London could be weird at night, sinister in the heart of the West End with dark figures loping about asking the way, and others standing in doorways flashing small red torches for rather obvious reasons. On quiet nights it could be a truly splendid experience to visit friends in a residential neighbourhood that so far had not suffered unduly, such as St John's Wood, Highgate or Belgravia: hearing your own footsteps in flat-heeled uniform shoes clattering metallically along the deserted streets, walking past elegant empty blacked-out houses, disturbing lonely cats left behind by their owners. These often struck up a quick excited acquaintanceship, following just as far as *they* wanted before disappearing in the night. I never felt that they were lonely: they seemed glad of their independence. Those nights when London was dark and silent, only the questing beams of searchlights radiating across the sky gave an awareness of danger and death.

The quiet nights or 'lulls' as they were called were a merciful relief, but oddly enough presented their own problems which affected service personnel, the press and sometimes the public. As far as I know nothing much could be done officially to enliven the tedious waiting game that sometimes had to be played when it was essential to keep crews at full strength in case of a sudden raid. A very old friend of mine, the distinguished historian and writer, David Green, reminded me recently of this strange situation and of one of the most extraordinary and successful efforts carried out by the men of a sub-station in the heart of the West End to beat boredom – as well as food shortage. With his permission, I will let David (as a serving fireman) tell the story in his own words:

'In the popular (sic) press, the London fireman was in times of Blitz a hero; but once let there be a lull in the bombing then the same fireman was branded as a layabout, who should be at the front fighting with "our brave boys". But of course, and as with any emergency service, there had to be lulls, times of inactivity when the firemen and firewomen themselves longed to be up and doing, instead of standing on patrol, scrubbing long flights of stairs or polishing and repolishing lamps and door-handles and other more or less antiquated bits of brass.

'Yet even from this boredom and waste of time sprang ideas which led to some surprising and very unfiremanlike activities. One of them was what came to be known as 'The Pig Farm' in Berners Street, a wide thoroughfare leading from the Middlesex Hospital to Oxford Street. We found ourselves in a garage next door to a very large hole in the ground, where before the Blitz an imposing office block had housed church vestments for priests. Every now and then we would find the odd biretta; and to see four firemen playing cards, themselves wearing birettas at various angles, was a sight not to be forgotten.

'One of these lighthearted firemen was a farmer and it was he who organised us into converting the bombed site into a small-holding in the very middle of London.

'At first it was decided to dig in manure and grow potatoes, tomatoes, lettuces and anything else edible which could be made to grow where only bricks and mortar had grown before. But at once we struck a snag: *manure*. Birettas were doffed and heads scratched until some bright fireman came up with the answer, which was *pigs*. The amazing thing was that it *worked*. The farm-that-couldn't-have-happened *did* happen and potatoes, tomatoes, and even succulent hams were produced. It was good for morale, and it made headlines in the newspapers, won over by enterprise. Of course as

Richard Dimbleby and David Green at Blenheim Palace, 1952

with all farms and gardens there were setbacks. In a sunless summer green tomatoes had to go for ketchup while, worse than that, when the bells went down for the latest conflagration, six pigs might find the daily mash hurled at them, while hens scattered to avoid the farmer-firemen racing for fire appliances.'

David Green and I served in the same District and at the same time, but we did not meet socially until long after the war. This was in much happier times, when Richard Dimbleby and I went to Blenheim Palace for a broadcast. David, as the authority on the reign of Queen Anne and on all things connected with Blenheim, took part in the programme and helped us in our researches. He is now one of my oldest friends.

I must confess that during the Blitz I rarely felt the 'exhilaration of purpose' in the mornings, as mentioned by one of my favourite modern poets, Cecil Day Lewis, and quoted at the head of this chapter. Perhaps I am unfair, as the lines come from his first published work as Poet Laureate – an office that often exerts a baleful moralising optimism on the holder in the early stages. Of course it depends what work you are given to do. Such an exhilaration must have been experienced countless times by the war leaders on both sides, but not so often by a dish-washing Dl. 113. However, the range of work was fairly wide and I was detailed in turn for some of it. I briefly became a 'Batman' to our senior Group Officer, Miss Willoughby. During that time the station was strengthened by a new intake of young firewomen from a poor district in London. They were a lively group of cockneys but they caused a certain discreet concern when it was alleged that they had introduced a small epidemic of parasitic insects – in other words, nits. This was not mentioned openly but a decision was taken to fumigate all the women's quarters, beginning with Group Officer Willoughby's bedroom (although none of the newcomers had had access to her flat).

Doors and windows were sealed up with sticky paper, but once the fumigator was well alight Group Officer Willoughby remembered she had left her Bible inside. She was very upset. I had often longed for an opportunity to test my gas-mask. Thankful there had never been a gas attack, I nevertheless resented the obligation to carry the thing. The episode suddenly became a hilarious joke. Everyone was laughing as I rushed in wearing that travesty of a black rubber face. In a matter of seconds I was overcome with a fit of coughing, spluttering and streaming eyes, which lasted for several hours. Yet it seemed to be worth it; the gas-mask had been on 'active service', however inappropriate the test, the Bible was retrieved, and we decided philosophically that all wars produce lice.

I also worked for a bit in the Paymaster's Office on a National Savings campaign, but this did not offer many excitements. Strange to relate, the job most coveted by most of us was to become a member of the canteen van team, touring the district during raids to dish out refreshments to the weary, sweating firemen. It was then we felt that we were covering ourselves with glory.

Exhilaration apart, I certainly discovered Day Lewis's 'new neighbourliness of danger' among my colleagues and friends in the National Fire Service. They were truly remarkable people, once things had settled down after the first flurry of recruitment and joining up when I had been so firmly rejected. They were dependable, efficient, and uncomplaining about the conditions in which we lived – accommodation during the Blitz appeared to be an afterthought and most of the girls in my section dossed down on the concrete floor of the basement when on call. That basement frequently became a first aid centre for injured cats and kittens (most firemen took pride in rescuing them and depositing them with us to be looked after). Sometimes there would be a trifling gift for each firewoman, as when the Pepsodent factory went up and hundreds of tubes of toothpaste were scattered across the street.

There were countless bizarre situations in the early days. A friend of mine on his first day of duty discovered that no dormitory had been allotted to him, yet his orders were to reside at the Station. Feeling peeved, he slipped out of the building in search of accommodation. Wandering down a nearby mews, he spotted a Rolls Royce parked on the pavement. The doors were unlocked so, taking a chance, he got in, sank into the superb upholstery and slept very well. At 8.30 a.m. he was wakened by a smart chauffeur, who touched his cap: 'I'm sorry to disturb you, sir, but her Ladyship wants me to drive her to Harrods.'

My regular companions in Baker Street were on surname terms with each other. We were a friendly and companionable cluster of women from the most diverse backgrounds imaginable, including a widow who owned a fine house in Manchester Square. In the mornings when the all clear went, she invariably got up to see if her home was still standing. We also had in our group a diplomat's daughter, a former parlourmaid, three factory machinists, a repertory actress from the Midlands and dozens of typists.

In times of stress it is not essential for people to have many interests in common to get on well together. For us, just one bond was sufficient: we were all in the same boat, we knew it was for the duration, and that seemed depressingly far away.

The curious thing was that Fate seemed to have taken a hand in creating an opportunity for me to escape the doldrums of National Service. It didn't actually happen until long after the Blitz – in June 1942 to be precise – but for well over a year before that a number of circumstances built up which unexpectedly gave me the chance to launch out on a completely new career. There were several unconnected reasons for this.

The District Headquarters of Manchester Square were but a few minutes away from Broadcasting House, where the BBC was fighting the first war in which radio was to become such a vital element. We had frequent visits from radio reporting teams, gathering news stories about the Blitz and experiences not only of fighting fires but of civil defence in general.

Unlike other fire stations, which feared that such diversions might obstruct the work in hand, our Superintendent rather liked the publicity of being interviewed; he welcomed the BBC with half-pints of bitter fetched on tin trays from the nearby pub, the 'Wallace Head'. As an ordinary firewoman I was lucky not to have been transferred to some far-away station that was never visited by the BBC at all. There is no doubt that our District had many advantages for the BBC, especially in the speed of getting there and back. News Bulletins and news magazines were being broadcast night and day, almost round the clock, on the Home and Overseas Services. Of course, when major incidents occurred further afield, they were covered by the BBC, but in those days before tape recordings were introduced, there were likely to be greater delays in transmission. At that time the BBC was using single turntable equipment on the mobile recording vans for cutting discs (like gramophone records). Tape recording came much later.

On one occasion I was detailed to fetch the beer for the Superintendent and his two BBC guests. One was Robin Duff and the other a well-known London actor, the late Terence de Marney. Robin was the first narrator of the famous war-time programme *Radio News Reel* and he later became better known as a 'Blitz reporter'. It would be more accurate to say 'observer', for BBC war reporters were officially called 'observers' then. I believe this to be a hangover from an idea of Sir John Reith, who decreed that there should be as little reference to journalism in the News Division as possible. The presence of Terence de Marney was an example of another policy that was to be greatly changed after the war. Here there was the feeling that it was immensely important for the News Division to employ people who could project the image of what was being said: it was considered that simply *because* someone was an actor he was likely to be able to broadcast well. The contrast today is, as we all know, very great. News staff are employed because they are journalists and it hardly matters if they have a cleft palate or not.

It was Terence de Marney who decided I should be interviewed there and then. I remember it as a very conventional interview on my impressions as a woman in the fire service, but as it was done in the august presence of the Superintendent, it could hardly have been anything else. It was a beginning that was to lead to much more exciting things. Gradually, I became a sort of tame firewoman to the BBC (unpaid), often called upon for a story. These were to include a description of the night of 10 May, 1941 (often now referred to as the worst raid on London, when the House of Commons was destroyed): I was on duty in a canteen van most of that night.

One of my recordings that was broadcast in *Radio News Reel* was heard by a high-ranking RAF officer who was in the studio, taking part in the same programme. It was reported to me that Air Commodore Harold Peake had said: 'I wish we had that girl at the Air Ministry', and of course I was flattered. But he meant it. To my astonishment, some arrangement was made between the NFS, the RAF and the BBC. I was seconded to the Air Ministry for six weeks to do six five-minute BBC talks on the work of the WAAF. The idea behind it was to contradict certain rumours that some of the duties in the WAAF were too arduous for women – particularly for those stationed on the barrage balloon sites in most of the cities and major airfields.

And so, still in the uniform of an ordinary firewoman, I was escorted halfway across Britain by a very elegantly tailored WAAF officer who was later to become Commandant of the WAAF and a Dame. We went to several stations of Fighter, Bomber and Coastal Command which included Biggin Hill, Waterbeach, Mildenhall and Poole, staying two nights in each. My AFS uniform caused a certain embarrassment to everyone, including myself, and at the first station we visited I messed with the other ranks and had little opportunity of talking on anything like equal terms with officers. I applied at once to be allowed to wear civilian clothes and the effect was electrifying. I was given a special pass and was permitted to travel without a conducting officer and was received as if I was someone important wherever I went!

One always felt very close to the war at an RAF station. This must have been because of the constant awareness that action could happen at any moment. On a visit to Biggin Hill I was greeted by the Station Commander with: 'Excuse me, there's a couple of Huns on the way over, but I will be back with you soon.' As he spoke we could hear the sound of two fighter planes of the stand-by patrol climbing into the sky. The stand-by patrol was always on the alert, pilots sitting in the cockpit with the engines running, able to take off within 30 seconds of a signal. The Huns turned tail on this occasion.

The atmosphere at bomber stations was no less alert, but the massive preparations for an attack seemed to me to make the tensions more long drawn out.

Outward behaviour at all RAF stations contrived to be lighthearted and often amusing, for morale was high. At the bomber station at Waterbeach the atmosphere was a splendid camouflage for the heavy responsibilities that lay on every individual directly concerned with Operations. The WAAF were integrated into almost every aspect of the preparations and carrying out of a bombing mission. It was the girls who packed the parachutes, who drove the aircrews to their aircraft, who worked in the Watch Office, in Signals, Codes and Ciphers, Intelligence, Meteorology, and who, as plotters, had their pictures more often in the papers than anyone else, perhaps because of the 'croupiers' rakes' they used to mark the movement of enemy aircraft and our own on the huge table map in the Ops Room. The information was derived from RDF (radar) and the Observer Corps. The domestic staff and the kitchen staff were also involved on night shift, laying tables and having a meal ready for the aircrews' return.

I look back especially on those evenings when, with small groups of the WAAF, we gathered near the perimeter of the airfield to watch the Lancaster Bombers taxi away into the dusk. We would screw up our eyes to catch the beautiful moment when the aircraft can just be seen to be airborne. When the last Lancaster was signalled off, the sky would be full of aircraft circling overhead before setting course for some devastating raid. The poignant beauty of the scene seemed only to add to the tension. Conversation was quiet and matter of fact. It was a synthetic calm. I would look at the faces beside me and know there was but one collective thought among the lot of us: how many will return?

The most difficult part of the whole assignment was that every time I came back to London I had to write a script. All my little items about the fire service were off the cuff. At Broadcasting House I met my first BBC Talks Producer, Donald Boyd, a famous figure in the News Division before and during the war – a very gruff kind of man, tweedy and pipe-smoking. As soon as you got out of the lift at the end of the corridor you knew if he was in or not from the smell of a terrible pipe, that seemed to be perpetually clenched between his teeth. He may have been happily married for all I know, but the impression was of a misogynist in his work, heaving weary sighs as he read through my scripts, but at the same time good-natured enough to tell me where I was going wrong in the difficult craft of writing to be heard rather than read. The six weeks flew by in a flash and I did my five minutes on the air every Sunday after the one o'clock news. At the end of the series, Donald Boyd gave me some serious broadcasting advice: 'I think you might get away with it if you cultivate a brogue. You were born in Dublin. Look at Priestley.' It was difficult to explain that most Anglo-Irish families like to think that they have hardly any brogue at all, and that I was sent to an English boarding school to lose any brogue I had. It seemed unfair to my parents even to think of it, but I often wonder what would have happened if I had taken Donald's kind advice.

Things were relatively quiet when I returned to the fire service. My friends had knitted a lot more socks and mufflers to send to the troops.

It was difficult to settle down after those six hectic, interesting weeks. I felt I wanted to know more about the techniques of broadcasting, of making words come across by voice alone. I was nearer to this than I imagined. A few weeks after my return I was offered a war-time appointment as an observer in the overseas service of the BBC, subject to being released from the fire service.

The formalities of the change-over took nearly seven months, partly because of my Irish birthplace, suspect at a time when Eire was neutral, and partly because my birth certificate could not be found. Inevitably I was vetted and screened by MI5 since the work would sometimes involve visits to places under strict security; but I did not have to face a BBC Appointments Board. All the details were worked out informally, often over a cup of coffee in a canteen. My starting salary was £645 a year.

I marvelled at my good fortune.

CHAPTER FIVE

200 Oxford Street

My first step after the vetting and screening of my credentials was to be sent on the BBC's staff training course, then held at Bedford College, Regent's Park. I remember very little about it, partly because in war-time it lasted only three weeks. Most of the lectures were concerned with the hierarchy of high-ranking officials, their grading and responsibilities, and who had to answer to whom. There was much emphasis on telling us that the BBC was an extremely good employer; details of insurance and pension schemes were explained by a benevolently mannered gentleman with white hair. We were each given a short private interview with him. He informed me that my salary was a very good one and that it should have been £620 per annum, but that owing to 'special circumstances' it was a starting salary of £645. I never discovered what the 'special circumstances' were.

The art of broadcasting was hardly mentioned, though there were several interesting if difficult talks on the techniques of BBC engineering, most of which went right above my head. There were between 30 and 40 men and women on the course and, as I remember, only one of them was to make his name. He was Gilbert Harding, who had come from the monitoring service (which he hated), and his career as a broadcasting personality was still quite a long way off. He had already acquired the habit of a very personal bluntness – especially to those who could not, or did not know how to, answer back. Such incidents were invariably followed by abject, almost tearful apologies, sometimes accompanied by gifts, which made everything all right until the next time.

During the last week of the course I found myself teamed up with Gilbert to play the chief parts in a feature programme which we were to rehearse and record. It was about the aftermath of air raids on provincial cities called, I believe, *The Stones Cry Out*. It was a serious subject but it was treated allegorically and, with Gilbert as Narrator, I found myself cast as 'Plymouth', conjuring up a statuesque maternal figure with many brave maritime sons. We both saw absurdity in this, and shared a joke about it for years. Whenever we met, or found ourselves in the same programme, he would cover his face in mock horror: 'Oh Lord, it's *Plymouth*.' I often wonder if he knew my real name.

The organisation that I joined in 1942 had changed out of recognition from the leisurely formalities of a peacetime broadcasting service with its highlights of nightingales singing in a Surrey wood and announcers wearing dinner jackets to read the news. Its work was scattered around in newly acquired premises all over London and elsewhere, to lessen the danger of a major breakdown through enemy action.

My new career made it essential for me to live as near to the BBC as possible. Reigate was rather far for a news reporter. So I acquired an unfurnished top floor of a house in Queen Anne Street. The first floor was already occupied by Miss Mary Pugh, the ophthalmologist and surgeon, who had been recently bombed out of her home and consulting room in Harley Street. We were then mere acquaintances and had gravitated

200 Oxford Street (*B.B.C. copyright*)

towards the same house in Queen Anne Street for company during the fire raids, little suspecting that this was to become a routine arrangement for the rest of her lifetime. From then on we always rented two flats in the same building. It was an unusual partnership of the arts and sciences. I regretted my total lack of any systematic and formulated knowledge, and Mary seemed to welcome being able to share in my many interests in the theatre and the arts. We saw eye to eye on all the fundamental ethics of daily life. We laughed a lot together and we both loved to travel, but in war time it was not often possible to do so together.

From Queen Anne Street I could walk every day to the office to which I was assigned at 200 Oxford Street, then housing the Overseas Service. I was a little disappointed not to be installed grandly at Broadcasting House, so carefully and elegantly planned as the first broadcasting headquarters in the world. '200', as it was always known for short, was something of an architectural mongrel. Originally it was the east block of Peter Robinson's – the department store – requisitioned in June 1941, and in spite of delays in conversion, owing to an unexploded parachute mine falling in the vicinity, it was occupied under a year later by the staffs of the most widely heard programmes in the world.

Editions of news went out every day of the year to the United States, Canada, South America, the Pacific, the Far East, Africa, and the British forces overseas: eight programmes over 24 hours. I was pleased to be associated straight away with the classic BBC programme, *Radio News Reel*.

I soon discovered that '200' was a very special building indeed. It was heavily protected by strong blast walls, all windows were blocked up and the street pavement level outside was raised to give several feet of concrete protection for the areas below. The basement included eight studios and recording rooms with a large control room, built to maximum security specifications so that the broadcasting services could continue as far as possible without interruption. The design of the building as a shop created certain problems in making suitable offices on the upper floors. Like most department stores of the period, it consisted of grandiose showrooms with very high ceilings in pseudo-banker's-Georgian style. Aesthetic considerations had to go overboard and the showrooms were divided up by seven foot high brick partitions. With the exception of a large painted hand on the wall pointing the 'customers' to 'Coats and Mantles' (which by some strange oversight never got painted over), the walls and cubicles were uniformly decorated the colour of cheddar cheese.

June 1942 could hardly have been a more stimulating time to become a member of the BBC's war-time staff. The landings in French North Africa were approaching. In the desert things were working up to a big offensive, and I had barely settled in before experiencing the heightened tensions in offices and studios as the first reports and sounds of the bombardments came in from the Battle of Alamein. By this time the news services were running like clockwork.

I came to know the editor, Peter Pooley, as the ablest immediate boss I ever worked for in the Corporation. His grasp of any political or rapidly changing war situation was quite remarkable, and his flair for recognising a weak spot or inaccuracy in a script was uncanny – as well as very helpful. He was an unusual figure, tall, very pale, with lanky fair hair and a slow lethargic walk. His clothes for the period were informal: he generally wore lightweight suits winter and summer in a range of whitish ashen colours – that I later discovered made some of his

The author (*Camera Press Limited*)

personal friends affectionately call him 'the monochrome young man.'

There was nothing monochromatic in his handling of staff. His team was a very diverse group of people brought together chiefly by the rather special way in which staff are recruited by the BBC to this day. The preference is nearly always for programme and broadcasting staff who have experience or qualifications in fields other than broadcasting, but who nevertheless make a contribution to the media. A number of professional broadcasters from the Commonwealth, from Canada, New Zealand and Australia, as well as from the States, were on attachment to *Radio News Reel*, but the newly appointed war-time staff belonged to a more conventional way of doing things. Taken out of context this must have made us look like a curious, unrelated bunch. Peter Pooley valued individuality and was quick to recognise it. He kindly left me to discover a technique of interviewing and scriptwriting on my own.

It happened that one of the producers (out to be helpful) felt he had a 'good little story' for me. A wholesale dressmaking firm in the City had been commissioned to manufacture khaki battledress instead of the beaded evening gowns that had been their stock-in-trade for years. The firm now called itself From Ballgown to Battledress. It was arranged for a recording car to take me to the factory. The producer said: 'There's the woman's angle here all right!'

The visit was a disaster. I couldn't think of any interesting questions for a burly foreman in charge of a row of electric sewing machines pounding down on the khaki fabric. I didn't help the answers either: 'Oh, we don't mind', 'The hours are just as long', 'Money's the same too', 'What's the difference?' 'People don't wear balldresses now'.

Next day Peter Pooley sent for me and said casually: 'Do you feel like going to St Mary's Hospital, Paddington, tomorrow at 9.30? It's about penicillin. *The Times* published a leading article a few days ago and now there's some sort of conference – so it's important. We do want an interview. It might be best if you can bring Professor Alexander Fleming back to the studio. Try and get him.' In spite of yesterday's flop I was cheered at the prospect of a second chance.

Fleming's publicity in *The Times* was enough to send every available reporter to St Mary's. When I arrived the lecture room was full of journalists and photographers clamouring for pictures, interviews and statements. Professor Fleming made a brief appearance, but quickly disappeared to some inner sanctum, stating that he did not wish to be interviewed. The press were immediately very put out and one could not help wondering if he had changed his mind on the spot. Handouts were then distributed which helped a little to make us understand what penicillin really was and what it could do. A senior consultant spoke briefly, welcoming the press, but there were no interviews from anyone.

The cameramen noisily packed up their equipment and left, grumbling about the waste of time. I decided to stay in the hope of catching Fleming when he went to lunch. He appeared punctually at one o'clock, a small neatly dressed man with a solemn look of determination on his face. He called out: 'Are you the girl from the BBC?' adding firmly: 'No interview, thank you,' as he walked to the door. He returned from luncheon without a glance in my direction. I then decided that some action must be taken and managed to contact the consultant who had welcomed the press that morning. He had described the conference as of national importance, so at once I pointed out that in broadcasting it was of both national and international interest. He looked thoughtful and almost pleased at this cliché and murmured: 'I'll have a quick word with the Professor.'

I could not believe that such a shy, self-effacing man would change his mind at this late stage, but at six o'clock he emerged in a different mood, sympathetic about the long tedious wait. We left the hospital at seven o'clock to drive to 200 Oxford Street. He made no attempt at conversation, and seemed reticent, modest and even nervous about the broadcast. There was a short delay before the studio was free and, sitting in my office, he doodled on a blotting pad stylishly signing his name several times.

The broadcast was what one would expect from a brilliant man, aware that he was speaking to an audience that could only take an elementary view of the almost miraculous curative properties of the new substance. The Professor became a celebrity almost overnight in 1942. He was knighted in 1944, for safety reasons in a basement room in Buckingham Palace. Then, in 1945, the Nobel Prize for Medicine was shared between the three medical scientists whose names are associated for ever with penicillin – Sir Alexander Fleming, Professor Florey and Dr Ernst Chain.

One of the experienced broadcasters was the one-time refugee from Austria, George Weiden, who came to this country in 1938 and spent nearly three years in the BBC's monitoring service as an Italian, French and German monitor. By the time he came to *News Reel* in 1942 his reputation was not only as a gifted linguist but as a man of outstanding ability. George Weiden was received with much respect in the department and justified it immediately by becoming a news commentator, brilliantly specialising in European politics. His background was something of a mystery to the staff but he was already surrounded by several versions of an endearing legend that when he fled to Britain at the age of nineteen he arrived with a postal order for 16/6 in his pocket and one light suitcase: all he was allowed to bring with him. He is better known today as Lord Weidenfeld, chairman of the publishing house of Weidenfeld & Nicolson and associate companies.

Perhaps the most unlikely person to find working with the BBC's early essay in tough radio journalism was the highly intelligent, distinguished Russian lady, the elegant Mrs Turia Campbell, *née* Princess Galitzine. I doubt if she had ever before submitted to the rigours of day-to-day office hours – hours that owing to the exigencies of a news programme were likely to be extended into the evenings. She became a very able senior member of the Talks producing staff, conscientious and wise.

Another of my friends came to the BBC through what should surely now be named 'the Corporation's Great Decision'. Rosemary Jellis graduated from Lady Margaret Hall at Oxford in 1940. This was when one of the several BBC committees studying the implications of war on broadcasting came to the momentous conclusion that it would be essential to try and employ more women than hitherto to replace male members of staff called up into the forces.

The prejudice against appointing women to any kind of senior post was widespread at the time in many organisations besides the BBC, so it was understandable that the first attempt to do so now seems a trifle limited – but it was a beginning. A few of the women's university colleges (including those at Oxford and Cambridge) were approached, asking the principals for a short list of about six likely candidates from each to form a staff pool of women. Rosemary Jellis was one of those chosen, and in due course she gravitated to the *Reel* as a producer.

This was at an intense phase of the war – and Rosemary Jellis appeared as one of the coolest and calmest of the entire team. It was often essential to scrap an entire programme to 'catch up with the news', devising a completely new edition with less than an hour to go before transmission. Ending the programme was even more difficult.

Rosemary, stop watch in hand, edited the reams of reports now pouring in by simply covering unwanted paragraphs with her hand as she sat by the sightreading narrator.

It was the exigencies of war that made professionals of us all, yet we remained a group of very unalike people, from different countries and backgrounds. I can think of a scriptwriter incapable of writing a script for a programme in the small hours (and who can blame him?) without a whisky bottle, full or empty, on the table in front of him. If it was full, he consumed a considerable amount. If empty, it was a solace to him to bemoan the fact. Yet, either way, he would turn in a lively accurate script, almost without fail.

Even these quick impressions of colleagues demonstrate that the whole unit was working well, and undistinguished as our surroundings were they suited us. 200 Oxford Street acquired a special atmosphere of informality; many people preferred to work there than in the loftier environment of Broadcasting House – and in war-time I felt the same. The studios were functional and non-committal in décor, quite unlike some of the remaining studio 'rooms' of early days in B H which were furnished to look like a gentleman's study or library, presumably in an attempt to make some speakers feel thoroughly at home.

I soon learnt that most of our contributors seemed pleased to dispense with formality. Once when the lifts were out of order I was slightly surprised to see King Haakon of Norway modestly step aside to allow a producer in a tearing hurry to go first down the stairs.

For me the place seemed an impregnable fortress. Most of my work was out of doors in night or day assignments with a recording truck. I never for one moment feared that '200' would be hit. Later, as a war correspondent returning from Europe, it felt the safest place I knew and, with such massive protection, this may well have been so.

As for my contributions, it was obvious that, being the first woman reporter, I must work my way up to the hard news stories gradually – indeed I was glad to be given the lesser news items in my first months on the staff. There was little or no prejudice against me among my male colleagues: they were friendly and helpful and only slightly patronising. This was due surely to the deep-down attitude at the time towards 'the woman's angle'. Some say it still prevails. This implies strict limitations on the kind of journalism open to women. I found myself dealing with war-time versions of fashion: 'how to get the best out of clothing coupons', 'an economic way of getting your hair cut' (it was known as the 'Liberty cut'). There were also the opening of day nurseries and crêches, flower shows, dog shows, cat shows, and endless ways of cooking war-time delicacies like snoek.

Luckily for me, the pressure of events and the departure of several more of our war correspondents to the battle fronts of North Africa and Italy, as well as a growing scarcity of dog and cat shows, brought me closer to more exciting assignments.

One of the most important was to report on the extent of damage to people and property caused by the flying bombs and later the rockets aimed to fall in and around London: the V1s and the V2s. This was a strange and macabre experience. We never knew in what district we might find ourselves at the end of each day. The rockets proved to be the more sinister of the two hazards. For some time they were surrounded in mystery. Entries in my diary reveal how little was known:

8 Sept, 1944. Friday. 49 Queen Anne Street. 11p.m. About 7p.m. this evening there was a very loud explosion in the distance. I was measuring a new rug for the flat. Various explanations put out in bulletins. It might have been a gas main explosion? Surely not. Or

The author talking to a lady whose home had been destroyed by a V. bomb (*B.B.C. copyright*)

a petrol barge blown up in the Thames? No alert.

12 Sept. At 6.15 this morning, awakened by a noise very like the Friday one. Rumour rife in London that three people were killed in Chiswick on Friday. It was officially stated that this morning's bang was 'an enemy projectile', but for some reason the name 'Flying Gas Main' seems to be catching on . . .

14 Sept. Am now authorised by MOI and the Min. of Home Security to make recordings at the scene of these incidents – so today have had my first look at what a 'V2' can do. Went with recording car to Walthamstow, the latest incident.

A nasty mess. About 600 houses damaged – about twenty totally demolished. Eight fatal casualties to date. ARP Controller was very calm – on the surface, at least. Helpful and remarkably free from red tape. Some people quite bitter that 'no one told us to go to the shelter'.

In all some 500 rockets hit London in seven months. In some ways our method of covering these incidents was a bit naïve. The routine procedure was to contact the engineer assigned to the job on arrival at the office, and then *wait*. Wait to hear an explosion and telephone the police for directions. Sometimes when the police had not yet been informed, we would start out in the direction of the bang. On one occasion, when *en route* for somewhere else on a Saturday afternoon, there was a terrifying explosion – we were barely four minutes away by car from probably the worst rocket incident in London. This was at New Cross, Deptford, a direct hit on Woolworth's killing over 100 people. Naturally I always dreaded what we would find when we got there.

There was a certain grim routine marking the beginning, the middle and the end of a mopping-up operation. There nearly always came a point when the extent of a tragedy seemed to be summed up by the number of utility sackcloth shrouds being unloaded from the equipment trucks. (For some years I was unable to look at that particular fabric without recoiling at the memory.)

Most civil defence workers by that time had been disciplined by nearly five years of war. As one of many eyewitnesses of countless London air raids, fire-bomb attacks, flying bombs and rockets, as well as the shelling of Dover (where I spent the best part of three months), I find it remarkable that in Britain I never encountered any worker who had been hardened or brutalised by the repetition of dreadful situations. Unfailingly, British rescuers dealt with fatalities with tact, dignity and skill.

We were constantly visiting areas of destruction. Much of what we recorded was banned for broadcasting by the censor, as revealing too much information to the enemy about the damage. I was puzzled when so much material was unused by the BBC that I continued to be sent on these melancholy assignments.

Some time later I discovered that these recordings were not entirely wasted. Many had been sent to the Home Office and/or the MOI for some kind of analysis of the morale of survivors spoken to soon after an occurrence. I believe this formed part of studies being made of rescue techniques and the speed with which the services could be mustered to help save lives. How curious to think that some fragment of a recording of a V2 incident could have played its part in the coining of the famous phrase 'Britain can take it'.

Looking back on those grim and momentous days of 1944, it should be remembered that things were not grim all the time: in fact it was possible to keep a sense of proportion as so many aspects of life in Britain went on in spite of the war. It was very civilised. I once spent a fascinating all-night session watching the 50,000th edition of *The Times* going to press in November 1944, an event which appears to have even greater historical significance now than it did at the time.

We began our recordings in the composing room, where for 159 years *The Times* had been published – without a day missed. Groups of compositors could be seen bending over large frames, locking up the final forme of tomorrow's newspaper and fitting the type that looked like 'looking-glass writing' at that stage.

With his eye on the clock, a senior official known as 'Imperial Father of the Chapel' was waiting to blow a whistle to indicate to the whole room that *The Times* had gone to press. His curious title goes back to ancient days when printing was carried out in monasteries. At the present time the title could be translated as Chief Shop Steward. The Father of the Chapel had worked at Printing House Square for nearly 30 years, and thought he had seen at least 10,000 editions through the press. Conversation with interesting information on the techniques of producing a newspaper was almost impossible for the throbbing of the machinery. The tapping and thundering in different keys was so great that we retreated to the office of the overseer for the long blowing of a whistle indicating the finish of that part of the job. The overseer came to the door having extracted the very first copy of the 50,000th issue as a souvenir for me. It was faultless and the ink was already dry! I immediately looked at the headlines – good news on the whole: AMERICANS AND FRENCH CROSS THE RHINE, THE THRUST AT STRASBOURG, TOKYO BOMBED BY DAY. Then a dignified voice called: 'Gentlemen, the first edition of the 50,000th issue of *The Times* has gone to press – long live *The Times*.'

The next sequence in the nightly routine was the swift packing of bundles of papers rolling down a chute to catch the train to Scotland at King's Cross. Someone next to me said loudly: 'We never miss trains – not even in the Blitz.' A great feeling of loyalty permeated the occasion and memories were sharp and clear whatever question was asked. I asked someone if he remembered any of the news stories at the time he joined the paper. Without a pause he rattled off: 'Oh, yes, there was Peter Painter and the Sydney Street Siege – Mr Churchill came out to see that, the loss of the Titanic, the outbreak of the 1914 war.' He paused. 'I think the strangest of all was the arrival of Rudolf Hess in Scotland.'

When London theatres opened again with regular five o'clock performances sometime towards the end of 1943, it was impossible not to feel the beginnings of normality returning. Mary Pugh and I went to as many shows as possible. In one of the theatre bars, I happened to meet George Speaight, well known as a collector of those attractive Victorian tinsel portraits of famous actors and actresses with model toy theatres to go with them. I had started a modest collection before the war, and searched the junk shops wherever I went, but toy theatres were far from my mind in 1943. George was bemoaning the fact that the most famous little shop that made such things, Pollock's, was about to close down.

This sent me flying to Hoxton in the hope of a little story that had nothing to do with the war, with the possibility that there might still be something to buy. I first went on a very cold January day. The battered shabby old shutters were up at 73 Hoxton Street, indicating that the closing down had already taken place. Someone in the neighbouring shop urged me to come back, with a vague: 'Yes, she's open sometimes.' I returned next day and waited, walking up and down the street for over an hour. Then an elderly woman across the street tripped on the kerbside and gashed her knee quite badly. I offered to take her home, stopping to buy iodine and a bandage on the way. She was cold and tired and irritable; I kept hoping that 'home' wasn't very far away. She stumbled on and suddenly stopped to find her keys – right outside the door of 73. It was

Miss Pollock herself, who with her sister had kept on the shop after the death of their father twelve years before.

After first aid to the knee, I found myself helping Miss Pollock to take down the shutters, remembering with some excitement that this was the place that had inspired Robert Louis Stevenson to write the charming essay 'Penny Plain Tuppence Coloured'. A first glance at the shop window showed that the sale of cardboard model theatres and tinsel portraits was now pretty limited. The Misses Pollock had turned to haberdashery. There were buttons on cards, thimbles, hair slides, bath caps and reels of thread in profusion jumbled up alongside the two remaining Pollock theatres left in the window. It was untidy, run-down and sad. Miss Pollock was incredulous that I had come from the BBC to see her. She offered to pay for the iodine and said she was much too busy to be interviewed. 'I am closing. I want to join my sister in the country – she's already there.' I was working with my own midget tape recorder, which was fortunate as I am sure she would have been too overawed to co-operate if there had been cables trailing out to a recording truck and engineer in the street outside. Gradually she became more friendly (though irritable about the knee), and this is part of the recording we made.

> *Miss Pollock*
> I worked with my father here from the beginning, but it was his father who started it all.
> *AR*
> How was the work done?
> *Miss Pollock*
> They used to print the stuff at the back of the shop. There were theatres and sets and the book of the play and the characters . . . and separate from that there were portraits of famous actors and actresses. The tinsels and spangles were kept in these drawers (*pointing to a bank of labelled drawers, like a chemist's shop*).
> *AR*
> And who coloured the black and white prints?
> *Miss Pollock*
> Well, they hired quite a number . . . mostly young people, and to save time, each person was given just one colour, and the prints were passed along – one person filling in all the reds, another the blue, another the green and so on. In my time, it was my brother and my sister and I used to do it all, but now my brother is on government service he's not able to get down here to do it.
> *AR*
> Have you any idea who the artists were who did the original designs?
> *Miss Pollock*
> They were sketched from all the different theatres in those days. And some of the customers that used to come in would tell me they could see a Cruikshank touch about the drawings.
> *AR*
> Tell me, there's one thing I am curious to know; what are those hooks in the ceiling?
> *Miss Pollock*
> Those are where the stages were hung about 60 years ago (*warming up*), and that is where Robert Louis Stevenson knocked his top hat.

I asked Miss Pollock if I might buy a few hand-coloured prints, if she still had any left. She refused, but then insisted on giving me two first pages of hand-coloured characters of two plays, *The Waterman* and *The Miller and his Men*. 'That's just instead of the iodine,' she said firmly.

By this time there was a crowd of children and grown-ups gathering in the street outside. Word had already got round that something mysterious was going on in the dark little shop. They flocked inside. Even the customers who wanted only a hair slide seemed aware that something precious from the Victorian age would soon be gone forever. For myself, I couldn't resist quoting Stevenson to wind up the BBC item, nor can I now. 'If you love art, folly and the bright eyes of children – speed to Pollock's.'

My broadcasting role on D Day was inevitably a very modest one. The war correspondents had been formed into a special War Reporting Unit, transcending department boundaries, and collaborating with departments concerning war news. Gradually, familiar faces were disappearing from offices and nearby pubs and the canteen, as one by one they left London for final training before the assault. Each BBC correspondent had a code name to be used during these critical days. They included Frank Gillard, Pierre Lefevre, Howard Marshall, Stewart Macpherson, Guy Byam, Chester Wilmot and others. To his chagrin and humiliation Kent Stevenson, a very professional Canadian correspondent, slightly older than the rest, was left out of the first-wave team. Just sixteen days later, on 22 June, he went on a bombing raid with the RAF and lost his life.

Although I had no accreditation I was surprised and pleased to be given the code name of 'Geranium': this made me feel on the fringe of things. In relation to the tremendous matters in the balance, my assignment bordered on triviality.

We were all on constant alert for over a week before 6 June. My instructions were these: when my telephone rang at home and a voice said 'Geranium', I was to proceed as quickly as possible to Trafalgar Square to meet a recording engineer and to interview street cleaners, dustmen, early commuters, indeed anyone around, on their reactions to the opening of the Second Front. I slept in my clothes most of those nights to be certain of getting there without a moment's delay (I was still living in Queen Anne Street at the time). Sure enough, on 6 June at around 4 a.m. the telephone rang and a rather nervous voice said 'Flower Bed'. I grabbed my coat and halfway down the stairs I remembered I wasn't 'Flower Bed', I was 'Geranium'. I nearly went back to bed. We had been told not to telephone the office on D Day, but I was desperate. I rang.

Yes, it was for me – and ever since I've been amused to think of the incident as a Freudian slip.

CHAPTER SIX

Orchids in a Tin Hat

I was pleased, perturbed and frightened all at once when it was suggested by Peter Pooley that the BBC should apply to the War Office for me to become a fully accredited war correspondent to go into Europe. Pleased, as I took it as a compliment, perturbed at the thought of tougher conditions than I had known before, and very frightened in spite of the experiences I had known in Britain. I had been scared stiff on many assignments here at home, not always of the enemy but of the things that had to be done . . . and of what people would think of you if you didn't do them well. Things like climbing ladders, particularly a rope ladder up the side of an American liberty ship in a rough sea off Milford Haven to report on the duties of the WRNS boarding officers. They went on board to check the documentation of merchant ships about to enter port. Sailing instructions were described as being given 'Officer by hand', which meant top secret, and the captain's confidential books had to be inspected to ensure that the correct up-to-date charts were available for entering the harbour. If necessary, a WRN petty officer could pilot the ship in to safety.

The ship we visited had never sailed into Milford Haven before. I felt the laborious climb up the ladder was worth doing to see the look of astonishment on the captain's face when he first saw women in smart naval uniform negotiating the ship's rails with agility to stand to attention before him. He was even more puzzled to see me, a flustered female *not* in uniform, slowly bringing up the rear. To celebrate, he gave us all a tot of rum, which made coming down for me a piece of cake.

While waiting for my accreditation to go abroad, I was fortunate to cover the most exciting part of one of the great stories of the war: Churchill's plan for prefabricated harbours, code name Mulberry, to be towed across the Channel to Arramanches and other French ports. It was to be ladders again for me but no matter, I wouldn't have missed it for anything. To this day the enterprise fills me with insular pride at what the services and British industry achieved at one of the most crucial phases of the war. In May 1940, after the fall of France, civil engineering designers and specialists on ports and harbours from the Royal Engineers began work together with a top secret organisation to make it possible for the project to be carried out. Work sites and accommodation had to be found or built, many along the west coast of Scotland, roads had to be widened, railway lines extended to dock sites for the assembly of materials and marshalling of resources.

The story was released to the British press on 30 October, 1944 — by then the Germans were well aware of its success and it was no longer a secret. I know little or nothing of civil engineering, but the time factor for the actual construction was certainly acute. Each section had a critical deadline and here British industry achieved the almost impossible. For example, in spite of all difficulties, the concrete floating caissons (breakwaters), aggregating 600,000 tons, were completed in only 26 working weeks.

To stand on the harbour top deck, to see part of the work being done on a caisson replacement and to meet dozens of people who had been working almost to a standstill for 26 weeks is one of my unforgettable recollections. There *was* a considerable height to be climbed up one of the caissons floating in a London dock. I was lent a donkey coat to keep warm and with a rope round my waist I clambered slowly upwards. It felt like climbing up the blank wall of a grey concrete block of flats.

At least I managed not to stop halfway: for me, the secret of ladders is to keep going, otherwise it may be necessary to send for the fire brigade to get me down – like a kitten up a tree. There was much more climbing to come, this time inside the caisson, down, down, down to a narrow platform running through the centre of the structure partitioned in bulkheads each side to prevent flooding. Here I met and recorded interviews with engineers, scaffolders, steel fixers, carpenters and concreters. Military and naval personnel apart, some 20,000 workmen were on the job in the wet or dry docks of the ports all over Britain.

It was amazing the way the project was kept secret. As each man got off the train at his work destination, he was met by a shop steward, vetted at a police station, given ration cards and passes for the district as well as the dock site, and then driven to a works Nissen hut camp, supervised by security police. They impressed on each individual that he must never talk about the work he was doing – not even to the folks at home. In fact very few of the men had more than an inkling of what they were building, except that it was likely to be something connected with the Second Front. Certainly they had no idea at all of what seems to me the most daring, audacious aspect of this risky undertaking. Parts of the structures had to be ready well in advance of D Day and were actually moved to the far shore at the same time as the first assault troops went in: this was to enable the building of the harbours to be carried out during the first days of the invasion. No wonder there was a hurry. One concreter told me that on occasions it was essential to work 28 hours without a stop except for meal breaks. Wet weather was a problem for the concreting: 'If it cleared at all, we would work right through the night to keep going so that we could start off on the right foot next day.'

At the industrial management level, the greatest factor in the carrying out of the stupendous task was that British consulting engineering firms agreed to pool their resources and pull together as one body. Eight leading firms of consulting engineers and over 25 contractors concentrated on the one great project. They incorporated experience, ingenuity, the will to co-operate and above all grim determination not to fail the country. With the exception of some imported timber all the material that went to the making of the Mulberry harbours was 'home grown' and included nearly 400,000 tons of crushed stone, 200,000 tons of sand, 100,000 tons of cement, 7,000,000 feet of scaffolding and 60 miles of steel wire rope! I suppose it could only happen in a war.

It is curious that some clothes, especially uniforms, need to get 'worn in' to look right. When I flew to Brussels, travelling in a Dakota of RAF Transport Command, I was wearing for the first time a khaki battle dress top that looked slightly too large and much too new. Happily the skirt and the beret and the brown calf shoes were fine and I was self-consciously pleased with the dark green and gold chevrons on the shoulders neatly indicating 'British War Correspondent' with the rank of Junior Commander. I felt rather new all round, for this was my first ever flight in an aeroplane, a bumpy one at that. The plane was stripped bare to the aluminium fuselage, for troop carrying. We sat on long benches facing each other, as in an old-fashioned tram. To my great good fortune, I found I was sitting opposite the very well-known novelist, biographer and then war correspondent Alan Moorehead and his wife, both in uniform. We soon began talking and they were flabbergasted that I was on my first flight. I had to explain that my father always insisted on boats and trains for me coming home from school or holidays before the war. They then invited me to dinner that evening to celebrate the flight. This was certainly a splendid beginning, for we also discovered we were to be billeted for one night in the same hotel, the four-star Palace, now requisitioned as an officers' leave hotel and also used as a one-night stand for people in transit. I was given a large double room with private bath, but the starriness ended there. There was no hot water, no mattress and no linen of any kind. The Germans had commandeered all the mattresses long ago, but the *valet de chambre* kept reiterating, with regard to the disappearance of sheets and towels, *'Ah, c'est les Canadiens qui ont volé le linge – comme souvenirs.'* He clearly felt this to be the greater crime of the two.

The Mooreheads took me to a small restaurant on the first floor of a house in a side street not far from the Palace Hotel. We were joined by friends of the Mooreheads, two Guards officers who had been in Brussels since the capital was liberated by the Guards Armoured Division on 3 September, 1944.

M. le Patron seemed overjoyed to see us and immediately produced two bottles of pink champagne to welcome us. (This was my first taste of the *pink* variety, but I said nothing; one first in a day seemed quite enough!) Someone said cynically: 'Don't forget he was probably dishing this out to the Germans in exactly the same way last August.' The evening was my introduction to the most extraordinary black market imaginable, in caviar, steak, asparagus, *marrons glacés* in syrup, and liqueurs. The restaurant was prepared for many eventualities. The room at one end looked nearly double its size thanks to a series of handsome panelled mirrors covering the wall from floor to ceiling. 'Each one is a screen really,' said one of the Guardees calmly. 'You see, British serving officers are supposed to eat in the officers' mess – here we could be raided by military police. It's said there is a room for at least 50 people behind those screens in an emergency. But raids don't happen very often, thank goodness. Apparently, the Germans would take over the whole of the space behind there as special private dining rooms equipped with *chaises longues*.'

It was an amusing and informative evening. When I went back to the Palace Hotel, I put my sleeping bag on the bare springs of the bed and slept well.

I was awakened early by the sound of crashing litter bins outside. Two skinny children were scavenging for any scraps of food they could find. The younger was concentrating on picking up a few bits of coal or coke that must have fallen off a lorry.

My first assignment was to go and stay a week with the first mixed ack-ack battery of the Royal Artillery, Battery 485, on a gun site. The public relations department of 21 Army Group sent me by utility truck accompanied by a handsome Guards officer as conducting officer. I still don't know where the gun site was but guess it was somewhere north of Liège, for I remember a journey there later in a lorry with about twenty ATS to visit the public baths – officially speaking, we were supposed not to know where we were.

This was the first time that British servicewomen had served as combatants in a war overseas. I had been to see them off at Southampton nearly three months before, but as my accreditation had not come through then I couldn't go with them. In this I was lucky, since I missed at least part of the worst winter of the war. On arrival, they found the site inches deep in snow. In the first few days there was a minute ration of coal. Then they had to forage for their own supplies. Sledges were improvised out of duckboards or

The author as a war correspondent, (*B.B.C. copyright*)

corrugated iron, and timber from a nearby wood was dragged back to the camp with the help of some of the local inhabitants. In no time at all there was a friendly relationship between the battery and the children and teenagers living in the district. They were always offering little souvenirs, such as small carved wooden sabots made at home, hopefully to be bartered for soap or chocolates. Eggs, too, were sometimes on offer, probably the most welcome transaction for the ATS. As for the snow, this was regularly melted down for washing; water was short and I was told enthusiastically that 'snow is lovely soft water – good for the hair'.

Like most gun sites, the one in Belgium was typical of the average ack-ack battery at home. Its very nature transformed the immediate area into something functional and bleak, rows and rows of rusty brown Nissen huts, a NAAFI block, a concrete command post surrounded by guns, with far distant views of a few fields and woods.

The snow had vanished. My problem now was a very high wind that made it difficult to record anything, especially in a Nissen hut: night and day it made a terrific row on the corrugated iron roofs. The wind, however, was welcomed by everyone else, as it helped to dry the mud. Mud really was the major problem; they had granite chippings laid down outside some doors, but even so it was ankle deep everywhere and knee deep in places. Even duckboards sank.

I need not have worried about wind and mud. The BBC was responsible for an insuperable difficulty. I had been supplied with one of the first models of a type of recording gear said to be 'portable'. It looked like an early portable gramophone with a handle to wind up the spring. With it was an issue of large blank acetate discs. The instructions said that a cutting needle was supplied as well as one to play back the recording. It was imperative for good results that the blank discs be kept at reasonable room temperature! I attempted to solve this by wearing about half a dozen discs under the blouse of my battle dress (the only time I was glad it was so roomy), but there was a lot of teasing in the camp about this because it made me look a very curious shape in front. I went on trying to make the thing work and it was really not very efficient. I had no engineer to help me. What I did not know was that all the men had rejected this terrible bit of equipment and refused to use it. There was even an apocryphal story that Richard Sharp, the war correspondent in Burma, threw one of these 'portables' out of a window down into a crowded street. Mercifully no one was killed but his gesture of frustration and rage put an end to it and nobody used them after that.

But this didn't solve my problem. I knew well that if I appealed to London they would probably send out an identical machine thinking: how like a woman, you see, she can't make it work, and so on. Then I remembered that Frank Gillard was in charge of the BBC forward area unit at Eindhoven. I sent him an SOS through Army Signals and sat down to wait. Within a day and a half, I suddenly saw the familiar and welcome sight of a War Reporting Unit recording truck lumbering cautiously over rough ground to dodge the mud. Even more welcome was the smiling face of one of the BBC's senior engineers, Harvey Sarney. We had frequently worked together during the shelling of Dover. He brought a message with him from Frank: 'When you've finished, why not join us here? Plenty of stories for you.'

Frank did me proud. We stayed on at the battery for several days and recorded again all the pieces I had tried to record without success. In fact we did much more than that. Everything was made easy for me without having to cope with the technical side. I got to know people better and to see the gun site as a little self-contained world of its own, getting on very successfully with its own little bit of the war.

I was beginning to understand how very different ethics could be in a country that had been occupied. For example, part of one Nissen hut was turned into a bar where the men and women could read the papers, listen to a radio and have a glass of beer or lemonade. Unlike the drab government issue furniture elsewhere, the 'bar' was furnished with several expensive, very ugly easy chairs and a sofa, all upholstered in a startling shade of green moquette. I enquired about their origin and found it hard to hide my astonishment when a young officer said briefly: 'Oh, Belgian collaborators with the Germans. One of the farmers round here told us about them. We needed chairs very badly for the bar – so we went and commandeered them. They took it quite well. Priceless.' We also made recordings at a dance held in a nearby village hall that was like something out of the French film *La Ronde* . . . the bit where the local boys were too shy to ask the girls to dance. Admittedly the ATS looked rather formidable muffled up against the cold in khaki.

What was much more important was that we were on the spot on several occasions when the guns went into action, generally at night. There were plenty of 'call-outs', usually in the daytime, but nearly always the targets crossed out of range or crashed before reaching our area.

There is no doubt that action has a tonic effect on morale, and the battery had a number of successes. Unfortunately I was not allowed to give exact figures then and, as for safety's sake I did not enter them in the little diary I was keeping at the time, I can't give them here, either.

When an alarm siren went, indicating the approach of enemy aircraft, it was impressive to see the gunners leap on to the gun platforms; with the sirens still sounding, the girls on operational duties would come tearing out from the ATS manning huts, struggling into greatcoats and rushing across to their instruments, either out in the cold night air on the predictors and view-finders and -sound rangers or with the radar section in the command post itself. It was said that sometimes it was possible to be ready for action in ten seconds.

The shattering sound of heavy guns firing together was enough to startle anyone, but the ATS on the gun sites were well used to it, for this battery had been defending London during the Blitz of 1941 and later, during the flying bomb attacks, many of the same young girls were on duty on the south coast of England.

To be on the operational side was exciting and interesting, but for most of the troops life seemed to be one long fight against wet, cold and monotony with a lot of hard work in very uncomfortable conditions. I mean the cooks, the clerks, the orderlies who fetched and carried and did unmentionable 'sanitary duties'. Yet in spite of everything I honestly believe that no one wanted to be anywhere else at that moment of the war. It was their St Crispin's Day.

London, I'm glad to say, were very pleased with our recordings. We sent back enough for two programmes and they were both used round the clock.

There was an unexpected sequel. A few days after leaving the battery I was astonished to hear large chunks of our recordings coming from a local radio station that frequently broadcast German propaganda to the British troops. The programme was introduced by a woman calling herself Mary of Arnhem. Her comments on the women of the ATS were scurrilous in the extreme: 'We all know the kind of services they are giving the British troops', and inferring that their presence in Belgium was a sure sign that decadent Britain was losing the war. Nation shall speak peace unto nation . . . At that time, to hear one's own voice coming back from a German station was positively macabre.

Harvey had been signalled on to another assignment when we finished at the gun site. My problem was how to get to Eindhoven. Once again I appealed to the public relations office and I was advised to get to Brussels somehow or other because yes, there was a jeep going to Eindhoven tomorrow with a war artist who wanted to make a detour if possible into Germany to do some sketches on the way. Did I mind a bit of a detour? No, I did not, and it turned out to be quite an exciting one. We met by arrangment early next morning in Brussels. The war artist was a short sturdy man, nearing middle age, with army cut features and a small bristly reddish moustache. He was one of the most well-known and popular figures in the world of journalistic art: Captain Bryan de Grineau, whose charcoal and pen and ink illustrations of battle scenes filled the pages of innumerable weekly magazines in Britain and America. His father had been a caricaturist and so Bryan as a youth had had a rigorous art training in etching and lithography. In the First World War, he served as a captain in the Royal Field Artillery, sketching and painting in his spare time. Then in 1939 he was commissioned as an official war artist to the *Illustrated London News*.

I think most people of that period remember seeing his illustrations in the pages of back numbers of the *Illustrated London News* in dentists' waiting rooms and elsewhere and wondering, as I did, how this artist, who could be accurate, factual and full of imagination at the same time, managed to keep photography at bay. His style was easily recognisable, faintly old-fashioned, and part of the tradition of depicting battles full of action: blazing tanks, mortar shells bursting in the sky, everything happening at once — crashing aeroplanes and for good measure a parachute or two descending gracefully to the torn-up earth. I often wondered if it was all thought up in the studio and now there was the chance that I might see how it was done.

By the time his drawing board and artist's materials, together with my kitbag and the dud recording machine, were stowed in the jeep there wasn't much room for us. Moreover we were accompanied by a Guards conducting officer (obligatory on such cross-country trips). Our driver was Corporal Green, to whom we were to owe a lot for his quick-wittedness in action when for a short while we found ourselves in a very awkward situation indeed.

The drive by a circuitous route to Eindhoven via Roermond, now in British hands, filled me with unexpected first impressions, for those days spent on the gun site had given me a sense of isolation from the cities. Civilian life was struggling on as best it could. On that early morning, at the door of almost every house women were going through the housework routine of shaking out the mats on the cobbles and scrubbing the front steps, although the streets had not been cleared of bomb damage. Bricks and pieces of concrete were scattered over pathways, broken glass lay in a green river along the pavements. With a monstrous insulting irony the only things that looked clean and new (and ugly) were the terracotta replicas of some of the statues and war memorials(!) put up by the Germans when they took away originals for the metal. There were other even odder contrasts to the look of British towns and cities. Some of the shop windows were full of expensive luxuries we hadn't seen for years: perfumes, jewellery, watches, and above all wonderful flower-shop windows filled with exotic plants that must have needed much hothouse cosseting, orchids, azaleas and poinsettias in baskets, dressed up with bows of coloured silk ribbons.

But the truth was that all these things were utterly subsidiary. Belgium and Holland were in the clutches of the great war machine that was rolling across them. We drove for miles along uneven cobbled roads, generally with two wheels in the gutter to give room for the stream of military traffic coming the other way. We bumped and jolted along, sometimes tacked on to the end of a convoy of British tanks going north. When the cobbles ran out we slithered and churned through potholes in the all-pervading mud.

I saw my first burnt-out German tank at Louvain. From then on the edges of the fields were strewn with burnt-out cars, German guns and the bloated corpses of cattle and sheep. We passed through Diest and Hasselt and caught a glimpse of women with shopping bags seemingly quite impervious to the endless stream of traffic and the ghastliness of their surroundings. We crossed the Meuse by a pontoon bridge and when we reached Sittard in Holland I had my first taste of ersatz coffee. It was brown and tasted faintly of senna, but it was hot and we were glad of it and the Dutch woman seemed so pleased to sell it to us that we all pretended it was very good indeed.

Soon after this we crossed the frontier. A large notice said: 'Germany ahead, beware spies. Drivers report all strangers in your car.' Already the area was signposted against every eventuality: 'Roads and verges cleared up to three feet'; then long stretches were cordoned off with white tape and the sinister warning: 'Mines'. We drove on through several small villages that were completely deserted, doors open, wagons half out of their sheds, as if there had been a sudden flight.

There was not a single civilian to be seen anywhere. As we drove on, the devastation and desolation were unbelievable: trees mutilated and torn up, the earth pitted with shell and mortar holes. We stopped at Geilenkirschen, which was literally razed to the ground. Bryan de Grineau, who had hardly said a word on the journey, began unstowing his gear and sat down on a canvas stool to work. I could feel he didn't want anyone looking over his shoulder, so I wandered off to read more notices and to look through a ruined window where a table was laid for a meal. A soldier's voice shouted: 'Don't touch anything, there are booby traps,' and sure enough, at my feet I saw a cheap metal fork with a thin wire attached to it, that buried itself in the earth.

De Grineau wanted more action so we drove on to Heinsberg. This was better. As we approached, three dazzlingly white parachutes were floating down to earth and a small party of US soldiers ran in front of the jeep carrying tommy guns. We had arrived as a British unit was being relieved by a company of Americans. De Grineau worked fast and with intense concentration, rather like the artists who do portrait sketches of tourists for a fiver outside the National Portrait Gallery. I thought: 'all we need now is a few shellbursts to complete the picture.' I had spotted another old notice that said 'No parking. Shelling at this point.' At once there was a sharp burst of artillery fire and I decided that perhaps it wasn't such an old notice after all. One of the GIs fixing a field telephone looked at me with mild curiosity. 'Lady, what are you doing here?' I said: 'Well, I think I'm sort of lost. Where is the front line?' He raised tired eyes and said: 'Just over that ridge about 2000 yards away. Yes, I'd say this is the front line.' There was some more 'nuisance shelling' (it was hardly a battle) and although it was now raining again de Grineau continued to work furiously, having retreated to the front seat of the jeep which at least gave some protection to his drawing, though the wet windscreen must have obscured the view. But everything was in the picture, the ruins, the running GIs, the parachutes and at least one shellburst.

Our conducting officer and Corporal Green were studying maps for the road to Eindhoven. 'Best way is straight through Roermond – it's now in British hands. Might get a cup of tea there!' I happened to have cut out one of those 'situation' maps from the *News Chronicle* that very morning. It showed Roermond in German hands. The conducting officer brushed it aside and off we started, taking the turn for Roermond. Suddenly Corporal Green pulled the driving wheel hard down to the right, the jeep swerved alarmingly and we shot down a narrow lane to slither into a conveniently shallow ditch. He turned off the engine. Nobody spoke – in fact we dared not move. Green had spotted what turned out to be three German lorries from Roermond in the oncoming traffic. I caught a glimpse of the last one as it passed and saw about ten bored-looking German soldiers standing up at the back. My relief at our lucky escape from being noticed was tremendous. I immediately thanked the corporal for his prompt action and congratulated him, but not much else was said. Our Guards officer's reputation was upheld: there was further consultation of maps and the route this time was chosen by Green. We continued down the lane and eventually took the road safely to Eindhoven. I always thought the *News Chronicle* was a reliable newspaper and much regretted its demise.

The billet at Eindhoven was a former youth hostel taken over by the British Army as billets for all the BBC men concerned with the advance of British troops through Holland. It was something of a bold undertaking for me to be there at all as the only woman, and I sensed a first slight embarrassment on my arrival. I felt sorry for myself too: it was as if I was invading the precincts of a broadcasting version of an exclusive men's club that had no ladies' entrance. But everyone was kind, solicitous and friendly and quickly understood that I needed a bath more than anything. I had not taken off my clothes for some nights at the gun site. There was no hot water, but in no time kettles were boiling in large numbers. My next essential was to wash my hair, but I didn't relish letting my hair dry slowly in rollers on a cold day in such company. But someone was very inventive. German officers had occupied the billets before us and had left behind a large number of electric pop-up toasters, far more than we needed, and a couple of these were quickly converted into an efficient if rather hazardous hairdryer. Somehow, this exercise made everyone relax. I was grateful, indeed from then on I enjoyed being there very much, and I believe my presence came to be accepted as I had worked with nearly everyone before. The correspondents' names were already famous: Frank Gillard, in charge the brilliant Australian strategist Chester Wilmot, Wynford Vaughan Thomas (an old friend), Howard Marshall, and several others who came and went on short assignments. It has always seemed to me to be the height of inequality that the names of engineers and cameramen should be less well known; their endurance and responsibilities were every bit as great as the broadcasters.' I intend to name some of them now, who were of that resolute band: the late Sid Gore, Robert (Noggs) Newman, Harvey Sarney and Bob Wade.

Among several other relics of German occupation at the hostel were some of a certain sociological interest. The hall and mess rooms were decorated with posters illustrating a number of well developed young women of the 'strength through joy' variety, bronzed by sun and wind, healthy-looking, tough good companions. Upstairs on the first floor (occupied for a short time by British gunners) decorations were less official. The girlie image here was more provocative: slender, very indoor young women, mostly nude save for a black suspender belt and becoming black stockings. It was surely rare to see the ideologies of the two combatants so close together.

At the time of my arrival the whole BBC unit was at its busiest. Preparations were in progress for the next major phase in the Holland campaign. The correspondents were attending daily briefings and confidential conferences on movements and plans for the crossing of the Rhine. Engineers and drivers were hard at work on the maintenance of vehicles and the 'tuning up' of recording equipment of all kinds. Then, in the evenings, one of the correspondents (generally Chester Wilmot, the expert on the art of war) would give those of us who were not entitled to attend the top secret meetings a simplified breakdown of what it was all about.

Of course the work I did at Eindhoven concerned background stories mostly, and the men were coping with hard news. There was one extraordinary story I discovered that showed how private enterprise could exist and thrive helpfully and successfully in that most organised of wars. In fact it is hard to imagine that anything could be achieved in rescue work or medical help without being attached to some official body or other, but it could and did. Two residents at Eindhoven, one an English woman who had previously worked with the Red Cross and the other an indomitable Dutch woman, realised the terrible fact that refugees flying from the enemy or a battle are quite likely to desert their elderly relatives to fend for themselves. Together these two women took over a half-ruined factory and scrounged beds and furniture of a sort from the townspeople. They then toured the district, searching for those who had been left behind. I was with them when they found a poor old blind man who had been without food and water in a cellar for some days – just left there; he hardly knew what was going on.

Food was provided by cooking anything they could find in a big tub, vegetables, fish, meat, anything: a sort of perpetual soup they called 'Soft Food'. The scene at the factory was a grim one. When I was there there were nearly 50 just-living people, senile, blind, deaf, mad and old. At least they died surrounded with compassion, and not alone. I did not stay long enough in Eindhoven to know how long this tremendous effort was kept up.

I was soon to be back on hard news again, this time on instructions direct from London in one of those cable-ese messages that can be so puzzling to interpret accurately:

AUDREY RUSSELL BBC CORRESPONDENT MQQYGR 21st ARMY GROUP PLEASE TRAVEL ANTWERPWARDS PROREPORT CITY'S FIGHT CONTRAVEE BOMBS ESPECIALLY GENERALLY RATHER THAN DETAILED PART PLAYED BY MIXED AA BATTERIES STOP ANXIOUS DESPATCHES DETAILED PARTICIPANT BATTLE STOP DEARTH HERE FACTS AND FIGURES IF VOICEABLE MATERIAL UNOBTAINABLE OTHERWISE SEND JUDICIOUS MIXTURE STOP ATTEMPT REPORTAGE EXPORT IF PERMITTED SECURITY STOP

Well, we knew for certain that Antwerp was by then in British hands but that the Germans had mounted a very heavy attack of flying bombs in a desperate attempt to put the port of Antwerp out of action. This was being magnificently defended by the Royal Artillery in much the same way as in Dover and the south coast of England, where a large number of V1s had been knocked out in the air before the fatal 'cut-out'. Unfortunately, in Antwerp many V1s 'strayed' from their targets, causing heavy casualties in the residential and commercial areas of the city. I remember counting as many as seven flying bombs at once against the sky converging towards the city and suburbs. Frank Gillard was against my going at all and even protested to London that it was 'just too tough'. But London was adamant; Harvey and I set off next morning and ran into the worst week of flying bomb attacks on Antwerp of the war. When we arrived the city was in a state of shock after a direct hit the day before on the Rex Cinema with the loss of 500 lives.

Chester Wilmot was anxious for news of some Belgian friends and gave me their

Antwerp address written on a large can of tinned milk to give them if we ever found them.

We were not allowed near the port to make recordings but, looking over the gates, we saw the place was crammed with ships, with goose-necked cranes moving steadily to and fro, and dock workers shifting heaving cargoes on to trucks and lorries. The port was being kept open, but the civilian side of the story was different. We drove to somewhere in the suburbs, parked the trucks and walked around the ruined streets to be appalled and horrified by the sounds of agonised cries coming sometimes loudly and sometimes faintly from the ruins. During the occupation the Belgian civil defence units had been curtailed and were now so limited that each 'incident' had to take its turn and generally help could only come too late. Worst of all, there appeared to be no proper air raid warden service. It was impossible not to compare it with our own organisation at home where wardens made it their business as far as possible to know how many people were living in the sector of the street they were looking after, how many of them stayed at home and how many went regularly to a shelter. To arrive at a scene of destruction with little or no idea of how many might be buried underneath did not bear thinking about. There was no attempt at setting up an Incident Enquiry Bureau either, as was carried out so magnificently by the WVS in Britain. Dazed civilians could be seen straggling around desperate for news of relatives and friends, and sometimes having to be restrained from scraping away at the rubble with their bare hands to reach the cries below.

The most cheerful discovery we made on that ghastly day was something to be proud of. We were directed to another quarter of the city to meet a British team of civil defence workers who had volunteered to help out the Belgians. Although a small contingent, they were veterans of London, Dover, Coventry, Edinburgh, Bristol and elsewhere, and they were expert at the job. The Belgians enthusiastically took instructions from our men, and the group leader summed up the difficulties: 'Most of the débris is just dust, powdered bricks. The continental brick is different from the English one; it becomes pulverised by the weight of the building and there are very few cavities made in the rubble to give anyone the chance of getting any life-giving air.' He was full of sympathy for the Belgians. 'They've been suppressed for nearly four years, they're undernourished and can't work long hours . . . but they do their best.'

Today we know the figures. British heavy ack-ack guns sent up over 531,000 rounds of ammunition and, a result, only 211 flying bombs fell in the port area. The civilians were not so lucky. About 4883 V1s were fired at Antwerp, with an occasional rocket thrown in. Of these, approximately 2000 were destroyed.

The attack we were in suddenly stopped after nearly 21 hours. I must say I was glad to be recalled to Eindhoven on a cold February day in 1945. When we had signed our names in the Town Major's office to say we were leaving, I suddenly remembered the tinned milk. The can had been rolling about the back of the truck throughout our visit. So we set off to find the house, which was in one of the main thoroughfares. It seemed to be empty. Looking through the ground floor windows we saw shining, well polished parquet floors, high ceilings and bare rooms. We were about to turn away when Harvey noticed a cellar door ajar. We ran down the steps and knocked. After a significant pause a grey-haired man appeared. He relaxed a bit when I gave Chester Wilmot's name. All the furniture was stored in the cellars and the family of four had been living in two basement rooms. It felt as if they had been living in silence together for months, for it was hard to make friendly conversation. They spoke good English but were very reserved and quiet. Their two children never spoke at all. You would have thought the Germans were still there — it was a strange private world they dared not leave. The mother was obviously very house-proud. She told me she often went upstairs during the night to polish the floors in the dark. They were now waiting for the V bombs to stop before moving back to normal. They both refused to be interviewed but said that, yes, the food problem was better, though there was no butter or margarine to be had yet. We were thanked politely for the milk, but I must say the large tin began to look very small for two adults and two children, a boy and a girl.

As we rose to leave, the father said: 'The schools are closed so we give the children lessons every day and go to bed before it gets dark so that we can sleep as long as possible. Like that, you see, we remain calm.' I have often wondered how long it took for that brave family to be released from the psychiatric distress caused by enemy occupation.

Not long after Antwerp I developed a throat infection that put me temporarily out of action, and as there was a chance to go home on leave I took it at once. It wasn't a serious infection but in a war you are either on duty or an official casualty, perhaps in hospital even.

I stayed the night once again at the Palace Hotel, feeling a bit of a humbug as the throat was much better. I had been asked out to dinner by a major whom I had met a few times – and liked. He was a regular Army officer and I assessed him as a confirmed bachelor.

I was sure we would have a delicious (black market) meal at the Fourchette d'Argent, but was amazed to find that the evening was to include a proposal of marriage as well. I thought it was a joke at first, but then felt abashed when I realised the poor man was serious. I extricated myself as gently and kindly as I could. We did not know each other at all well. In spite of promises to see me off the next day, he was evidently too crushed to do so and sent his driver instead. He turned out to be the intelligent, courageous young Corporal Green of the Roermond incident. When we got to the airport he dealt with my baggage, saluted, and produced from under a seat in the jeep a superb spray of Odontoglossum orchids – indeed, a bouquet. He then made a little speech: 'Madam, I am very sorry things are turning out like this. The Major has asked me to give you these, Madam. May I say it has been a pleasure for me to meet you and I hope perhaps you may be coming back to us sometime.' We shook hands and I nearly kissed the Corporal.

On the journey home, I whiled away the time arranging the flowers in my tin hat. One of the RAF aircrew found some cottonwool in a first aid box and he suggested moistening it with water to wrap around the stems to keep them fresh. It was an unusual and spectacular display when we'd done but, on landing at Northolt, I overheard a customs official say disparagingly: 'That's how women go to war. I ask you – orchids in a tin hat.'

CHAPTER SEVEN

Happy Days

There may be a few 'armchair warriors' who consider that by returning to Britain in March 1945 I missed being on the spot for one of the most important campaigns of the Western Front, the great simultaneous drive by British, Canadian and American troops across the Rhine. It was coincidental that I wasn't there, but I shall always believe that there is a limit to how useful a woman war correspondent can be — in fact, I have sometimes felt that it is a kind of self-indulgence to try to push oneself too much into the thick of things for the sake of being there. Indeed, I have sometimes been embarrassed by the concern shown to me by people who have possibly risked their lives to escort me or to point out some hazard I hadn't spotted.

So I have few regrets about it. The sore throat turned to 'flu on my return, and when I got well I worked at 200 Oxford Street again, chiefly interviewing the immense floating population of Commonwealth visitors from other broadcasting organisations over here for consultations on future plans. There were also plenty of stories to be gathered from nameless resistance workers and survivors of Auschwitz and Belsen, and there were tales of great scientific achievement. One future celebrity was the inventor of the jet engine, Frank Whittle. Peter Pooley kept a visitors' book that became packed with signatures of people both famous and unknown, whose voices were heard all over the world. The last entry was made by Dame Laura Knight who came to describe her experiences as a war artist at the Nuremberg trials. She had been impressed by the demeanour of Goering. Pen in hand she impulsively asked me: 'Would you like a sketch? *Dare* I do it straight on the page?' I assured her that she should and the result was subtle and very like. I returned the visitors' book to Peter's office and he was most pleased about the Goering sketch. Unfortunately, someone forgot to put this unique record of 1940–46 under lock and key that evening. The album was never seen again.

I went on various short missions by air with the RAF into Europe. By spring the tasks were changing from the belligerent to the merciful and the celebratory. We went dropping food parcels to the hungry civilians in Holland; we attended Allied Nations' Day in liberated Norway when King Haakon took the salute at a march past of British, American and Russian troops in Oslo. The Russian soldiers had been held prisoners in northern Norway by the Germans and were liberated in June by the Americans.

A Victory party in Oslo went on for days and as many nights. We were showered with flowers and invitations to return to Oslo on holiday, once things got back to normal. Anyone in a British uniform found it impossible to walk down a street without shaking hands or being hilariously hugged and kissed by the public at large. One feature of the celebrations was a Norwegian concert held in honour of the Allies. They persuaded a few of the Russians to dance, and a group of Americans to sing negro spirituals. The tribute to Britain was fairly solemn and a little dated. A star Norwegian actor recited Kipling's 'If' with background music of 'Land of Hope and Glory' to accompany him.

One very important assignment led me to what most of my friends think is probably the most laughable *contretemps* of my career – at the time it was rather unnerving. It concerned my loss of identity when I flew in a procession of Lancaster bombers sent to collect small parties of British ex-prisoners of war, who because of some mishap or other had missed the main convoys bringing them home. They were waiting to be repatriated at airstrips in various parts of France and Germany.

We landed first at Juvincourt in France to pick up a small group of about fifteen ex-prisoners who were waiting for us, standing in line on the tarmac. Each man had been provided with a small kitbag that easily held all he possessed. Some seemed unwilling to part with the bundles they had carried with them out of captivity, attaching importance to bits and pieces they might never need again, such as an empty cardboard box and rusty tin kettle. They watched their belongings being loaded into a bomb rack and then relaxed, though their smiles did not hide their intense fatigue. We stopped off at three or four airstrips in Holland and Germany and made for home when we had a full load.

Owing to bad weather we were diverted from Northolt to Bovington in Oxfordshire. This was the beginning of my troubles. It had been arranged for a recording car team to meet me at Northolt and I had no means of communicating this change to London when we were in flight. I admit I must have looked scruffy on arrival. My uniform beret had been carried away by the slipstream at some stage. I wore a khaki tunic with a borrowed pair of blue WAAF slacks as the captain insisted on parachute regulations being observed (an impossibility if wearing a skirt).

We helped our passengers disembark and, as I left the plane, I suddenly found myself at the receiving end of a lavish distribution of cigarettes, chocolate bars and biscuits from kind ladies of the Red Cross and WVS. A tall wing commander approached, took my arm and said: 'You are our first *girl* ex-prisoner. We must make special arrangements for you to be de-loused.' Nobody would listen to me or even glance at my papers which I tried to get out of the breast pocket of my tunic. 'Please, I left England only the day before yesterday and I *must* now telephone the BBC.' There was nothing but soothing, kindly replies.

'Ah, now you are home . . . you can listen to the BBC at any time you like, and after supper you can telephone your family and say you are safe.' A screen was put round me in the hangar, my clothes were swiftly removed and I was sprayed with something all over. I was then invited to lie down on a sofa, wrapped only in a tartan rug.

The rest of the Lancasters were landing in quick succession and the hangar was getting crowded with new arrivals all needing attention of some kind. Everyone was madly busy and I kept begging for the return of my clothes. The arrival of the BBC car diverted from Northolt saved the day and led an RAMC woman doctor to believe that what I said was true. The engineers were flabbergasted to find me on a sofa wearing nothing but a tartan rug. I got my clothes back in about an hour's time – by then the ex-prisoners I wanted to interview had all heard of the ridiculous situation. In spite of great fatigue, their contributions to the BBC programme were sparkling with amusement. It became the joke of the evening.

I had always hoped that when Victory Day came I would be working in London rather than abroad. When Churchill broadcast that Germany had unconditionally surrendered, it was one minute after midnight in the early morning of 8 May, 1945. Not only was I in London, but I had little or nothing to do on that day. So I spent VE day celebrating with family and friends and wandering around various parts of London seeing what other people were doing. Overnight, flags and bunting sprouted on damaged buildings and ruins, especially in the East End. There had evidently been some forethought about official decorations. Whitehall was ablaze with the grandeur of huge 'Ministry'-size Union Jacks; in the City the Lord Mayor's residence, the Mansion House, was one of the first buildings to be 'dressed overall' with crimson banners. With shops and offices closed, the city was given up to leisure. The scene was of holiday-makers on a warm, sunny day strolling round the narrow streets, looking relieved and relaxed. There was a quiet spontaneity about everything and the strongest inclination was a wish to give thanks. People flocked to the churches. The most impressive evidence of this was at St Paul's Cathedral, where all day long informal hourly services were held. Everyone was welcome, there were no reserved seats and every seat was filled at almost every service. It must have been a marathon for the Dean, Dr W. R. Matthews, the clergy and the organist, Dr Dykes Bower. The Lord Mayor attended at midday and the final service included a relay of the King's broadcast at 9 p.m.

The Members of the House of Lords attended a service in Westminster Abbey, and the House of Commons walked in procession to their special service at St Margaret's. Here the names of MPs who had lost their lives were read out slowly and quietly by one of the Westminster canons. This roll call and the singing of the metrical version of Psalm 124 deepened the awareness of the peril from which we had been delivered.

> Ev'n as a bird out of the fowler's snare
> Escapes away, so is our soul set free.
> Broken are their nets and thus escaped me
> Therefore our help is in the Lord's great name
> Who Heaven and Earth by His great power did frame.

I have never seen anything like the crowds along the Mall and outside Buckingham Palace. Every man, woman and child was wearing a bit of red, white and blue. Once again that afternoon was quiet, gentle and relaxed. Families sat in groups on the grass in between the formal flower beds of tall, stiff, red, pink and white tulips in front of the Palace. But in spite of a vast sauntering multitude, none of the flowers were touched or trampled on. People waited patiently for the regular appearances on the balcony of the King and Queen and the two Princesses, to give them the greatest ovation they had ever known.

The mood of British crowds on VE day could never be forgotten by anyone who was part of it. There was no arrogance or rancour or jingoism in that mood: next day *The Times* described the event as 'a holiday which had been duly arranged and was to be sanely and soberly enjoyed'. Although no one was aware of it at the time, in retrospect I often wonder if it was also one of the most special days in the lives of the two youthful Princesses. It was on VE night when darkness fell and the crowds began dancing in the streets that they actually went out to join the throng, escorted by a group of friends (most of them young Guards officers), to experience liberty, freedom and anonymity on a triumphant occasion, among the people for the first and only time in their lives.

The close of the war against Japan was still some three months away and British forces were deeply committed until the end, but it was understandable that most of us in temporary war-time jobs with the BBC were already speculating on the future. My own feelings were mixed. It felt as though my life was now in two separate halves. After three

The author on the second V.E. day, 9th May 1945, recording a commentary at Ilford when the King and Queen visited the East End (*B.B.C.* copyright)

years' absence from the precarious little foothold I had been struggling to gain in the theatre, I was well aware that to go back meant starting again from scratch. However much I loved the theatre, I was a nobody there. The war forced me to exchange fantasy and fiction for real life – grim as it was. It had taught me a craft, and already I had a few ideas on the career I would like to make in the BBC.

As a stepping stone I gladly accepted an appointment on the established staff as a reporter in the newly formed Home Service reporting unit. I was the first woman to be appointed, and moved over to the first floor of Broadcasting House to share an office with Richard Sharp, Douglas Willis, Roland Fox and Richard Williams. It meant, of course, that once again I was back on minor news stories. As the war correspondents returned one by one, there was a good deal of jockeying for position in the department. However, I had other ideas. Even before I joined the Corporation I was fascinated by a much more difficult kind of broadcasting when I first heard a spontaneous description of an aerial dog fight over the Channel at Dover in July 1940. Charles Gardner was the BBC's air correspondent at that time, watching the scene from somewhere on the cliffs of Dover. Seven German aircraft were attacking a convoy of ten British ships struggling to sail up the Channel. The arrival of five Spitfires sent one Messerschmitt out of control to fall in the sea. The aircraft zoomed and veered around each other, a parachute could be seen coming through the clouds and eventually three Spitfires chased the Germans back across the Channel and the ships got through. Charles, with much emotion, reacted to the scene, but with a selective and fastidious choice of words that created a remarkable effect. It was one of the few war-time recordings to be broadcast that had not been scripted beforehand and is now preserved in Sound Archives, acknowledged to be classic radio.

When peace came, I heard superb descriptions of royal occasions by Richard Dimbleby and others, and I decided that this was what broadcasting was all about for me and that I would aim to become a commentator. I got little encouragement from my colleagues, dyed-in-the-wool news reporters to a man. Even Richard Dimbleby was prejudiced. 'Audrey, do give up this idea. There will never be a successful woman commentator. Why? They haven't got the stamina.'

The Outside Broadcast department (OBs for short) was directed by the popular Seymour Joly de Lotbiniere, known to all as 'Lobby'. I applied for any job that was suitable in OBs to come up on the BBC notice board, and while at least I was always shortlisted I consistently failed the Boards. I know that more than once I lost to a better candidate, notably to Raymond Baxter. Maybe, too, I was over-anxious at the interviews. Then happily, and very conveniently for me, the engagement was announced of Princess Elizabeth and Prince Philip on 10 July, 1947. The Royal Wedding was to take place about four months later, on 20 November. There was suddenly a quick change of opinion in the BBC hierarchy; perhaps it would be a good idea to have a woman somewhere along the route in the Outside Broadcast team – after all, someone had to describe the *wedding dress*! It was arranged that I was to be 'lent' from the News Division for this very purpose.

I was allotted one of the less important positions along the route in the Mall. This was on a roof parapet of the ivy-covered Citadel, the building where many of Churchill's defence meetings were held. To get away from the immediate war-time connotation, it was decided to say in the *Radio Times* that I was on top of Admiralty Arch (which was only a few feet away anyway). 'I do hope', said Lobby in a kindly but somewhat complacent way, 'that you will get some sort of view of the *dress*. Whatever you do

The Wedding of Princess Elizabeth and Prince Philip in 1947 (*Hulton Picture Library*)

don't get too excited as the carriage comes past and say "I can just see the bride's knees from here." ' In fact this was just about all I could see on the outward journey in the Irish State Coach, a quick glimpse of HRH the bride, pale, very dignified and serious, with her father, the King, in Admiral's uniform sitting beside her. It was easier on the return journey when the Glass Coach came spanking through the centre archway of Admiralty Arch with the bride and groom leaning forward smiling happily to respond to the cheers of the immense crowds on either side of the Mall. A live commentary is a different proposition to the work of a sound reporter. The scene before one must be closely followed and the action described *as it happens* – whether one is watching on a television monitor or looking at the real thing.

There were several meetings concerned with the format of the broadcast, the timings, and how the handovers from one speaker to another should be done, but as a newcomer I received no further instruction on how the broadcast itself should be tackled. I began to devise what I felt should be my own technique and soon discovered that commentating is a very personal *métier* and that most commentators work in their own way.

I became smothered in background information, even walking up and down the Mall trying to assess if the leaves on the plane trees would have fallen by the wedding day or were likely to obscure the view. I interviewed the florist, Mr Martin Longman, Master of the Worshipful Company of Gardeners, whose Company, by tradition, would be presenting the bridal bouquet of orchids. He told me that he had been asked to include a sprig of rosemary from a bunch that had been planted by Queen Victoria at Osborne in the Isle of Wight.

As this was the first time since the war that full dress uniforms would be worn by troops lining the route and by the mounted Escorts of the Household Cavalry, I was invited to watch troopers of the Life Guards and the Blues (Royal Horse Guards) rehearsing in 'Full dress'. Helmets were falling off in all directions in the Riding School at Knightsbridge Barracks. This made me appreciate the immense difficulty (especially for young soldiers who had known nothing but battle dress) of mounting and riding a charger, wearing a very tight scarlet or dark blue tunic with white buckskin breeches and long heavy black jackboots. To complete the picture and the problem there must be added white gauntlet gloves, shining breastplates, plumed helmet and sword. I can only say that on the wedding day the Divisions of the Escorts, riding in the famous cavalry sitting trot, presented an impeccable, faultless display.

In the weeks before the wedding, frantic efforts were made by the press and the ready-to-wear dress trade of the world to obtain details of the Princess's wedding dress. Some American newspapers speculated with sketches, labelled 'the Wedding Gown of the Year'. Naturally, by tradition, it was to stay a well-kept secret. The greatest strain fell on the shoulders of the designer, Norman Hartnell, and his staff, literally beleaguered in Bruton Street. They were not only pestered by journalists but were offered money by certain industrialists for details. There was a rumour that the landlord of the building opposite refused a large sum of money to allow photographers with telescopic lenses to stand in his windows on the chance of glimpsing even the fabric of the dress – a fitting was too much to hope for.

I collected what information I could from press reports including a small sketch, cut out of a Rome newspaper and sent to me by a friend. There seemed little else to do about it.

Having now been present as commentator at all British Royal Weddings since the war in Westminster Abbey, York Minster and St. Paul's Cathedral, I still consider that Princess Elizabeth's dress was the most romantic and becoming of them all. It was inspired by a Botticelli painting, in heavy Duchess ivory satin with embroidered designs of stars and ears of corn worked on to it with 10,000 seed pearls. Lightness was given to the whole effect by a long veil and full shoulder train of delicate silk tulle, also embroidered and appliquéd with designs of the roses of York, star flowers and orange blossom. Unlike the wedding dresses in old photographs, which often date into dowdiness, Princess Elizabeth's is an enchanting masterpiece.

Needless to say I did not have these interesting details on 20 November, but I did attend a Hartnell press conference the afternoon before the wedding, which was unexpectedly helpful. Mr Hartnell did his best to help us, but few details were given and no sketches were issued at all. We were shown some patterns of the fabrics used and also one small example of the embroidery of a star flower. The questions went on and on, over and over again; Mr Hartnell was patient almost to the last. Someone piped up: 'Will you be going to Westminster Abbey tomorrow?' 'Oh yes – behind the West Door, with my mouth full of pins.'

As I went home, I kept thinking: I've seen that star flower before. I fished out the Rome newspaper cutting and there were several stars embroidered on the train. I took a chance. A charming glimpse of the Princess confirmed the newspaper sketch from Rome, and the broadcast became what I hoped was a vague but romantic impression of 'the wedding gown of the year'. I am glad to say it was not far wrong.

CHAPTER EIGHT

On Contract

> I can never be grateful enough for my first acquaintance with words, not as dead objects to be thrown around promiscuously, but as a living essence from age to age, from nation to nation; precise and lightfooted dancers in and out of the meanings of man.

Freya Stark

My first commentary on a royal occasion fortunately led to some more outside broadcasts, including a very important one with Wynford Vaughan Thomas in September 1948: the Inauguration of Queen Juliana in Nieuwe Kerk in Amsterdam. 'The New Church' happens to be the oldest but one of all Amsterdam churches, dating from 1408, and the Inauguration is approximately the equivalent of a Coronation in Britain.

I owe a great deal to Wynford for he is one of those rare people who is generous with information. It is so easy to generously invite someone to dinner or for a drink, but it's much more difficult for some folk to impart valuable 'know-how' to a beginner. I was faced with a long stretch on the air outside the church (Dutch ceremonial goes rather more slowly than ours), and Wynford mapped everything out in stages and showed me how to fill it. He also took me with him to the Press Office, to memorise from photographs the faces of famous Dutch personalities we had never seen and Wynford emphasised the need for a rich vocabulary: 'Just throw words into the air like confetti,' he would say with his irrepressible enthusiasm. I could never emulate Wynford's flow of language but I have tried to follow most of his advice ever since.

We had invitations to many of the main functions after the Inauguration, including a State Ball at the Palace. During the visit we had fleeting glimpses of Princess Margaret, then aged eighteen, on her first official engagement abroad, representing her father, the King. With Princess Alice of Athlone accompanying her and Captain Peter Townsend as her 'Master of the Household' we were, I suspect, seeing the first blossoming of the sad romance.

In the next few years there were several chances for me to be versatile. For the News Division I found myself reporting on the last day of the trial of William Joyce, Lord Haw Haw. This was a miscalculation on the part of the news editor; he had not anticipated that the trial would fold up so quickly. I was there to send back short paragraphs on the legal aspects for the news bulletins, hourly if necessary. The summing up ended rather abruptly after one hour and ten minutes, the judge ruling that Joyce without a shadow of doubt owed allegiance to the King. The jury retired. I immediately telephoned the office but it was too late to send a senior legal or political correspondent down to the Old Bailey for the final scene, so it had to be me. No time was wasted. The jury were back in just under twenty minutes. Joyce stood to hear the verdict and by then

The author with Wynford Vaughan Thomas (*B.B.C. copyright*)

he was very pale. When the foreman announced the verdict of 'Guilty' I thought Joyce was going to speak – but we never heard Lord Haw Haw's voice that day.

The awesome moment came at once. The judge, Mr Justice Tucker, placed a small black square of cloth on top of his wig and in a steady, low, compassionate voice pronounced sentence of death. Joyce refused the warder's arm. The scar on the right-hand side of his mouth now gave the impression of a twisted bitter grin. He attempted a wave of his right hand to someone in court and was then quickly escorted below.

Occasionally a broadcast can bring a most unlikely sequel. In 1947 the sea froze in Whitstable, Kent, and I was sent there by the BBC. The sight at low tide was astonishing. The beach was fringed with boulders of snow and the sands had a crazy pavement of ice strewn across them. A strip of whiteness in the distance showed that the ice field had receded with the tide, and the harbour was a sheet of ice with static marks of swirling waves – there were dozens of little boats quite immovable in this strange petrified sea.

Instead of staying sensibly indoors before a nice fire, most of Whitstable's fishermen were leaning against a jetty wall in a biting wind. The most forthright in the group was a Mr Harold Rowden, expressing the view that there was nothing to do 'until the wind changes. At present it's nor'east; we must have the wind sou'west. It don't look very happy without a southerly wind and we shall have ice here for weeks. We don't know the damage done to the oyster beds yet, do we?' I commiserated suitably and waited to see the frozen tide coming in, when the boats and ice rose together rigid against the harbour wall. I recorded a brief interview with Mr Rowden, and went home.

To my surprise, a few days later I received a letter from Harold Rowden. He was having a new boat built and he would like to name it after me. Would I give permission? It would be an honour. At the end of the page he added: 'PS Mrs Rowden doesn't mind.'

I was the one to be honoured and can only say now that it is a strange feeling to think of a boat setting out in a rough sea with one's name on the side. There was no official launching and naming when she was finished, but I went for a long weekend later and joined in the festivities. There was much jocularity in the local press that *Audrey Russell* was broad-beamed and clinker-built. The fishermen just pushed the boat down a slipway and I was given a short cruise around the bay, which brought us to a famous landmark called Pudding Pan Rock seven miles north of Herne Bay.

Harold's boat has had many adventures and I've closely followed her fortunes. She was sunk on 1 August, 1953, by fouling an uncharted wreck from the war. Harold and his crew were rescued after being in the water for several hours. About twenty local fishermen salvaged *Audrey Russell* and towed her home and Harold was lent another boat as the repairs took over six weeks. Then, in 1956, Harold himself went to the rescue of a sailing yacht with a man and his wife on board in a hurricane force gale. For this he received the RNLI Bronze Medal for Gallantry. With Harold's wife and son I was invited to watch the presentation of this award by the late Princess Marina, Duchess of Kent, at the Central Hall, Westminster. ('You see,' he wrote to me afterwards, 'Audrey behaved very well on this occasion – that's where her broad beam came in handy.')

At the end of the same year Harold Rowden retired, and by selling what he described as 'my very good boat' he was able to buy a nice bungalow with no financial worries. A subsequent owner, Mr Marshall, wrote to him about her later history: 'She toured the Fleet gathered at Spithead many times on the occasion of the Silver Jubilee Review in 1977. It was very dirty weather throughout and she took it like a lady, which pleased the

The author on the Flying Scotsman, October 1952 (*Barratt's*)

numerous sightseers she took round. I'm throwing this information in because, if my memory serves me correctly, Miss Russell is involved quite closely with this kind of occasion.'

The late forties were gimmicky times. For Woman's Hour I travelled on the footplate of a mainline London–Edinburgh express train, the famous Flying Scotsman. I am told I was the first woman ever to do so. I am not surprised – it was an incredibly tough experience. The vibration from the footplate made my teeth chatter, the front of me was freezing cold from the draught at high speed, the reverse was true of my backside which was nearly scorched every time the fireman stoked the fire. I discovered that the perspective of a rail track ahead, coming to a point in the far far distance, has a strange hypnotic effect: I could not take my eyes off it, otherwise I would have turned round more often to even things up. The experience left me with unfading admiration for the stoical engine drivers and firemen of all steam locomotives.

Then for Outside Broadcasts, in a feature programme with Richard Dimbleby about famous buildings by the upper reaches of the Thames, I was locked, alone in the dark, in the Haunted Gallery of Hampton Court Palace. It was on the anniversary of the execution of Katherine Howard, the fifth wife of King Henry VIII. Her little ghost was said to be last seen in the Gallery in 1917. The engineers and all their equipment were outside in Kitchen Court and a long cable was attached to the microphone to give me as much freedom of movement as possible. Suddenly, just before the broadcast, the engineers heard footsteps. They became so alarmed that they nearly rescued me by unlocking the doors before we went on the air. I had been holding the microphone close to my chest for comfort as it grew darker and darker in that long corridor . . . luckily the footsteps were merely the beating of my heart and the Rose without a Thorn did not appear.

With a Princess as heir to the throne, opinions were at last changing slowly about the necessity of having a full-time woman commentator. There was still a hard core of male chauvinism in both departments for which I now worked. Both were hesitant about the reaction of the rest of the male staff if I began to compete with them.

I found myself in a tug of war between Outside Broadcasts and the News Division. The latter did not encourage versatility of any kind at that time and begrudged 'lending' me for the occasional commentary.

My friends, Wynford, Raymond Glendenning and Richard (now a supporter), urged me to leave the comfortable security of a staff job, and the prospect of a pension. They were all on contracts. 'You will walk it,' said Wynford, always optimistic and courageous. Eventually I took the plunge and gave notice; I felt Wynford had been right when the very next day I was put on contract to Outside Broadcasts at almost double my staff salary. The immediate sense of freedom was very sweet indeed and, allowing for the ups and downs that I have since experienced, I have had no regrets and have lurched from contract to contract ever since.

Lobby treated me generously. I had been on the staff for nine and a half years, and he pointed out that if I waited six months I would be entitled to a small ten-year golden handshake. He promised to keep the job open.

On the other hand he reminded me of the immediate possibilities of the coming Festival of Britain, for which there were extensive broadcasting plans. I decided this could be a wonderful landmark in my career and accepted the contract at once. Many people have been critical of the Festival – I enjoyed every moment of it. I was involved in most of the broadcasting, which made it a real 'break-through'. Here are some

Royal group on the steps of St. Paul's Cathedral, 3rd May 1951, for the Opening of the Festival of Britain (*Hulton Picture Library*)

impressions of those hectic and refreshing days.

It was stimulating from the start. It was the first time since the war that things were being planned, designed and created because they were decorative and imaginative rather than useful and economical.

At early press conferences, held primarily to whip up interest and enthusiasm, the mass media cautiously watched the Festival grow. While the project had to run counter to the harsh economies of the time, even the most grudging of newsmen and women found it difficult not to get swept along by the explosion of ideas that emerged at these meetings on how to commemorate the Great Exhibition of 1851 and pull ourselves up by our own bootstraps at the same time. Clearly it was to be an enterprise of complexity and sophistication, together with a charming simplicity.

During a long meeting on street decoration plans, one of the young designers on the platform said: 'I would like to have a bunch of flowers put in the hands of all female statues on the day of the Opening Ceremony.' The prospect of including, say, Florence Nightingale, Mrs Pankhurst and Lady Godiva in the festivities seemed irresistible but, in the sheer volume of notions flying around, I fear this idea was one that got away.

The BBC made extensive plans for full coverage. There was to be a radio and TV centre built into a converted garage somewhere at the South Bank Exhibition. It was also to serve the Pleasure Gardens at Battersea Park. Nearly all the main Exhibition buildings were equipped with 'plug-in' Outside Broadcast points for on-the-spot broadcasts, all of which were used extensively by broadcasters from overseas, as well as ourselves. The fact that the whole of Britain was involved in the celebrations made it a broadcasting marathon of Arts and Music Festivals, Pageants, Gymkhanas and Carnivals from Aberdeen to Brighton. The word 'Festival' must have appeared more frequently than any other word in the language in issues of the *Radio Times* that summer.

On 3 May, on the Home Service, Richard Dimbleby and I were the commentators at St Paul's Cathedral for the Service of Dedication and the Opening Ceremony by HM King George VI from the steps of the Cathedral. He was surrounded by senior civic and Church dignitaries and the rest of the Royal Family: the Queen, Princess Elizabeth, Prince Philip, Princess Margaret and the outstandingly tall upright figure of HM Queen Mary, who followed her son's speech with rapt attention and a certain anxiety for his ordeal as a public speaker. Although it was a cloudy grey day, it was a brilliant psychological stroke that the King should perform the ceremony *out of doors*. It really felt that the occasion belonged to the whole of Britain and not merely to the capital. As a broadcast, it was an international event, described in more than 30 languages by visiting broadcasters from all over the world.

The South Bank was ready on time and waiting for the visitors and their opinions. The first impact on me was that the overall design of the terraces made me more aware of the river frontage than ever before, with water buses plying to and fro between the South Bank and the Pleasure Gardens at Battersea. Because the river was so much part of the scene, a great many outside broadcasts were done from high-speed motor launches (and they always seemed to go too fast for all the words I had to describe the animated scene on the Bank). It is sad and perhaps curious that the great potential of the River Thames revealed at that time has not been realised since, to the same degree.

Most exhibition architecture tends to remind me of a boy on a bicycle crying out: 'Look, no hands'. The Festival architecture had its full share of new materials, with exciting shapes of strange angles that stood up without visible means of support. The

Princess Elizabeth and Prince Philip during their tour of the South Bank Exhibition (*Hulton Picture Library*)

Exhibition emblem led the way in this: 'the skylon' was a silvery splinter of light against the night sky. Looking back now, I see it as a prophetic glimpse of soaring rockets at Cape Canaveral. The extensive use of glass was new to most of us at that time, giving a transparency to entire buildings and creating fantastic vistas of a luminous, sparkling city by the river at night.

The most important and the only permanent structure on the site, the Royal Festival Hall, was the first public building to be built in Britain after the war. The first concert was held on the evening of 3 May in the presence of the King and Queen and other members of the Royal Family. The King unveiled a small commemorative plaque in the entrance hall. With his careful attention to formality and ceremony he pointed out that this unveiling was *not* the official opening. 'I opened the whole Festival of Britain this morning,' he declared; 'I don't have to open anything else now; I am just attending the first concert.'

It was an evening of elation and exhilaration. Few people had ever been in a British building with glass walls and split-level floors. Everyone marvelled that the concert hall could be so successfully insulated from the noise made a few yards away by the trains on Hungerford Bridge, and the architects, Robert Mathew and Dr J. L. Martin, explained that the hall itself 'sat cushioned within the outside walls, like an egg in an eggbox.'

The programme of music was familiar, patriotically triumphant and magnificently performed, with Sir Adrian Boult and Sir Malcolm Sargent conducting players from no fewer than five very distinguished orchestras, with combined choirs. The clarity of sound was astonishing. As *The Times* put it next day: 'the words of the choirs were actually intelligible.' It was a bravura performance that included Handel's 'Zadok the Priest', Sir Malcolm Sargent's arrangement of Arne's 'Rule Britannia,' Vaughan Williams' 'Serenade to Music,' Elgar's 'Pomp and Circumstance No. 1' and the 'Hallelujah Chorus' and 'Amen' from Handel's *Messiah*. Everything went quite beautifully . . . everything, that is, except for a small hitch that may well have been engraved like Calais on the hearts of house engineers and others concerned. On that great occasion, on his way to the Mayoral box the Lord Mayor of London, Sir Denys Lowson, with his Lady Mayoress and all the aldermen and sheriffs, got stuck in a Festival Hall lift. It came about because everyone wanted to be in the same lift as the Lord Mayor. The apparatus rebelled at the overloading and it took the engineers at least fifteen minutes to wind the lift down to ground level. By then the concert was under way and very few members of the audience were aware of what was happening. Perhaps it was only Richard and I who spotted the unusual sight of a mayoral party tiptoeing into the auditorium as unobtrusively as possible.

After the historic opening of the whole Festival, the South Bank Exhibition immediately drew the London crowds; from the start it was the aluminium Dome of Discovery that created the greatest impression. This held pointers to things we now accept without question and on looking back it would seem that an awful lot has happened since then. I remember wondering incredulously if man would ever walk on the moon. There was a first glimpse of the new science of radio astronomy with a huge caption: THE EXPLORERS OF OUTER SPACE ARE THE ASTRONOMERS. It was impressive — and puzzling — to watch the return of radar impulses from the moon, beamed from the top of the old Shot Tower (now demolished), and to see the impulses reflected on a screen in the Dome.

Another pavilion that was also ahead of its time, in an entirely different way, was fanciful and amusing. It managed to express abstract ideas about our attitudes to life and, above all, the ability of the different social strata in Britain to be amused at the antics of each other. Bits of it were like a copy of *Punch* in the round, for it relied on the funny men for much of the content. Writers and artists such as Stephen Potter, Laurie Lee, Heath Robinson, Pont, Edward Lear, Rowlandson and Max Beerbohm were all represented.

It might be thought that only the intelligentsia would be charmed by all this, but there was an unerring touch in the choice of exhibits and their juxtaposition. There were things there that everyone could like and be proud of. In no particular order, I remember a 365-day clock by Thomas Tompion, an original edition of Dr Johnson's dictionary, a first folio Shakespeare, the Bible of King James I, a model of the White Knight, with acknowledgements to Sir John Tenniel, a corrected page proof of Winston Churchill's *History of the Second World War*, and – of all things – a pair of tailor's pinking scissors. The display achieved greatness by the inclusion of four masterpieces of English painting, for ever to be remembered: Gainsborough, Constable, Turner and, unexpectedly, a work by the contemporary painter, Paul Nash, who stood up well in such august company with *Vernal Equinox*, lent from the Queen's own small but fine collection of modern art.

This pavilion, appropriately named The Lion and the Unicorn, really did fulfil the organisers' claim that the Festival was an autobiography of the British people, written by the nation itself. I believe it reflected what we were like at that particular time: We were even hopeful for the future.

When the Festival closed on 30 September, 1951, an auction sale of fittings and fixtures was held on the South Bank during the dismantling of the pavilions. I had my eye on one of the most imaginative features of the décor. This was a clever illusion that a flock of doves were in flight out of the Lion and Unicorn Pavilion. The impression was that they were flying straight through the glass, in defiance of the vitreous walls. I managed to acquire two plaster doves for a guinea apiece. One was for Richard Dimbleby as a souvenir of the many broadcasts we had shared. I also bought an elegant white wrought-iron garden chair, but when I received my purchases I soon realised how fragile were the plaster doves and how heavy the chair. There were no taxis to be seen anywhere and halfway across the now deserted concourse the chair had to be left behind. The dove still hangs in the hall of my flat as a precious reminder of the Festival. I often wonder what happened to the chair.

The year 1951 had been dominated by many factors: we were still in the age of austerity, the war in Korea continued to ebb and flow, there was also the threat of an economic crisis. Above all these things there was a deep concern for the King's health. Even back in 1948, the year in which the King and the Queen celebrated their silver wedding with a service of thanksgiving in St Paul's Cathedral, there were signs that he was far from well. It was said he had not recovered yet from the strain of the war years. A Royal tour proposed for the following spring to Australia and New Zealand had to be postponed.

The King's condition was diagnosed as 'early arteriosclerosis' with symptoms of severe cramp, and there was fear that the right leg might have to be amputated. Later, with skilful medical care, including some surgery, King George recovered sufficiently to consider making new dates for the tour. If all went well, it was proposed that he should go sometime in early 1952, but this was not to be. The serious lung condition was then developing and, in spite of a successful operation by the leading surgical authority on malignant diseases of the chest, it was apparent that cancellation was inevitable. Disappointment was allayed by the decision that Princess Elizabeth and her husband should go instead. The journey was to take them to East Africa, Ceylon, Australia and New Zealand.

Frank Gillard, Wynford Vaughan Thomas and I had been included in the BBC's plans for the original tour; so towards the end of January 1952 we found ourselves travelling across the world a few days ahead of the Royal party, Frank to Kenya, myself to Ceylon (now Sri Lanka) by turbo-prop Argonaut on the longest flight I had so far undertaken, with Wynford bound for Australia. Little did I think that I was destined to make the journey to Colombo and back again in under one week.

This was my first Royal tour and first glimpse of the tropics. We arrived at dawn and I was so entranced with the sights and sounds that I dumped my luggage, scorned sleep and went out again to drive round the city. The decorations for the Royal visit were unlike anything I had seen before: magnificent triumphal arches spanned the streets of Royal routes. These arches, constructed of bamboo, were festooned with coconuts, pineapples, plantains, branches of green tea leaves, lotus flowers and masses of indigenous flora intertwined with emblems of the British crown and the turban-like coronets of the ancient Sinhalese kings. They presented a feeling of great national pride in the products of Ceylon and the splendours of its past.

The headquarters of Radio Ceylon, which I visited that morning, were a legacy of the last war, built by the British during the South East Asia campaign as a radio station and communications centre. It had probably been enlarged and certainly converted into one of the most elegant small radio stations I have seen in the Commonwealth. Shady colonnades enclosed an inner courtyard with an ornamental lake and a small fountain playing in the middle. There were no reminders of the perilous days of its origin.

My first objective in Colombo was to see and describe the Royal apartments at the Governor General's residence, prophetically named The Queen's House, presumably after Queen Victoria. I was fortunate to be granted a preview that afternoon. I arrived in the middle of a rehearsal. A group of solemn officials watched an Arachi guard opening and closing a car door, then handing an imaginary Princess down the step as the thin strains of the National Anthem were played a little uncertainly by an orchestra on the lawn.

The rehearsal was repeated over and over as I was being shown the Royal apartments. The rooms were large and lofty with polished wood floors. Some of the bedroom furniture was new, and looked as if it hadn't quite settled down. The reception rooms gave the impression of the interior of a lacquer cabinet. I suddenly felt tired and even depressed: I had never heard the National Anthem sound so sad.

I left The Queen's House just after four o'clock and at four fifteen Colombo time the news was flashed by Reuters to Ceylon that King George VI had died. Colombo came to a standstill. To a westerner, the brilliant profusion of rich colours in that city seemed heartless in the sun.

We went into reverse at once. There were cables to be sent to London and I thought it best to go in person to the main cable office. To my surprise, this showed me how little I knew of social custom and behaviour in Asia, even in time of tragedy. The office was crammed with excitable houseboys and messengers clamouring for attention. I soon realised that my presence was a grave solecism. I learnt that women, especially Europeans, do not send their own cables. It is just not done. They must employ a servant or perhaps one of the ragged urchins who hopefully hang around that office. It is

The King waving off Princess Elizabeth and Prince Philip on their Royal Tour in 1952 (*British Airways*)

no exaggeration to say that I created something near pandemonium. The underlings of many households and offices took a poor view of the situation and I was pestered for custom. I quickly hired one of the urchin Ariels, who immediately disappeared in the crowd to emerge in triumph at the counter ahead of every one else in the queue in no time at all. I was then rescued by a young Scotsman in charge of the office, who took me behind the counter for the sake of peace.

Then an odd thing happened. A large direct printing machine was working on a beamed circuit to London; single letters were being typed out on a paper ribbon. I watched my Christian name appear, jerkily, letter by letter and realised the cable was for me: 'RETURN SOONEST FUNERAL BROADCAST FLIGHT BOOKED BOAC 771': I caught the plane in the small hours and slept most of the way home.

I don't believe my thoughts, impressions and emotions have ever been so tightly compressed by time as on that journey across the world, at first so full of hope then back again to sorrow. We arrived at Heathrow early next morning and, to my delight, Mother and a friend were there to meet me. It was an emotional reunion. Mother, who had a great sense of occasion in keeping with the times, was as practical as ever. She handed me a small parcel, saying: 'You can't drive into London even at this hour in that yellow cotton frock. Go to the cloakroom and change – I have brought you your black dress.'

CHAPTER NINE

Strew the Laureate Hearse

Bring the rathe primrose that forsaken dies,
The tufted crow-toe, and pale jessamine,
The white pink, and the pansy freakt with jet,
The glowing violet . . .
And every flower that sad embroidery wears.
Bid amaranthus all his beauty shed,
And daffadillies fill their cups with tears,
To strew the laureate hearse where Lycid lies.

John Milton, 'Lycidas'

When I left Colombo the city was in a state of shock at the sudden news of the King's death. A few hours after the announcement many of the well-to-do Sinhalese and Tamil people were wearing white for mourning; but there had not yet been time to remove the triumphal arches, still looking cheerfully colourful against the blue skies and viridian sea of that lovely island. As we drove to the airport we were twice stopped by groups of bewildered workmen standing by their handiwork, questioning us as though in disbelief of the news. 'It must be a rumour!' one of them declared and stoutly maintained his intention of guarding his own archway all night. (And this despite the fact that the Governor, Lord Soulbury, had already, on the air, confirmed the death of the King.)

In the cycle of emotions, London was at the next stage of bereavement: quiet, saddened and subdued. Everyone I saw had responded to the official suggestion that mourning should be observed. Some made it merely a black tie or a black armband; but the majority were entirely in black, while bands of purple or black draped the shop windows. There was a feeling of unnatural stillness, with a strong undercurrent of great activity behind the scenes. Already, on the first day of the lying-in-state, 76,000 people were paying quiet homage to the late King in Westminster Hall. The total file-past before the funeral was 305,806.

The Duke of Edinburgh and other members of the Royal Family and household, together with officials of the Lord Chamberlain's office, were fully occupied at airports and railway stations greeting the Heads of State, Kings and Queens, Princes and Presidents, and official delegations from many countries, some of them very distant, all converging on London for the funeral.

On 13 February, two days before the funeral, at 7.15p.m., Queen Mary, then 85, accompanied by the Duke of Windsor, went to Westminster Hall. The Duke had arrived earlier in the day by air from New York, to stay with his mother at Marlborough House. When they reached the main entrance to Westminster Hall, the queue of mourners filing down on the right-hand side was checked; and as the Royal couple entered the Duke, with bowed head, dropped to one knee where he remained for several seconds. He then rose and stood at the Queen's left hand for about twenty minutes. When the Watch was due to be changed the Duke, after speaking to his mother, called over a police officer; the mourners who had been waiting again began to file past. Before leaving, the Queen and her son watched the sentries of the Gentlemen-at-Arms and the King's Bodyguard change the Watch. The Duke knelt once again before leaving.

On that same day, at the BBC, a briefing meeting for the commentators was called by the Head of Outside Broadcasts. It began as a kind of cheerful travellers' reunion as we took our seats. Wynford, halfway to Australia, had made the turn-around; Frank Gillard was back from Kenya; and I believe I was the last to arrive. I own that the two long journeys by turbo-prop, in such quick succession, had made me feel like a long sleeve pulled inside out.

Lobby waited patiently for the end of more or less exaggerated anecdotes of nearly missed planes and lost luggage before giving us a broad outline of his plans for the funeral broadcast. At the same time we were all given a short but cogent memorandum as a reminder of the proceedings. I was secretly thrilled to read that my own position was an important one; at Windsor, watching the scene from the windows of a house in Horseshoe Cloisters. Richard Dimbleby was to be in St George's Chapel for the service. In London Howard Marshall would open the broadcast as the cortège left Westminster Hall; while Wynford would be outside St James's Palace, with the heavy responsibility of naming the foreign and Commonwealth representatives in the procession (for the programme was being transmitted worldwide). Frank Gillard would be watching the King's remains leaving London, from Paddington station.

Lobby's recommendations were to make this broadcast an impressive reflection of what people on the spot saw and felt and heard. I was sure that his final advice would be appreciated by many a listener: 'Please don't talk too much. Make the maximum use of sound. On such an occasion as this the gentle handling of effects can "make" the broadcast, provided commentators will only allow the necessary pauses.'

The broadcasting at short notice of a great state occasion such as a state funeral inevitably presents difficulties for the commentator; not least, gathering quickly all the information bound to be needed. Too often one has largely to rely on official snippets as they happen to be published. In this case Lobby arranged for the press agencies' tickertape to be 'fed' to our meeting, and there were many interruptions with stop-press news which he read out to us, for example, 'Queen Mary will not be attending the funeral. She is quite well, but it is felt that she should not be exposed to the strain and ordeal of the long procession.' Another detail that had been bothering me reached us through the same channel: 'The late King's widow will in future hold the style and title of Queen Elizabeth the Queen Mother.' How strange now to think that this title ever sounded unfamiliar!

Lobby's outline of the programme made me set off immediately by train for Windsor; for there was little enough time to memorise details and to have a good look at what could be seen from my vantage points in the house in Horseshoe Cloisters. This was one of a row of Tudor oak-beamed houses that screened off the entrance to St George's Chapel from the public gaze, creating a small enclosure with a green lawn to one side. My instructions from Lobby indicated that I was to begin broadcasting from a window looking out on to the sloping path leading from the Round Tower. Then, as the cortège approached the entrance into the cloister, I was to walk across the room to a window facing the steps of the chapel, to describe the lifting of the coffin from the gun-carriage;

the disappearance of the cortège through the west door was to be the cue for the service in the chapel.

There could be no doubt but that Windsor was at the very heart of public sorrow. On the day I went down there I watched a military rehearsal for the procession through the streets; and even then the pavements were thronged with people. Everyone who spoke to me recalled how often the King had been in residence at the castle or at Royal Lodge; many of them seemed to consider that they knew him well and indeed counted him as a friend. Formations of troops in service dress escorted 142 gunners, hauling the drag-ropes of the bare gun-carriage from the railway station, where the iron pillars supporting the roof were already swathed in purple fabric. Troops lined the whole route, through the streets into Windsor Great Park and the grounds of the castle, all the way to the steps of St George's Chapel. There was no music at this rehearsal, but drum-taps (to mark the steps) gave a moving foretaste of the morrow.

The colonel in command of the troops at Windsor then held a useful and informative press conference. He had, it seemed, been a close personal friend of the King's. With typical British dread of overdoing things emotionally he addressed us in a clipped tone of voice, apologising for bringing the press to Windsor at short notice and on such a very wet night; and then, in a voice half-strangled with grief, said: 'But I feel sure that, just as much as we do, you will all of you want everything to be ticketyboo on the day of the race.'

Next day Frank Anderson, the Outside Broadcast Manager, called for me at 7.30a.m. It was a wise precaution, for even at that hour there were traffic diversions in London, while the town centre of Windsor was to be closed to traffic at 10. More snippets of information kept coming through to us on the car radio, one of the most unusual being a tribute to the King from the RAF. I sometimes wonder if that was the first time in history that this was ordered and carried out. As the instruction ran, on the day of the funeral, 15 February, no RAF aircraft would fly anywhere over the United Kingdom from the hours of 6a.m. until the same time on the following morning. Should there be any emergency, the Air Ministry was first to be consulted.

At 9.20 we heard the deep voice of Howard Marshall, outside Westminster Hall, opening the programme with his impressions of the first stages of that long and poignant day. When we arrived at Windsor Great Park, it looked from a distance as though someone had drawn a thick charcoal line along the edge of the grass on either side of the Royal Mile. Huge crowds had been waiting for hours, stamping their feet to try to keep warm. We walked down the processional route and, turning the corner by the Round Tower, had our first view of the thousands of flowers spread out on the sloping lawns outside the chapel. St George's, with its sheer lines of Perpendicular architecture soaring above, was surrounded by what looked like a mammoth flower bed. Between the buttresses the wreaths and crosses covered the grass to the edge of the pathway. But of course there were more — much more — than wreaths and crosses. There were crowns, there were vast cushions, there were the floral coats of arms of the cities that had sent them; there was even a battleship made entirely of chrysanthemums. Collectively they were magnificent and, though some of the more mountainous 'tributes' were a little overwhelming, there were a great many beautiful and delicate flower-arrangements too.

As we were making our way back to the commentary point in Horseshoe Cloisters, I suddenly spotted something rather special; as it was so small, I thought at first it must have fallen from something else. I stooped to look more closely; and there, sure enough, on that flamboyant verge, lay a minute bunch of flowers: just five small primroses and a single snowdrop. The fragile stems had been tied together with white knitting-wool bearing a small label inscribed in a round hand: 'A tribute from a Shropshire garden'. It was something I knew listeners would like to hear about when I described the flowers because – homely gesture that it was – it clearly came from someone who knew that its simplicity would not be misunderstood. It came from two sisters who had travelled from Wellington by milk train to lay the flowers personally on the grass at Windsor. They had intended to stand in the street to watch the procession pass, but the weather deteriorated and they were tired, so they went to a Windsor hotel to rest and to listen to the radio.

The mention of 'a tribute from a Shropshire garden' on the air brought me a charming letter from one of the sisters and for many years afterwards they sent me a replica of that little bunch of flowers on 6 February, the anniversary of the King's death.

The broadcast from Windsor began at about 1.45, and it was a calming influence for me to hear Richard's steady voice setting the scene in the chapel. By the time he had finished indicating the Order of Service, the head of the procession could be seen passing the silent crowds by the Round Tower, as it moved down the hill to the Lower Ward.

As for my own impressions, they stay like vivid snapshots in the mind. At first I was surprised at the unexpected richness of colour at the head of the procession: the scarlet cloaks of a division of the Life Guards on foot. Then the tall troopers, their shining helmets enriched with white plumes hanging limp and still: a contrast indeed to the flurry and jingle of mounted escorts on happier occasions. But I remember too searching for words to do justice to a particularly dazzling moment on that grey day when suddenly, as the coffin drew level with me, the sun came and blazed on the diamonds set in the Imperial State Crown. At that instant it seemed as though the crown itself was the very source of light.

Of course I shall never forget the arrival of that closed landau with half-seen, veiled figures within. Quickly the door was opened and we saw the young Queen, taking precedence over her mother for the first time. She was swiftly followed by three figures in deep mourning, all heavily veiled: the King's widow, his younger daughter Princess Margaret, and his only sister, the Princess Royal. They and the four Royal Dukes (Kent, Windsor, Gloucester and Edinburgh, who had walked behind the Queen's carriage the whole way in the procession, both morning and afternoon) then followed the coffin up the long flight of steps, to vanish into the shadowy interior of St George's Chapel for the service.

As the simple, twenty-minute funeral service began, those of us outside were aware of a sudden serenity and peace. The maximum use of sounds, as counselled by Lobby with his flair for such things, had been very telling, but it had meant too a deep emotional strain ... the perpetual slow marching tramp of feet, the clatter of horses' hooves (slightly muted by sanded roadways), the bands, the bells, the gun salutes, and above all the full naval honours accorded by the bos'n's pipes plaintively piping the Admiral alongside and ashore, as the bearers of the coffin slowly climbed the steps to the resting place of the King.

Now the listeners (and ourselves on headphones) came to the climax of the splendours of all those moving sounds: the choirs and the organ music of the service itself.

The Queen reverently placed the neatly folded King's Colour of the King's Company, Grenadier Guards, on the coffin. Known as the Royal Standard of the Regiment, by tradition this is eventually taken to hang in Windsor Castle among the standards of other sovereigns. As the coffin was lowered to the vault, the Queen

The Dukes of Edinburgh, Gloucester, Windsor and Kent marching in the Royal Procession at the funeral of King George VI (*Hulton Picture Library*)

scattered earth from a gilded bowl, while the Archbishop of Canterbury, Dr. Fisher, committed the body to the ground.

It is often said that funerals can give the impression of ending abruptly; and this indeed can with some truth be said of military funerals, where ceremonial drill rather sharply goes into reverse. As the troops disperse, solemn music gives way to a brisk march; the message seems to be : 'The living must carry on.' At all events, so it seemed to me at Windsor on that momentous day. With a minimum of ceremony or delay the Royal Family left in motor cars, while the congregation dispersed and walked to the car parks.

We were not quite so speedy. After a broadcast of that magnitude there were many people to be thanked for kind and expert help. At the same time congratulations reaching us from Broadcasting House were cheering and pleasing.

Quite unexpectedly, an official who all along had been particularly helpful, approached me and asked quietly, 'Would you like to go into the chapel?' We entered by a side door, where I met a verger. Already a few workmen were dismantling the specially built stands, and I heard the unceremonious sound of planks being shifted and stacked. Then I was led to the dark oblong hole in the floor below the high altar. And there, down in the vault, now bereft of crown and regalia and no longer guarded by anyone, the coffin lay wrapped in the Royal Standard, with the Queen Mother's spray of white flowers at its head. In silence the three of us walked past and away, aware that quite possibly we chanced to be the very last of a good King's subjects to pay our personal respects to him.

CHAPTER TEN

Coronation Prelude

It is generally accepted that a formal ceremony is a way of letting as many people as possible know what you intend to do. It is a declaration of intent having various forms from, say, the signing of a peace treaty, to getting married or buried or crowned. For the British it is significant that every King and Queen regnant has been crowned in Westminster Abbey since William the Conquerer in 1066. Queen Elizabeth II can trace her descent from Egbert in AD829, and the Coronation service in its main outlines is the same as it was for the crowning of King Edgar at Bath in AD973.

The aura of this antiquity gives us the pride of knowing that the complex solemn rites of the sacred and the secular, the civil and the ecclesiastical, have been evolved (however confusingly) over 1100 years of history and tradition. In a sentence, the English Coronation symbolises our national continuity – in spite of the Cromwellian interlude of eleven years!

I first learned that I had been given a place in the BBC's broadcasting team for the Coronation about six months before 2 June. Naturally I was overjoyed to be told that I was to be in Westminster Abbey to describe the processions. John Snagge and Howard Marshall were to be up in the Triforium annotating the service.

During the six months' period, it was arranged that all my broadcasts were to be about the history of and the preparations for the Coronation, which was an immense help in the research work. Most of the Overseas Services wanted short, snappy little pieces about almost every aspect of the preparations, and I was also commissioned for six months to do a weekly 'Coronation Report' for transmission on several American networks. The most exciting of the pre-Coronation programmes for me was a fifteen-minute live broadcast from a heavily guarded workshop in the West End of London. It was arranged with Messrs Garrard, the Crown Jewellers, that we should do a piece about the remodelling of the Imperial State Crown for the Queen. Although the Sovereign is crowned with the very heavy St Edward's Crown, weighing nearly five pounds, to most people the lighter Imperial Crown (a mere two pounds thirteen ounces) has become the real symbol of monarchy as it is always worn during Coronation processions and at the State Openings of Parliament. It is also, sadly, secured to the Sovereign's coffin at funerals.

The late Mr Cecil Mann, the Crown Jeweller, who was supervising not only the work on the crown but also the refurbishing and restoration of the entire regalia from the Tower of London, took these responsibilities with a calm enthusiasm and quiet charm. He suggested that two senior craftsmen should reassemble the framework of the crown during the fifteen-minute broadcast. The workroom was a top-floor room, well lit with skylights and tall windows and resembling a studio rather than a place strewn with curiously shaped machines and tools with names I had never heard of. Several other craftsmen had stayed on after work to watch the proceedings.

The two men sat side by side, wearing leather aprons that were anchored to the bench to prevent the gems falling on the floor. They began assembling part of the circlet of fine gold open-work, studded with diamonds, emeralds and sapphires, bordered with pearls set together as closely as possible – in fact the pearls were strung together as a necklace, and I watched this being carefully fitted round the base. The crown had been completely dismantled 'to lower the arches to lighten it for the Queen'. 31 years ago I had the impression that this meant to reduce the weight still further, but checking with Garrards recently I was assured that the weight had not been reduced: the work had been done to make the crown *look* lighter and, to quote the official description, 'more feminine'. The arches are now one inch lower than before, but none of the gems have been removed.

The Imperial State Crown is a fabulous, dazzling object – but for me the word 'beautiful' does not quite apply to it. The frame is an oakleaf pattern, thickly set with over 3000 precious stones. It has a tremendous magnificence and one is overawed by the emanation of history around it. This crown was made for Queen Victoria in 1838 and worn by her throughout her Coronation, including the moment of crowning.

When the framework had been assembled during the broadcast I was allowed to hold the crown in my hands and the diamonds flashed and blazed under the lights. The best was yet to come. Cecil Mann produced four white cardboard boxes and carefully opened them. They contained what I would hazard are the four most historic jewels in the world. The Victorian jewellers of 1838 had assembled some of the priceless objects which, in the fatal year of the execution of Charles I, were noted in an inventory dated 1649 as 'totally broken and defaced'. As everyone knows, mysteriously, some of them turned up again in excellent condition at the Restoration of 1660. The first box revealed the Stuart Sapphire, taken by James II in his flight from England and eventually bequeathed to King George III by the last of the Stuart exiles, Cardinal York. Then there was a smaller sapphire, probably the oldest crown jewel of them all, for it is said to be the stone from a ring belonging to Edward the Confessor, removed from his dead finger as a holy relic when his tomb was opened in the twelfth century. Most conspicuous of all is the great irregularly shaped spinel, the ruby given to the Black Prince by Pedro the Cruel in 1367 and said to have adorned the helmet-crown of Henry V at Agincourt. The latest addition to this extraordinary collection is the second stone of the Star of Africa (the Cullinan diamond) given to King Edward VII but not set into the crown until 1911 for the Coronation of King George V.

If the craftsmen's work had been further advanced and the gems reset I would never have had the unique opportunity as an outsider of seeing and touching each stone in turn. Cecil Mann asked me to describe each one and I felt excited at being so tangibly close to these symbols of English history. My personal memory of handling the gems in quick succession is that I was aware of the weight, texture and feel of each one: the crystal hardness of the Cullinan, the dark blue corundum of the sapphires. Although I know that mineralogists might not agree, the most romantic of them all – the Black Prince's ruby – did not feel cold and hard; it was an indented crimson large polished pebble, smooth and warm as amber.

As we came off the air, the watching craftsmen applauded their colleagues' performances (and it was something of an achievement for the experts to put a crown together in fifteen minutes); then it was suggested that I should try on the crown! There was quite a chorus – 'Try it on now . . . Try it on.' I quickly declined, fearing that a great experience might turn into a giggling charade.

The time had come to lock up for the night. The armed security guards assembled to

The author outside Broadcasting House (*Camera Press Limited*)

escort us to a lift. 'Would you like to see the crown being put to bed?' This was a complicated procedure of signing and countersigning ledgers as we progressed along the dark corridors of a basement. We passed heavily barred strongrooms brightly lit inside, as well as anonymous closed steel doors, all the way to the crown's destination. I remember nothing of the room in which it was housed, only more signing and countersigning and the clanking of keys. The crown had been packed in a leather case that resembed an old-fashioned travelling hatbox. It was still labelled HM THE KING.

All manner of likely and unlikely preparations were going on behind the scenes in the last months of 1952. What might have been a serious problem arose over the oil with which the Archbishop of Canterbury would anoint the Queen. In the Abbey muniment file on the subject a letter from Her Majesty's Apothecary, dated October 1952, states that 'a small quantity of the original oil used for Queen Victoria is available'. This was inaccurate as unfortunately, but not surprisingly, it was unusably rancid over 100 years after her Coronation. The letter adds little information about the Ampulla, or Golden Eagle containing the oil. 'The capacity of the stomach will take five ounces ... I think that two ounces should be ample.'

The custom has been for the anointing oil to be made up in quantities to last several reigns. A batch of oil used for King Edward VII and later for King George V, together with another batch for King Edward VIII and used for King George VI in 1937, had been destroyed when the Deanery was bombed in the Second World War. The real shock came when it was discovered that the Royal Appointment Pharmacists, Messrs Squires of Bond Street, had gone out of business.

Enquiries for the prescription were made all over Britain and extended as far as Australia. It was discovered in the possession of a Mrs Keep, *née* Squires, living in East Fremantle, Perth, Australia. Mr Jamieson, a chemist and distant relative of the Squires family, made a fresh supply from this prescription, said to contain identical ingredients to those in the oil made for King Charles I in the seventeenth century. The King was a carefully selective man for it has been described as 'rich in aroma ... a mixture of sesame and olive oil, perfumed with roses, orange flowers, jasmine, cinnamon, flowers of Benzoin, musk, civet and ambergris'.

Some years later, on the death in 1975 of her husband, also a pharmacologist, Mrs Keep presented the original prescription to Westminster Abbey. It is now carefully stored with other documents relating to it in an Abbey safe. It is a pleasant thought that, in spite of loss and mischance surrounding the holy oil, there still exists a small quantity of a reserve portion of unconsecrated oil made in 1902 by Sir P. W. Squires and now held by the Keep family in Perth as a treasured heirloom.

As I delved into books and various documents and records, mostly stored in the Muniment Room of Westminster Abbey, I soon discovered that in a ceremony of such general interest, small incidents were bound to be discussed and written about in contemporary letters and journals — and that this made for a long tale of mishaps. On more than one occasion St Edward's crown was placed back to front on the Sovereign's head, the last time as recently as the Coronation of King Edward VII, and there are even some doubts as to what happened when King George VI was crowned: it is believed that 'some officious person removed a small piece of wool tied to the back of the crown for guidance.'

At Queen Victoria's Coronation in 1838 (which lasted over five hours) the Archbishop of Canterbury put the Coronation ring on the wrong finger and, at the reception afterwards, the poor young Queen had to keep her right hand in a finger bowl of iced water to reduce the painful swelling. Coronations may have been lavish affairs but very little planning went into them. At another point in the service the Dean records that the Queen whispered to him, 'Pray, tell me what to do next. The Bishops know nothing.'

For the many hundreds of years before broadcasting, ceremonies were just allowed to happen. Tradition was upheld from memory and ritual was rarely, if ever, rehearsed. There was an element of secrecy in the arrangements. The Establishment had always been cautious and withdrawn and had shunned what we would call publicity. Is it not a strange thing that only one contemporary artist's impression of the Coronation of Queen Elizabeth I exists? This is a series of pen and ink sketches made by an amateur artist who was present in the Abbey in his office as one of the Heralds of the College of Arms. Presumably no professional artist was engaged to illustrate the scene on the spot as it happened. Fortunately the amateur sketches are very charming and were acquired by the British Museum about 30 years ago.

Leaping ahead to nearer our own times, we know that photography was already a 'going concern' by the middle of the reign of Queen Victoria, yet no photographer was allowed to take pictures in Westminster Abbey at the Coronation of her son, King Edward VII, in 1902. Was this because it was felt to be 'unseemly'? Or was it to preserve some hierophantic mystery of kingship?

The first still photograph of a British Coronation was at the crowning of King George V in 1911. The record states that 'Sir Benjamin Stone, Court Photographer, was permitted to expose a number of negatives from a hidden view-point opposite the Royal Gallery.' Sir Benjamin's predicament deserves our sympathy, but astonishingly the results are excellent. King George and Queen Mary can be seen surrounded by the clergy and Officers of State. Both are seen seated in the Chairs of Estate before the service began; a second picture was taken just before the ritual of the Recognition (the pictures are in the Sir Benjamin Stone Collection, Birmingham Reference Library).

The breakthrough for broadcasting a Coronation came in 1937 when King George VI and Queen Elizabeth were crowned in Westminster Abbey on 12 May, the day that had been chosen some fifteen months before for the Coronation of King Edward VIII. Such circumstances are without parallel in the history of our country: the date was a bare five months after the gloomy memories of the Abdication and it was decided that the original date for King Edward VIII should be taken over by his brother, the Duke of York. The ceremony alone was a tremendous assignment with little time for preparations, yet the new King and his Queen approached it with humanity, dedication and devotion.

The problems of Coronation arrangements lie entirely with the Earl Marshal, who virtually takes over the Abbey on such an occasion. After all, the Monarch is head of the Church!

In 1953 I was to appreciate that this situation was accepted with formality, when on 1 June the Dean, Dr Don, handed the Earl Marshal, the Duke of Norfolk, all Abbey keys giving access to the Abbey from outside. There were two witnesses present, Mr Hebron the Registrar and Mr Bishop, Clerk of the Works. I was told the keys would be returned on the afternoon of 2 June, when the Earl Marshal's responsibilities came to an end.

So far as concerns the sound radio coverage of the 1937 Coronation, the Earl Marshal was certainly puzzled and perturbed about adding a team of reporters and equipment to an Abbey that already seemed overflowing with important people who had to be on the invitation list, to say nothing of the journalists from all over the world clamouring to be present. Fortunately, the Earl Marshal remembered being up in the north-west frontier in India at the time of Princess Marina's wedding and listening to the broadcast of the service, with Howard Marshall's commentary, on the BBC's Empire Service as it was then known. He had been impressed and therefore decided to consult the King, who without hesitation said that the service must be fully broadcast to reach all the people of the Empire and that the BBC must have all the facilities that it needed, provided that the microphones could be concealed and that they could be controlled in a way that would minimise the possibilities of any 'asides' to do with the ceremony reaching the listeners. I think the King must have been aware of an historic incident at the Coronation of William and Mary in 1689. The Princess Anne, observing that her sister was somewhat discomposed by the variety of ceremonies and weight of the crown and regalia, whispered: 'Madam, I pity your fatigue' – a kind thought, not well received for the two were not on the best of terms. The Queen snapped back: 'A crown, sister, is not so heavy as it seems.'

The Earl Marshal gave the BBC wonderful facilities; microphones were hidden in faldstools, on lecterns, from light fittings and under the arms of chairs, with cables tucked along skirting boards and under carpets.

In those days of sound broadcasting it was customary for all or part of the broadcast to be relayed to the crowds in the streets. According to a patient, detailed diary written by the King on the evening of the great day: 'We were woken up very early at about 3a.m. by the testing of the loudspeakers which had been placed on Constitution Hill: one of them might have been in our room. Bands and marching troops for lining the streets arrived at 5a.m. so sleep was impossible . . .' Later that morning, when driving in her coach to the Abbey, Queen Mary had great reservations about the broadcast in general. On arrival at the Annexe she despatched an elderly member of her household 'to speak to the BBC'. This gentleman found a short ladder that led to the commentary box in the Annexe. Michael Standing, who was about to go on the air, heard heavy footsteps and jingling medals approaching – he was confronted by a stern voice telling him that 'Queen Mary could hear the broadcast as she drove in her carriage; it must be stopped immediately.' I believe after some discussion things smoothed over and arrangements continued as planned.

As it turned out, the broadcast went without a hitch. It was so successful that it paved the way for the infinitely more complicated television coverage of the Queen's Coronation on 2 June, 1953. Here again there were even greater problems of space; these were coupled with genuine anxieties about the extra strain that our live cameras might impose on the Queen. At first the authorities went as far as deciding that there should be television cameras in the Abbey but only as far as the Choir screen, which meant that viewers would see the procession going up and down the Nave but absolutely nothing of the ceremony itself. This was to be left to description on sound radio. The adviser on public relations to the Prime Minister and Government had all along favoured full sound and television coverage. He hoped to draft the announcement in such a way that the public would protest against being deprived of the most important element of the service. This is exactly what happened.

When the decision was reversed it led to the organisation of one of the most expressive and beautiful occasions of its kind. All the old shibboleths disappeared. Nothing was left to chance. The movements of all those taking part were timed down to minutes and even half-minutes . . . and they weren't far out at the end of the day. The Earl Marshal, the Duke of Norfolk, had shown himself to be a brilliant organiser of the

Coronation of 1937. This time he surprised many who were participating in the Queen's ceremony by announcing that everyone must dress up for the final rehearsal on 29 May. He had observed that robes of state, mantles, full dress uniforms, swords, even decorations and Collars of the Orders of Knighthood slowed up proceedings considerably. At the final rehearsal, therefore, peers were asked to wear robes of state over a lounge suit and Officers of Arms their tabards ditto. Bishops were to don their copes over purple cassocks and all pages to rehearse in full uniform.

The exceptional quality of the Coronation of 1953 was basically caused by modern technology. With the prospect of a world congregation of millions of people, who with the help of the camera's eye would see and hear more and in greater detail than even a guest in the Abbey itself, it became imperative for everyone taking part (including broadcasters!) to know exactly what was happening and what was expected of them individually. All played their parts with confidence, dignity and reverence: and because they knew what they had to do they were more deeply integrated into the solemn significance of it all.

In this century, at least, it is no longer considered sacrilegious to rehearse ceremonial. There were, of course, several rehearsals of essential importance, held in private for the Queen and the Duke of Edinburgh and the Archbishop of Canterbury. As well as this there were daily rehearsals for everyone concerned in the Abbey for a fortnight preceding 2 June.

As a general rule the Duchess of Norfolk, wife of the Earl Marshal, deputised for the Queen, but on a number of occasions the Queen and the Duke were present in the Abbey, and Her Majesty sometimes took part, walking diagonally across the Annexe with an even, steady tread, never varying the pace by one iota, and joining the long procession already on the move to escort Her Majesty to her chair of Estate in the sacrarium.

Small sections of every aspect of the service were made clear to the participants, from the sequence of processions to instruction on the carrying of the regalia by the Officers of State. Lesser problems were also tackled. The Royal Duchesses and their trainbearers and dressmakers spent several jolly afternoons manipulating yards and yards of toile 'mock up' trains pinned to their shoulders. No detail was too small for attention. Even I was approached by a tactful official from the Earl Marshal's office: 'We are a little worried about you,' he said diffidently. 'We hope you will dress very unobtrusively?' In the event, I wore a long grey chiffon dress, long matching gloves and the obligatory head-covering, a confection of grey velvet and tulle; as grey is not a becoming colour for me I am sure I looked very unobtrusive. Like Michael Standing I was to be situated in the Annexe of the Abbey. This was a temporary structure built on to the ancient West door, creating a vestibule where the great processions could be marshalled and where the Crown Jewels were set out on a damask-covered table, before being carried by the Officers of State in procession before the Queen. The Annexe was the Royal entrance and led to an octagonal lobby with a series of robing rooms alongside for the Queen and the Royal Family.

The first time an Annexe was used was for the Coronation of William IV in 1831. In 1953 no attempt was made to emulate the Abbey architecture for the Annexe. It was courageously built in a modern style: plain white walls with a ceiling of vermilion studded with gold stars. The west side looking on to the street was glazed with engraved glass from top to bottom and, on the day, through it could be seen the silhouettes of swaying black umbrellas outside in the rain. A vast expanse of deep blue carpet matching the carpet in the Nave was the final touch of a brilliant prelude to the Coronation.

CHAPTER ELEVEN

The Coronation

A day which the oldest are proud to have lived to see and the youngest will remember all their lives.

Winston Churchill 2 June, 1953

On 2 June I arrived at the Annexe of the Abbey just after 5.30a.m. accompanied by one of the broadcasters from the Commonwealth, all of whom were sharing commentary positions with the British team, for space and lines of communication were scarce. My companion was Captain Briggs of the Canadian Broadcasting Corporation. We both thought we must be among the first to arrive, but the Abbey doors were already open and manned by Gold Staff Officers directing those taking part in the processions. It didn't seem early once you got there – guests were already filling the Annexe with the brilliance of crimson robes of state, shimmering jewels and full dress uniforms or velvet court dress. Everyone looked so pink and well and at their best, all so calm, composed and untheatrical, as if dressing up like that at such a very early hour was the most usual occurrence in the world.

Unlike Sir Benjamin Stone and his 'hidden viewpoint', our commentary box was the best vantage point I have ever had in my whole career. Situated about ten feet from the ground, almost immediately above the Queen's retiring room and close to the Royal entrance, it consisted of a small rectangular room with a wide glass-fronted window giving a perfect view of the assembling processions, and the damask-covered table for the regalia. Admittedly, we had our backs to the Royal entrance so our first glimpse of the Queen was bound to be the top of her head, but even this difficulty was to be unexpectedly solved in a rather remarkable way.

As in 1937, the approach to our box was by a short ladder which, as the early waiting hours went by, aroused curiosity among friends and the many acquaintances whom I had come to know during rehearsals. I received several visitors including Dermot Morrah, Arundel Herald Extraordinary (and also a *Times* correspondent), who came to wish me good luck and brought the news that Everest had been conquered. This was being whispered right round the Abbey. Later he came back with one small ducal page who unfortunately had been sick with nerves and had refused to go to the first aid post. We sat him down on the floor of my commentary box and, as he revived, he began to show interest in a cardboard luncheon box kindly provided by the BBC. I was too nervous to eat much that day, except perhaps the fruit, but I still treasure the typewritten list of contents with its friendly greeting from the BBC canteen staff:

This luncheon box contains:

> 3 rounds of Sandwiches : Cream cheese and gherkin, Ham and sweet pickle, Tongue.
> Finger Rolls: Cream chicken and ham.
> 1 Buttered Bap.
> 1 Individual Meat Pie.
> 1 Hard-boiled Egg. Tomatoes.
> 1 portion Gruyère or Demi sel.
> Salt.
> 1 portion Fruit Cake.
> Penguin Chocolate Biscuit.
> Apple, Pear, Banana.
> 1 Bar of Chocolate.
> 2 oz Barley Sugar.
> 2 paper serviettes.
> 2 paper cups, 2 drinking straws.
> And this will, we hope, keep body and soul together from 6a.m. to 5p.m.
> Signed, *The canteen staff*, 2 June, 1953.

The traffic of processions between 7.30 (when the Yeomen Warders of the Tower came on duty) and 11 was prodigious. There were between twelve and fourteen progresses from the Jerusalem Chamber to the Annexe, to the High Altar, to the Chapel of St Edward and back again to the Annexe as every detail of the pageant and its appurtenances was set into place. All was being watched intently but with a calm assurance by the Earl Marshal. The Duke of Norfolk spent those early hours strolling among the guests, chatting to friends before they were shown to their seats by one of the Gold Staff Officers. Before the Abbey doors closed at 8.30 to individual guests (except those arriving later by outside processions), the Duke was informally dressed in what I can only describe as a splendid padded smoking jacket worn over his white buckskin knee breeches and white silk stockings, with black velvet slippers monogrammed in gold.

The first duty of the Dean of Westminster, Dr Don, was at 9.30 when, accompanied by the Abbey clergy, he walked in procession to the altar of St Edward's Chapel for the consecration of the Ampulla, the spoon and the newly made oil for the anointing . As has been done for centuries, the oil was then duly poured into what may well be part of the original regalia that escaped destruction during the Cromwellian period: The Golden Eagle or Ampulla. The Dean and Chapter then returned to the Annexe, now presenting an animated scene that was a catalogue of *Burke's Peerage, Debrett* and *Who's Who.*

The arrival of Winston Churchill in his new finery as Knight of the Garter created a stir. As he was to walk in the Queen's Procession he was asked to stay in the vestibule while Lady Churchill was escorted to her seat in the front row of the eastern end of the Choir. Churchill would have none of this. There was nearly an argument – and, of course, he got his way. They walked up the Nave together, Lady Churchill wearing the becoming rose pink silk mantle as Dame Grand Cross of the Order of the British Empire. I had never seen her ageless beauty look so radiant.

Churchill proudly returned to the Annexe, now in his element. He became much preoccupied with the Crown Jewels set out on the regalia table, looking at them piece by piece. He actually picked up the Sceptre with the Cross and pointing to the second stone of the Cullinan diamond at the top of its stem – the Star of Africa – he turned to Dr

Malan, then Prime Minister of South Africa, and was heard to say: 'Your country has been generous to us in the past. I trust such generosity in other ways may continue.'

I was due to go on the air as the Queen and the Duke were about to enter the Annexe. When the procession was a matter of minutes away a little incident occurred that might have been calamitous for the State Trumpeters and me. It looked as if 1953 was to have its well-meaning 'officious person' as well as 1937. For the benefit of timing the exact moment when the opening fanfares of the Coronation service should sound and when my introduction to the service should end, a small piece of red ribbon was sewn into the rich blue carpet at a point ten yards away from the West door. The fanfare was of 55 seconds' duration and it was reckoned that it would take about that time to walk from the marked point to the Gothic archway (Her Majesty's pace had never varied at any rehearsals).

Imagine my alarm, and the alarm of a young Gold Staff Officer waiting to flick an electrical signal to the Trumpeters in the Triforium, when we saw someone in a white overall stride quickly across the Annexe, kneel down and with a shiny pair of scissors cut the ribbon from the carpet. We were bereft of guidance. I felt as if my heart really missed a beat. But the cheers were coming closer and closer; there was no time to do anything but brace oneself, keep calm and trust to luck.

The fates were kind in more ways than one. I suddenly noticed Sir Winston Churchill deliberately coming from his place in the procession to take up a position facing the Royal entrance. He stood gazing transfixed at the open door. The cheers were overwhelming but I could not yet see the Queen. Indeed, it was Sir Winston's look, the smile on his expressive old face, that told me when Her Majesty had reached the top of the steps outside. It was as if he had been waiting to see the young Queen on Coronation Day all his life.

As the Queen and the Duke went to their robing rooms, the Earl Marshal gave a signal and the head of the procession slowly began to move. The Duke entered the vestibule first, taking his place in the space left clear for him. This was almost a precedent: Queen Anne is the only other English Queen regnant who was already married when she was crowned but not much is known of the part played by her husband, Prince George of Denmark, at the ceremony. There were several innovations for the Duke, including prayers offered for him by the Archbishop of Canterbury.

A total silence fell over the vestibule as we waited for the entrance of the Queen. Only a swishing sound could be heard in the Nave as the congregation rose to its feet with what the painter Haydon once described as 'a sort of feathered silken thunder'.

Her Majesty was suddenly before us in the vestibule, supported by the two Bishops and attended by her six very pretty young train bearers, who did not need to grasp the fabric of the heavy long train but held it effortlessly by means of loops of silken cord sewn on to each side of the hem. A few paces behind came the tall authoritative figure of the Dowager Duchess of Devonshire, Mistress of the Robes.

The Queen entered the Annexe with her hands clasped lightly before her. I think she must have been the only woman in the Abbey not to be wearing long white gloves — somehow it simplified the grandeur of her crimson parliamentary robes, so richly embroidered, with the collar of the Garter worn with a parure of diamonds, as well as the famous Diadem, the badge of sovereignty – worn by Queen Victoria in 1838. Queen Elizabeth II was very calm. Her unselfconsciousness and dignity emphasised the serious, forthright approach to the whole of the great service of her consecration and crowning.

(Top) A scene in Westminster Abbey during the Coronation Ceremony 2nd June 1953 (*Hulton Picture Library*)
(Bottom) Dr. Fisher, Archbishop of Canterbury, about to place the Crown of St. Edward on the head of the Queen (*Hulton Picture Library*)

As for the crucial signals to be given as the Queen walked across the vast expanse of carpet, the rehearsals stood us in good stead and the position of the now unmarked point was accurately assessed by nothing but guesswork. Faultlessly the Trumpeters sounded the beautiful opening fanfare specially composed by Sir Ernest Bullock, and directed by Major Meredith, and it ended precisely as Her Majesty stood framed by the Gothic archway of the great West door. The organ and the singing began immediately: 'I was glad when they said unto me: We will go into the house of the Lord', Psalm 122.

It might be thought that as the procession disappeared from our sight there would be a relaxation of tension in the Annexe. Not so. The few who remained on duty were as still and absorbed as the vast congregation witnessing the scene. In particular the officer commanding the Annexe party, the Queen's Company of Grenadier Guards and a small detachment of the Queen's Bodyguard of the Yeomen of the Guard, was much concerned that these men should in some way observe the moment of the Queen's crowning. The service was not being relayed to the Annexe and no instructions had been issued, but I was listening on headphones. The Colonel and I devised a hand signal for me to give the Guardsmen and the Yeomen in the almost empty Annexe in order that they might come to attention at the *moment critique* of that historic day. Later, I received a letter from the officer telling me he had written to the Earl Marshal pointing out the oversight and that this protocol had now been written into the arrangements for future Coronations!

The many facets of the complicated symbolism of the Coronation proceeded with an unhurried precision, from the laying of the regalia upon the High Altar to the Recognition and the Oath, then to the anointing of the Sovereign on the palms of both hands, on the breast, and on the crown of the head. The climax of putting on the crown, and the Homage to follow, were heard all over the Abbey with the loud and repeated acclamations of 'God Save the Queen'.

I was then given the marvellous opportunity of climbing the stairs to the Triforium for a brief glimpse of the scene at the High Altar. Over the heads of guests sitting tier upon tier in the steeply ranged seats I looked down at the golden carpet of what was called the Coronation Theatre. I could just see the lovely eminence of the old wooden Coronation Chair, used at every Coronation since Edward II in 1308.

At this moment magnificence seemed to have been withdrawn. The Queen, divested of all insignia, including the crown, was kneeling before the High Altar at her private devotions, with Prince Philip beside her. They had just received Holy Communion.

For this, the prying eyes of television had been turned away and viewers waited at home for the final episode in the Abbey.

The Queen's great procession was reformed and Her Majesty, wearing the Imperial Crown, received from the Archbishop the Sceptre with the Cross into her right hand and, into her left, the Orb. The procession came slowly down the Nave. I noticed that my Canadian colleague, Captain Briggs, was so moved at the sight of the Queen approaching us that tears rolled down his cheeks as he described the scene. The Queen, very self-contained, serious and calm, did not reveal the inner exaltation that surely must have been there.

Richard Dimbleby had been the commentator for television. Already a well-known broadcaster and war correspondent, on that day he first established his pre-eminence over us all in the craft of what was then being called 'the new profession of commentating'. He wrote afterwards that, from his vantage point high up in the Triforium, 'the whole pageant on the floor of the Abbey moved with a slow irresistible

The scene on the Balcony at Buckingham Palace after the Coronation (*Hulton Picture Library*)

rhythm that seemed to lift it out of time altogether. I thought at one moment as I half closed my eyes and watched the measured ceremony being carried through that I might have been watching something that had happened a thousand years before.'

Personally, I felt that to be present as a broadcaster was to have experienced something rare and precious that no one can ever take away.

The Queen's Coronation has been a model for ceremonial ever since . . . only the weather did not play fair. It must have been one of the wettest June days for years. So wet indeed that, for the sake of the troops taking part in the Queen's procession to Buckingham Palace, the departure was held up for a little while in the hope of a clearer sky.

There was more broadcasting to do and I spent some time describing the orderly pandemonium that broke out as heads of government, colonial rulers and Commonwealth Prime Ministers swarmed into the vestibule, not willing to brave the torrents to walk the short distance to Deane Yard where luncheon was being served in the Hall of Westminster School.

This was an unexpected extra and I remember very little about it except that there was one outstanding personality in all that throng. She was wearing the rose-coloured satin mantle of a Dame Grand Cross of the Order of the British Empire, with an unusual head-dress whose tall, bright red feather did not quite match the rose pink of the mantle. She towered good-humouredly over everyone and waited patiently for emergency transport to lunch. She was later cheerfully to get very wet in an open carriage driving to Buckingham Palace. It was Queen Salote of Tonga.

The VIPs gradually solved their problems and got away to lunch. I realised that I had certainly missed the BBC transport that was to take me home. (I don't know what happened to Captain Briggs, he must have slipped away when I was on the air.) As the congregation thinned out I found that with the exception of the security branch and some of the vergers I was suddenly almost alone in Westminster Abbey. The clergy were all at luncheon.

It was a bonus to be left behind. My senses were uplifted and I walked up the Nave nearly as far as the High Altar, past rows of empty blue velvet chairs. Already a few cleaners were beginning to tidy up, to straighten the chairs and clear away litter left behind, before the public were permitted to see the setting built into the Abbey for the Coronation, the barriers covered with blue silk damask creating gangways between the rows of seats which filled the entire Nave and rose tier upon tier almost to the ceiling of the Triforium for the congregation of 7000 people.

A very great deal has been said over the centuries about litter left behind at Coronations (refreshments have always been a problem). Richard Dimbleby, as he left the Abbey, said he was shocked to see sandwich wrappings, toffee papers, morning newspapers ('All this and Everest too'), and even miniature gin bottles under some of the chairs. As I wandered about ahead of the cleaners I saw relatively little mess and have put it down to typical journalistic exaggeration. Admittedly, on that day I had not yet heard how someone had asked the Lord Great Chamberlain if packets of sandwiches could be carried in a coronet. The reply was that 'it is undesirable but permissible'. One peer at least must have regretted taking advantage of this pronouncement, for when he joined his fellow peers simultaneously putting on their caps and coronets he heard a soft thud and, looking down, saw a plastic-covered triangular package at his feet.

I returned to the Annexe. The swirling crowds outside the huge West window were now allowed much closer to the glass and there was a great sea of faces looking in at emptiness: the Queen had left the Abbey to drive through the wet streets to Buckingham Palace.

The heavy curtains leading to the robing rooms were now pulled back. Greatly daring and feeling like Alice going through the looking glass into another world, I went in. The now empty dressing rooms had a faintly theatrical look with big mirrors and strong electric lights. The Queen's robing room looked very tidy and quite bare save for an arrangement of golden roses set on a small table near the looking glass. In the room shared by the Queen Mother and Princess Margaret there were some sheets of discarded tissue paper about, and a beautiful spray of Odontoglossum orchids nestled in an open cardboard box on the dressing table. Was this a gift sent direct to the Abbey? More likely, a case of second thoughts . . . 'how beautiful, but no, not to be worn on this occasion.'

I could hear the sound of some clearing up, the chink of silver and the clatter of plates, and exploring further discovered a small octagonal dining room in the Royal private apartments. It was here that the Queen and the close members of her family had enjoyed what was later described to me officially as 'a very simple packed lunch brought from the Palace'.

A footman was clearing a large round table, covered with a white damask cloth. In the centre of the table was the perfect still life of flowers, a simple bunch of philadelphus in a small basket, a few petals already dropping from the little cup-shaped flowers. The fragrance was reminiscent of orange blossom.

The table was laid for ten, perhaps twelve, people, and chairs were now pushed back; there were crumpled table napkins around, empty glasses and quite a lot of crumbs. I believe it would be plain to anyone where the Queen had been sitting at that round table, and the young footman shyly confirmed it when I asked if I was right. Characteristically, Her Majesty's chair was set quite straight, her table napkin had not even been unfolded, there were no crumbs and a wine glass was still three-quarters full of champagne.

CHAPTER TWELVE

The First World Tour

Just five months after the Coronation, in November 1953, the Queen and the Duke of Edinburgh set out on their epic journey of six months round the world, to visit ten countries of the Commonwealth and two foreign States, making the Queen the first reigning Sovereign to circumnavigate the globe. I was delighted to be chosen as one of the BBC commentary team. The Royal Yacht *Britannia* was still under construction. As the tour was planned as a round the world voyage by sea, another vessel had to be chosen for the first part of the journey. The Shaw Saville liner *Gothic* was selected chiefly because the route was a familiar one for her captain and crew. She was a comfortable ship of 15,911 tons and had worked regularly in Australasian waters as a passenger cargo ship.

The welcome, everywhere out of doors, was overwhelming — we brought the atmosphere of Coronation day with us, and very often the acclamation and adulation verged on wild hysteria. We who had been close to the solemnities in Westminster Abbey wished sometimes that there could have been a deeper understanding of all that these rites stood for. The atmosphere at official functions, by contrast, was of stifling formality and awe. My first impressions were of social *mores* belonging to another age and maybe to other Royal tours — even as far back as 1901, when King George V, as Duke of York, with his Duchess, Princess May of Teck, made a similar visit to Australia. The record states that he laid 21 foundation stones, received 544 addresses of welcome, presented 4329 medals and shook hands with 24,855 people at official functions alone.

For Queen Elizabeth II, in New Zealand and Australia there were long presentation lines in every city, each vying with the others in the number of handshakes bestowed. In Australia it was observed that the presentation lines were mysteriously getting longer and longer as the tour progressed. Apparently, certain 'top people' of influence and wealth were travelling from state to state, where they knew other 'top people' and therefore soon found themselves on other presentation lists: apparently it was not enough to shake hands once with the Royal couple. It was all very different from the unscheduled 'walkabout' visits of today, when the Queen and other members of the Royal Family mingle with the crowds and chat to whom they please.

We travelled westwards around the world from Britain with several short stops *en route* for New Zealand and Australia. The BBC team of broadcasters and engineers split up to be ahead at Bermuda, Jamaica, Panama, Fiji and Tonga.

I was on my own in Bermuda. For the first 24 hours my head was full of the prettiness and charm of the place, which is the oldest English-speaking country in the western hemisphere. As we came in to land at Kindley Airport, I remember looking down in the moonlight at the semi-circular chain of islands strung out like a necklace sparkling with lights across a dark sea. As we came low over the rooftops, I spotted one of Bermuda's most distinctive features. As there are no rivers, the roofs are universally painted with white limestone to catch rainwater rolling down the sloping tiles. The water is then purified for domestic use.

The opening of the tour was my first experience of working with a commercial radio station and, because it was so utterly different from anything I had known in the broadcasting world, I enjoyed it enormously. They were understaffed and overworked but with a relaxed efficiency, and were anxious to be friendly and helpful. Station ZBM had its premises in a small shop in Front Street, Hamilton. The shop window was dressed with postcards of pop stars and long-playing records that could be purchased at a counter inside. Beyond a glass partition, a very tired-looking young man could be seen sitting at a bank of turntables churning out a non-stop live music programme that began at 8a.m. and went on all day until late into the evening. Next door there was a very small office-cum-studio, packed with discs and packets of tapes belonging to customers who had recorded birthday greetings as well as weddings and even funerals.

It was arranged for me to be present in the Bermuda Assembly Hall where the Queen was to attend a special session of the Legislative Assembly and make the first important speech of the tour, which was being recorded in the local station. I was a bit apprehensive about getting this first recording back to London with all possible speed, not being acquainted with the local station's technique. Owing to the shortage of equipment, it was necessary for me to return to the studio to record my impressions before transmitting the whole speech to London. I raced back when it was over but on reaching the shop door realised that something had gone awry. 'I'm sorry,' said the Manager. 'We thought we might get short of tape so we wiped a lot of tapes clean – they were funerals mostly. I'm afraid the Queen's speech has been scrubbed.' I was aghast. 'Not to worry, we are making an announcement . . .'. Sure enough, at the end of 'Oh what a beautiful morning', the tired young man playing the records told the listeners what had happened and appealed to anyone who happened to have recorded the Queen's speech at home to bring it in, adding that the British Broadcasting people would be much obliged. Within about ten minutes, people began arriving on bicycles, in donkey carts, carriages and cars, and we soon had fourteen recordings to choose from. Frankly, there was no time to sort out the best-quality recordings. London was already on the line. I snatched a tape from someone who seemed to know most about recording, ad-libbed my opening piece and was thankful when London congratulated ZBM on the excellence of the first broadcast of the Royal tour. I have recently heard that ZBM is still working from the shop in Front Street, but it is also well established in radio and television in a spendid purpose-built headquarters building larger than our own Television Centre at the White City in London.

I hopped by air from Bermuda to Fiji and then to Auckland to stay in an old-fashioned and claustrophobic hotel with a faded grandeur and portrait of Lord Tennyson in the hall. This was certainly unexpected – but I could sense that the hotel management were proud of him. It seemed to be right in the context of the youngest, smallest and most remote of the original British Dominions: '1200 miles east of Australia, 6500 miles west of America and 12,000 miles away from Britain.' They were still calling it the Mother Country. At that moment, I felt very far away from home, especially as it was Christmas time.

I had introductions to two Auckland families, and both were immensely kind and hospitable in a simple, domesticated way. In 1953 there were no restaurants to speak of in Auckland, or anywhere else in New Zealand, and they were surprisingly complacent about this. There was good home cooking if one was invited out, but dinner in the hotel invariably consisted of roast hogget (tough mutton), boiled potatoes and cabbage, served simultaneously with a pot of tea and an ice cream — all had to be consumed before 7p.m. when the hotel dining room closed punctually to let the Maori staff go off duty.

Everyone was knowledgeable about New Zealand history, and made it all sound as if it had happened yesterday. When I was on my way to do the traditional thing and sign my name in the Visitors' Book at Government House, I was told they had already entertained another Duke of Edinburgh there. He was Queen Victoria's second son 'Affie', who had been able to make a career in the Royal Navy; as captain of HMS *Galatea* he went round the world in 1867 and was enthusiastically received by many colonial territories. The Governor had a ballroom built on to Government House for his visit. 'Affie' may not have been a member of the House of Windsor, but a Saxe-Coburg-Gotha is near enough. He greatly impressed the New Zealanders by playing a violin solo at a dance given in his honour, and next day by successfully driving a coach and four horses up and down the hilly streets of Auckland at a gallop.

The day before the Royal arrival in Auckland (23 December) I met the Governor General, Sir Willoughby Norrie, and his wife, Lady Norrie, themselves preoccupied with the last-minute arrangements for receiving the first British sovereign to stay in Government House, Auckland. New Zealand engineers were working to install cables for the Queen's Christmas broadcast message, to come from outside Britain for the first time. Sir Willoughby was speculating whether the five-acre garden was big enough for a garden party for 2000 guests and Lady Norrie was determined that everything should be as 'Christmassy' as possible. 200 school-children were rehearsing to sing a surprise carol for the Queen, and being told to talk in whispers and tiptoe in single file through the trees to the lawn where at a signal they were to break into the familiar downright rhythm of 'Hark the Herald Angels Sing' early on Christmas morning. It was a genuine surprise and the Queen was charmed.

Perhaps the nicest and most typically New Zealand personal touch was an amusing gesture to see that the Queen and Prince Philip each had a Christmas stocking. Lady Norrie showed me a pair of brightly coloured striped socks and began filling them with inexpensive grown-up toys: novelty trinkets, things like key rings, a compass, pencil sharpeners and, emerging at the top, two small toy ponies — white and woolly, complete with model harness and saddle.

The SS *Gothic* berthed punctually at Central Wharf West on 23 December. In spite of a continuous drizzling rain, over 100,000 people in the streets of Auckland acclaimed and applauded the Queen and Prince Philip and when the Queen replied to the Address of Welcome at the Town Hall, she said just what the people wanted to hear at that moment: 'It has been an inspiring experience for us to travel across two vast oceans from one side of the world to the other and to find ourselves not in a foreign land and among alien people, but at home with our kinsmen.'

It was a magnificent start which, alas, was about to be overshadowed by a national tragedy in the early hours of Christmas Day, in which, unexpectedly, I was to become involved. I was due to leave Auckland almost immediately after the arrival of the Royal party, following BBC policy that someone must go ahead to make all broadcasting arrangements at the next town or city to be visited by the Queen. (I'm glad to say that we all took it in turns to do this chore!) With Frank Gallaher, my engineer for the tour, I was bound for Wanganui, the 'river city' on the west coast of the North Island.

The State Opening of the New Zealand Parliament by Her Majesty the Queen, January 1954 (*Hulton Picture Library*)

Her Majesty the Queen and the Duke of Edinburgh at Pukekura Park, New Plymouth, New Zealand, January 1954 (*Hulton Picture Library*)

Sheep shearing explained to Her Majesty the Queen and the Duke of Edinburgh at Mclean Park, Napier, New Zealand (*Hulton Picture Library*)

We arrived at Wanganui about half an hour after the pubs had opened, a time known in those days as 'the six o'clock swill', and this was a particularly earnest swill as it was Christmas Eve. In 1953 New Zealand licensing hours were brief, which did not help sobriety. Scores of the inhabitants were already half seas over, tottering along the pavements attempting to sing carols. It was a depressing sight. We had an evening meal at our hotel. Frank went to a Christmas Mass at a Roman Catholic church. I unpacked and went to bed.

Three hours later I was awakened by a telephone call from Auckland giving me the news of a terrible train disaster, known to this day as the worst rail crash ever to hit New Zealand. A train from Auckland to Wellington, packed with office workers going home for Christmas, was wrecked because a railway bridge had been swept away by a raging torrent of water at a desolate place near an extinct volcano. The voice on the telephone said encouragingly, 'I think you and Frank are the nearest to it. It's a place called Tangiwai, but I don't quite know where it is.'

We left as soon as possible, at about 4.30a.m., and drove mostly in darkness for over 60 miles. Whenever we saw a lighted window we stopped to ask the way – curiously, people simply couldn't believe us when we told them about the accident. 'We would have heard,' they said. Even when I discovered I was talking to a postmaster and immediately asked him to open up lines to Wellington for the BBC, he refused with a 'Surely not on Christmas Day?' Fortunately he later changed his mind. We drove on, and it was almost daylight when we spotted groups of soldiers crawling over the roofs of train compartments broken and scattered across soggy, wet ground. It was an appalling and to us a totally unfamiliar sight.

Owing to the torrential rains the side of a deep crater lake broke at the top of the extinct volcano called Mount Ruapehu, and a torrent of ash-grey water gushed down the mountainside carrying with it ice, boulders and débris, sweeping away the bridge that was spanning the Whangaehu river and hurling the engine and all but three carriages as far as 40 yards in several directions. As the waters subsided everything was coated with an ashy sediment, as grey as concrete. Dozens of people had been flung clear of the carriages, but were then submerged by the water; their twisted and distorted bodies lay like broken grey statues in a nightmare. The Prime Minister, Mr Sidney Holland, flew by helicopter to the scene at once, arriving shortly after us. Fortunately, a detachment of Army engineers was on a training course nine miles away and so rescue work was almost immediate and very efficient. Casualties were shocking. Out of 285 persons known to be on the train, 151 lost their lives. The Prime Minister worked in shirt sleeves, co-ordinating the rescue effort and trying to keep track of the figures of injured and dead.

Our problem was communication with the outside world in that deserted spot, so we drove back to the Postmaster's house and eventually managed to persuade the man in charge to open up the lines to cable reports to Wellington and London. We were the first to break the story to London in the six o'clock news.

The shock of such a calamity at Christmas, so close to the happy celebrations for the Queen's arrival, was cruel indeed in a small country, though the sad aftermath revealed the Duke of Edinburgh's aptitude for the right word at the right time. He visited relatives and friends in their homes, went to several funerals and later attended a mass interdenominational funeral for 21 victims whose remains were unidentifiable. It was most harrowing. The Duke laid a wreath from the Queen and unhesitatingly joined the bereaved for the rest of the service. One would think it was impossible to bring comfort to those who did not even know if the one they mourned was among those being buried, but the Duke's presence was clearly appreciated, for his gentleness, infinite tact and sincerity.

Time swiftly wipes disaster headlines off the front pages and the trauma and misery of the sufferers quickly become a personal matter for them alone. In a matter of days, the Royal tour was on its triumphant way.

The Queen left Auckland on 28 December to begin a series of brief visits by car and by air to small towns *en route* for the great Maori centre at Rotorua. The names of the towns were unknown to most of us from Britain but as they were the first to bask in the excitement and glory of Royal 'whistle stop' visits of fifteen to twenty minutes, here they are! They included Warworth, Pukekohe, Huntly, Te Kuiti, Te Awamutu, (with luncheon at Cambridge), Karapiro, Tirau and on to the beautiful private house overlooking a lake, Moose Lodge, the property of Mr and Mrs Noël Cole, who were waiting to greet the Queen and the Duke on arrival but then disappeared to stay with friends so that their guests could have complete privacy and rest for three days.

On the first tour of New Zealand I had the opportunity several times of staying in the same hotel as the Queen. It was particularly interesting to do so at the Law Courts Hotel, Dunedin, for this was the only occasion that the visit was more than a one-night stand. We were there for four nights — and were to be perpetually and pleasantly besieged. Extra passes were issued, a pink card to be allowed to go out of the hotel and a blue one to return. Looking back, I know that the security measures were much more informal and friendly than would be required today. One became acclimatised to the non-stop chant of the crowds outside — 'We want the Queen' — whenever she returned from an engagement. This did not intrude in the daytime, but on one occasion (in another hotel this time, near the end of the New Zealand visit, at Invercargill) the police were unable to move on a small group of misguided loyalists who kept up the racket after 2a.m. The Queen had to move to the only corner available that was quiet. This was a small 'ironing room' that happened to have a single metal bedstead kept in case of an emergency. Next morning after breakfast the manageress showed me the room — she was outraged that what she called the 'luxury Royal Suite' had to be abandoned in the middle of the night.

The stay in Dunedin taught me that the work of a Royal tour never finishes for the principal participants. In between functions someone was nearly always to be seen waiting for the Queen's return to be given a special audience — a delegation with something to say about a worthy cause, or an eminent descendant of someone who won a medal in the Maori wars but was now too decrepit to meet the Queen at a garden party. Last, but not least, there were the red despatch boxes from London, said to be kept to the minimum on tour, but nevertheless to be seen daily in a shuttle in and out of the Law Courts Hotel.

*   *   *

Canberra and its Parliament have been close to the Royal Family since 1901, when the future King George V inspected the beautiful territory that was being mapped out as the site for a parliamentary city for the several states of Australia. Today it is a twentieth-century garden city with modern architecture, conventional but handsome in style, surrounded with carefully planned open spaces and parks, enhanced by numerous statues. The largest structure is probably the imposing War Memorial, known as the

Hall of Memory and dedicated to those Australians who lost their lives in the World Wars.

The Queen and the Duke of Edinburgh spent five days in Canberra in 1954, and in their crowded programme were two outstanding ceremonies. The people of Australia paid a magnificent tribute (through public subscription) to the United States Armed Forces who gave their lives with valiant Australians in a common cause. The memorial design is unique and imaginative, a slim octagonal aluminium shaft rising 258 feet above its surroundings of green fields and trees. After moving speeches by several persons closely associated with the project, Her Majesty unveiled the monument which, standing apart in its lonely grandeur, is now a witness to Australia's gratitude to America for timely help in days of peril.

The other highlight of the Royal visit in 1954 was the opening of Parliament on 15 February. The Queen was wearing the bejewelled Coronation gown designed by Norman Hartnell and described in one newspaper as 'the most beautiful dress of the century'. It was an historic scene and the first occasion that a reigning sovereign had performed the ceremony in the federal capital.

* * *

After Canberra, to get to Kalgoorlie, we put the BBC car on the Trans-Australian Railway at Port Pirie to cross the Nullarbor Plain. This is a distance of 300 miles and is the longest stretch of single railway track in the world without a curve anywhere in the whole distance. We were encapsulated for 28 hours in an air-conditioned compartment with large windows. There were no landmarks anywhere – not a house, not a tree, nor a hill – and at night the blue-white and grey-green salt bush (the only vegetation) looked even more ghost-like by moonlight than by day.

The famous goldmining town of Kalgoorlie appeared abruptly on the horizon. There were no straggling suburbs. The salt bush stopped and there we were in a neat Victorian station almost in the centre of town. Parts of Kalgoorlie are still shabbily picturesque: rows of terraced houses with decorative cast-iron balconies supported by slim rusty pillars, all of the same design as if they had been manufactured to be sold by the yard.

We stayed at the best hotel, The Palace, where in the nineties, it is said, all the barmaids wore very décolleté glittering evening dresses from breakfast onwards, presumably for the benefit of goldminers coming off night shifts! The ground floor consisted mainly of two huge bars on either side of a rather spendid horseshoe staircase, which was once used on the stage of the Gaiety Theatre in London. This was brought out by a stage-struck peer who had joined the gold rush of 1892. At the top of the staircase, the first-floor landing dwindled to a dark narrow corridor leading to a few bedrooms built on as an afterthought, for drunks.

To this day, Kalgoorlie depends for its life on a single slender pipeline which carries the city's water from the Mundaring Weir, over 350 miles away just outside Perth. In spite of this, I knew that after the rail journey I needed a bath more than anything in the world. The taps were padlocked. I obtained the key, only to discover that there was no plug in the bath. I called down over the elegant banisters to the proprietor, who shouted back 'We can't waste water – use your heel.'

The Queen and the Duke were due by air from Adelaide next day for a brief visit of two hours and twenty minutes (which was to include a drive to Kalgoorlie's twin town, Boulder, three miles away).

Most of the time was taken up with presentations, beginning with the Governor of

Her Majesty the Queen and the Duke of Edinburgh at the Lord Mayor's Ball in the Town Hall, Sydney, February 1954 (*Hulton Picture Library*)

A Certain Voice

Her Majesty the Queen dubbing Sir Garfield Barwick at Government House, Sydney, February 1954 (*Hulton Picture Library*)

(Top) A Civic Reception for Her Majesty the Queen and the Duke of Edinburgh at Echo Point, Katooba (*Hulton Picture Library*)
(Bottom) Her Majesty the Queen and the Duke of Edinburgh viewing the Blue Mountains from Echo Point, New South Wales, February 1954 (*Hulton Picture Library*)

Her Majesty the Queen and the Duke of Edinburgh visiting the Flag Ship of the Australian Navy, HMAS Australia during their visit to Cairns, North Queensland, March 1954 (*Hulton Picture Library*)

Western Australia, then local dignitaries, mayors of outlying districts, municipal councillors, railway officials, chairmen of the goldmining industries and all of their wives. A bouquet was presented. There was a drive round the Oval packed with children. 'The Golden Mile' was not visited at all. Yet this area was the richest square mile of gold-bearing country in the world; the men worked in tiers of galleries as deep as 4000 feet, and the output was a quarter of an ounce of gold to a ton.

The visit to Boulder was a carbon copy of that to Kalgoorlie. Another bouquet, more presentations, another Oval packed with children. Not for the first time, I found that the followers of a Royal tour can have more fun than the two principal guests. Kalgoorlie is a romantic Australian period piece. They saw none of it.

The programme for Western Australia had to be slightly amended as an outbreak of poliomyelitis had given the medical profession cause for anxiety. At one point there was even the possibility that the visit might be cancelled as most of the cities in the state were affected. But the Queen strongly disapproved of any cancellations or of any measure that was being taken for her sake. We were seeing an early sign of one of Her Majesty's most forceful characteristics. As we all now know, like her father, King George VI, the Queen considers it her duty to take things as they come, whatever the hazards.

There are several examples. In 1961, it was finally agreed with her ministers that she should go to Ghana at a time when the dictator, Nkrumah, was in danger of assassination and a stray bullet was a dreadful possibility. In the event, the Queen was his best protection and the visit was a great success.

Then there was the visit to the troubled area of Northern Ireland, of which one of her household is reported to have said afterwards: 'We hoped to carry it through with honour; in the event it was a triumph.' The same can be said of Her Majesty's determination to go into the thick of things in the French-Canadian campaign in Ottawa and Quebec.

Nevertheless, in Perth a children's rally was wisely cancelled and a medical officer advised that there should be no more handshakes with the presentations. On arrival at Perth, this unusual procedure was self-consciously kept by the Australians, then the Duke forgot the advice and started shaking hands vigorously with everyone. It became a sort of joke, smiles were broader than ever and imperturbably the Queen joined in.

The SS *Gothic* was waiting at Fremantle for the final stage of the Australian tour. The Royal Party lived on board during the Perth visit, a foretaste of the plans to come when the Royal Yacht *Britannia* was commissioned and ready to become a floating home on most Royal tours.

CHAPTER THIRTEEN

The Travelling House of Windsor

The new plan was put into action for the second tour of New Zealand and Australia ten years later, in 1963. It involved a different sort of geographical planning and extensive use of the Royal Yacht *Britannia*. One-night stops in different Government Houses, palaces or hotels are now cut to the minimum, together with the laborious shifting of Royal Household baggage, radio-telephone equipment, the Queen's wardrobe (including ironing boards!) office files and furniture and the equipment needed by the Secretariat.

The general plan these days is for the royal party to leave by air for the first long leg of the tour. They land as nearly as possible equidistant from the capital city they are bound for and a harbour where the Royal Yacht, fully equipped, is waiting.

Whenever geographically practical, the Queen and the Duke return each evening to this beautiful ship. She must be the best-run ship in the world, manned by a hand-picked company of officers and men of the Royal Navy who, once chosen, spend their whole naval career with the ship. As far as possible orders on the upper deck are executed by hand signals, without spoken words of command. Seamen wear a special No. 1 uniform, with their jumpers inside the tops of their trousers, which are finished at the back with a black silk bow. On other blue uniforms all seamen wear white badges instead of the red badges which are customary in the Royal Navy, so they are instantly recognisable when on shore. The Royal Yacht is commanded in person by the Flag Officer, Royal Yachts, who is the only admiral in the Royal Navy to be also captain of a ship. The present captain is Rear Admiral Paul Greening.

It is surely appropriate that the Queen of a maritime nation should travel in her own ship, where everything is done in such style — in fact, as well as it can be done. Great interest and admiration are shown when the ship, floodlit from stem to stern, lies at anchor in the bays and harbours of the world's capital cities. Crowds gather to watch and wait to see Her Majesty coming ashore in evening dress to attend an evening function. It must be a more restful way to travel, for there is some privacy and opportunity for relaxation when cruising from one place to another.

On these tours, the Queen and the Duke entertain extensively on board. Visitors get a glimpse of the way things are done at home in Buckingham Palace. The Queen is surrounded by her own staff in her own ship. I've been to a great many of these informal receptions and will just say they are both marvellous hosts.

Royal Yacht *Britannia* was to make a grand first entrance almost at the end of the Coronation tour of 1953/4. When newly commissioned she sailed to Tobruk and waited there to bring the Queen and the Duke home after the arduous tour. For them it may well have been the most perfect moment of the journey as it was here, on board *Britannia*, that they were reunited after a separation of nearly six months with Prince Charles and Princess Anne, then aged six and four, who with their nannies had come to greet them (a reminder that Prince William was not the first Royal child to get a glimpse of a Royal tour!).

The accredited correspondents attached to a tour do not travel in the Royal Yacht — whatever some of the newspapers say! There is a detailed itinerary laid down for us, involving massive airlifts from place to place to get us a few hours or minutes ahead of the Royal party. These plans include accommodation, generally paid for by the host government, as well as transport to take us from function to function. It is nowadays essential to submit to a rigorous time-table as disciplined as that of the Royal party. To miss a Royal tour plane can be awkward — all the commercial airlines are heavily booked by the sightseers and it could take days to get back on the tour. Some of us are not used to living a life mapped out for weeks, even months, ahead. I was rather agitated in India once to read that, at 3.15p.m. some eight weeks ahead, 'Elephant 16 has been allocated to Audrey Russell (BBC) for the State Entry into Benares'. This was during the Royal tour of India and Pakistan in 1961.

This was the first Royal visit to the independent nations of India and Pakistan, and was followed by State visits to Nepal and Iran, a journey of some 20,000 miles and at least 150 engagements. I well remembered the excitement and pride of my entire family, 40 years earlier, when my beloved Uncle Dudley, "Fruity" Metcalfe, having got through the First World War in France and Mesopotamia without a scratch, was appointed to the staff of the Prince of Wales for his long tour of India, Burma, Ceylon, Singapore and Japan in 1921/1922. That had been a luxury tour for the early twenties. The Indian Government provided three trains, an elaborate train for the Prince, a pilot train for the press and a third for carriage horses and landaus as well as no fewer than 25 polo ponies lent by the Indian Princes. There was also an efficient if complicated organisation of a travelling Post Office. Letters were delivered anywhere on the vast continent if addressed simply to "Prince of Wales Camp, India". Little did I imagine that 40 years later I too would have a magic postal address, "Queen Press, India".

Since childhood I had had a picture in my own mind of what I felt India must be like, through the many stories Fruity used to tell us of romantic customs and traditions when he was serving in the Indian Army. Would the people have changed considerably in the fourteen years since Independence? How would the Queen be received? Would she enjoy it?

I was already in New Delhi waiting for the arrival of the plane from London. The answer was almost immediate. As Her Majesty stepped from the plane she said: 'I am thrilled to be here. To all India I bring a greeting of goodwill and affection from the people of Britain'. It was the first visit by a British monarch since 1911, when King George V held his Delhi Durbar, accompanied by Queen Mary.

If there was any apprehension about the reception, it was quickly dispelled by Delhi's incredible welcome. Thousands of people assembled from dawn onwards, having driven overnight in bullock carts to greet the Queen. They kept on coming and the numbers went up and up . . . by the time the Queen's car began its hour-long journey to the President's palace, driving at the processional pace of under five miles an hour, the traffic experts were estimating that there could be almost 2,000,000 people lining the route.

I had been allotted a commentary point near Air India, close to the grand entrance of the President's residence. Originally designed by the famous British architect, Sir Edwin Lutyens, to be the home of the Viceroys of India, it was built between the years 1921 and 1929. The press criticised it for its sheer size, to which Sir Edwin airily replied: 'I am building this palace to impress – as well as for other architectural reasons.' There are a mile and a half of corridors and 340 rooms, of which 63 are living rooms and eight are enormous state rooms. These proportions were certainly impressive.

The Queen's suite was on the first floor in a wing known as a 'Dwarka suite', and consisted of huge bedrooms and bathrooms, and a private sitting room panelled in dark teak rather like the boardroom of an exclusive London club. White carved pilasters flanked the many portraits of Viceroys of the past: Minto, Reading, Hardinge, Halifax and others. There were four portraits of royalty in the corridor outside the Royal apartments, as well as more Viceroys and Vicereines in a series of works done in the academic style of the early twenties by Indian artists, instructed or certainly influenced by someone like Sir William Orpen. I was indebted to staff members of Air India for a lightning tour in the early morning of Rashthrapati Bhavan, a superb building with constant reminders of its British past.

There was so much to see of great interest that I nearly forgot that London wanted to experiment with the idea (time permitting) of going live into the 8a.m. News in London sometime during its ten minute duration. Miraculously, the timing did not let us down. The procession passed us at just the right moment, and I was able to describe the scene for four minutes, not only to the World Service but also to home.

The most complicated and difficult manoeuvre of the great occasion was when, due to go on the air, I had to clamber up a ladder to the domed roof of an ornamental pillared structure that reminded me of the domes of the Royal Pavilion, Brighton. The circular ledge of the dome was too narrow for my feet to stand on, so I managed to balance on the dome itself.

The Queen and the Duke were waving vigorously to the vast crowd and looked relaxed and even happy after their 18-hour flight from London. After luncheon in the Queen's private suite at Rashthrapati Bhavan (which is said to be twice as large as Buckingham Palace) following a short rest the Queen's first act was to drive to Rajghat to lay a wreath on the memorial to Mahatma Gandhi, who devoted his life to ending British rule in India. It is the custom for visitors to approach the shrine unshod, but as a concession the Royal party wore slip-on red velvet sandals. The Queen planted a sapling near by, and then received the first of the many gifts of the tour, this one presented appropriately by Gandhi's fifteen-year-old grandson. It was a spinning wheel, symbol of the non-violent campaign of rural cottage industries which led to India's freedom. The first day in India ended with a state banquet and a short speech of thanks by the Queen. The rest of the evening was devoted to meeting the guests, nearly 100 in number and including Sherpa Tensing of Everest fame.

I was suddenly aware that the Queen was looking at me and got ready to curtsey in case she came closer. She began to smile broadly and I was astonished when I heard her voice: 'I saw you up on that perch today – do you have to be so high?' I nodded, and I think I shrugged my shoulders.

When the Benares visit came, it was a great thrill. My processional elephant was elderly and well trained, and automatically knelt down to make mounting easier. The young son of his owner was already installed and appeared to be sitting almost on the head. It was a long elephant procession with Her Majesty and HRH bringing up the rear, sitting in the most decorative and lavishly equipped *howdah* of them all.

It was a marvellous way to enter the holy city of the Hindus: Benares claims to have 1500 temples that give it a solemnity unmatched in any other city I have ever seen. The crowds thronging the route were on the whole dignified and quiet, and enthralled when they saw the Queen and the Duke.

Later that afternoon, I escaped the ceremonial formalities to explore another neighbourhood, which was the greatest contrast imaginable. The River Ganges sweeps through the city for about four miles. The scene was macabre and tumultuous. The banks of the river are lined with stone, with landing places (or *ghats*) built along the wall by pious devotees and worshippers. The whole area was crowded with bathers, young and old and dying, who had come to wash away their sins in the sacred river. The smoke of funeral pyres on the bank rose like a series of grey-black clouds across the water. These pyres of 'bonfire wood and bones' are built and attended by young boy relatives of the dead or dying. It was a tragic, repetitive scene when viewed from a boat on the Ganges. Small groups of families surrounded their loved ones, sometimes carrying them to the edge of the water as a final blessing. It was noisy, with the commotion of a multitude of beggars hoping to live on the alms distributed by rich Hindus and *always* on the look-out for a tourist. I found it difficult to evade a repulsive Indian mendicant who kept following me, chanting: 'I show you dead body . . . one rupee.'

There were a number of diplomatic complexities when, after the tours of India and Pakistan, there was a State visit to Nepal. Katmandu was in a frenzy of preparations right up to the morning of the Royal arrival. All the temples and shrines (said to number 2000) in the city were regilded and the carvings of both Hindu and Buddhist deities were newly painted in the bright primary colours of folk art. The paint was hardly dry before the faces of the most popular deities were smeared with clarified butter and red ochre powder. This appeared to be a devout form of worship inextricably mixed with the elation of a festival. There had been some political unrest caused by the temporary suspension of the constitution; this gradually calmed down as the atmosphere of festival and carnival built up. King Mahendra of Nepal made full use of his autocratic powers to expedite the work of widening the streets of the Royal routes. Houses were knocked down and compensation was paid summarily on the spot. The finishing touches included banners and welcoming arches with greetings in English: 'Heartiest Welcomes' and, though Christmas was long past, 'Peace on Earth, Goodwill towards All'. 'Welcome to Bess and Phil' was removed at the last moment and so was 'Good Hunting', for reasons to become apparent at the airport.

As an absolute ruler, King Mahendra, with his consort Queen Ratna, sat under a shady canopy at the airport a little back from the tarmac surrounded by a number of notables in flamboyant full dress uniforms. The Royal party were travelling in two Dakotas, taken out of mothballs by the RAF as being the safest for the mountainous journey and short runway at Katmandu. I was doing a commentary relayed to New Delhi and was thankful and relieved to see the small planes land safely and taxi to the stopping place about 50 yards from the King. (These aircraft already have a place in history, as they were used extensively in the last world war by the late Lord Louis Mountbatten during the Burma campaign.)

The doors opened and we waited. I spotted a senior member of the Household at an aircraft window looking at King Mahendra, who remained seated. It became clear that he expected the Queen to disembark and walk up to him. It was nearly ten minutes before he 'got the message' and slowly rose to his feet. The Queen and the Duke appeared immediately and they all met, smiling, on the tarmac.

During the playing of the anthems, it was noticed by most people that Prince Philip's right-hand index-finger was bandaged and in a finger stall. I could almost feel the wave of consternation sweeping though the crowd. Tiger shooting in Nepal was considered to be the grandest form of entertainment for Royalty and the Duke had contracted an infection in the trigger finger. It was unlikely there would be 'Good Hunting' for him. Like the Queen, he was to be a spectator at the huge camp created in the jungle for the tiger shoot.

The arrangements for this event were elaborate. An airstrip had been built. Acres of land were cleared to create a tented camp and the whole area was scooped out to a depth of nearly a foot to eradicate scorpions, prolific in that region. The site was returfed, rolled and watered: they actually brought a steam roller and a fire engine into the jungle to do it. Nepal had entertained no fewer than six members of the British Royal Family to tiger shoots in 91 years. It was announced that 325 elephants were to be used in the drive, five of them carrying refreshments and known as the 'bar elephants.'

It was all in a great tradition belonging to an age that showed little concern for the preservation of wild animals. Prince Philip had been criticised in the British press when he went tiger shooting on the private visit to the Maharajah of Jaipur a few weeks before arriving in Nepal. It was a delicate as well as an incongruous situation. At that time the Duke was President of the British National Appeal for the World Wildlife Fund. For the Nepalese the tiger shoot was to be the highlight of the entire State visit. To refuse to take part except on medical grounds would have been incomprehensible to most indigents. The problem was partly solved (except for the tiger) by a compromise. It meant a diplomatic whitlow for the Duke, which he carried off very well, and the shooting party was restricted to members of the Queen's entourage. Lord Home, then Foreign Secretary, was one of them. He aimed and fired but it missed. The tiger fell to Mark Bonham Carter, the Duke's equerry.

Prince Philip is now the International President of the Fund. He must be relieved that this was to be the last shoot of its kind, for the whole area of the camp is now one of three Nepalese tiger reserves.

I really enjoyed every moment of the visit to Nepal. It was exhilarating to be breathing the thin clear air of the Himalayan range, and I was lucky enough to have been invited to stay with friends at the American Embassy. Unexpectedly, I found myself with the whole of one evening free: a rare occurrence. Owing to certain limited resources and the huge size of the press party, a ballot had been held for media invitations to the King's banquet and I had drawn a blank.

With mixed feelings I watched the departure in full fig of my friends, the Ambassador and his English wife. As the official car swept down the drive it felt strange to be alone in the now silent house. Dinner was served for me in the large ambassadorial dining room by two dignified barefooted stewards, who did not speak English. Halfway through the meal, all the electric lights went out. The servants made no comment. I opened the French windows and in total darkness walked to the gates, half hoping to get some information from the sentry, who spoke a little English. His head was bent in sleep although he was standing up, one shoulder leaning against the side of the sentry box. I walked on down the rough road to a turning. The darkness was uncanny, but I came on the remnants of a market where a few stall-holders were patiently extinguishing naptha flares as if ordered to do so. Then, looking north, I saw a splendid sight. There was a blaze of steadfast lights along the length of a big building somewhere in the foothills. I asked questions all round and eventually learned that this was a romantic if autocratic gesture by the Queen's host. King Mahendra had decreed that when Queen Elizabeth II had dinner with him, the Banqueting Hall should be the only place in Katmandu to be illuminated, like a star.

I had visited fifteen different countries on royal engagements before setting out again on the second tour around the world in 1963. The return journeys to New Zealand and Australia were very different — and not merely in the tour organisation; there were changes in the countries themselves. In New Zealand, there was a strong feeling of greater self-sufficiency — a certain hardening of attitudes at the prospect of Common Market considerations. But the same values and democratic principles prevailed and although the welcome was less hectic there was, I believe, a deeper appreciation, understanding and affection for the Queen and all she stands for: it was a more natural and mature relationship.

Australia was also greatly changed. Again there was the feeling of self-sufficiency, but the most notable change was in a much greater sophistication at almost all levels of society, brought about through the integration into Australian life of European migrants. We saw a great many of them at special reception centres in 1954, sad, worried foreigners, most of them unable to speak English, desperately anxious to start a new life. By 1963 the majority were already running successful businesses and were now part of the country's professional life. They forged ahead — to the good of Australia. It was said that catering and the rag trade were almost entirely in their hands

Perhaps the greatest difference that was to affect the Royal visit in 1963 was the introduction of television for the very first time. It felt as if the cameras never left the Queen all day. Certainly everyone wanted to see her, and families with children could not do so without the hazards of standing for hours in a blazingly hot sun. This is what gave rise to the press comments that the crowds were smaller and that the tour was 'a flop'. Many Australians were deeply hurt about this. Everyone was hiring, buying or borrowing television sets or crowding the hotels to watch, solely to see the Queen. 'We thought we gave her a nice welcome; anyway, we'd like her to enjoy herself.'

Even in 1963 I do not think any of us would have believed that in 1973 the Queen would be able to go to Sydney just for a week-end to open the new Opera House.

In spite of the evolution in the development of the Commonwealth and the breaking of some of the bonds that held the colonies to Britain, we are fortunate that the Queen and the Duke are very 'Commonwealth-minded'. There is no doubt that Her Majesty regards the upholding of Commonwealth ideals as one of her most important responsibilities. As country after country approaches freedom, it seems that we have been learning how this independence can be achieved with some peace and dignity. That independent countries can still retain stable links with Britain and the modern Crown is surely due to the extensive travels of the Queen and other members of the House of Windsor.

To quote an American philosopher, 'The years teach much that the days do not show.'

CHAPTER FOURTEEN

With Dimbleby in Monte Carlo

After the war Richard Dimbleby was undoubtedly the most accomplished, elegant broadcaster in the BBC. He had been the Corporation's first fully accredited war correspondent, travelling abroad most of the time; now he settled down to a busy life in a series of lightweight programmes, including 'Twenty Questions', as well as the more serious productions such as 'Panorama' and the inevitable all-night coverage of General Elections. They all suited his strong, suave personality very well. He had already distinguished himself as a commentator on ceremonial occasions and could not fail to be aware that he was certain to be included in the OB team — at ceremony after ceremony. In this specialised section, however, he did develop a hushed reverence for Royalty that some people began to find affected. But I don't think it changed his great popularity — he was very talented.

As far as I remember, he never undertook the very long Royal tours. A Royal State visit of three or four days was about his limit. There was the inherited family business to be cared for — the *Richmond and Twickenham Times*, and other local newspapers.

In 1954, news broke of a story that had a fairytale quality to it and which immediately attracted Richard's interest. This was the announcement of the engagement of Prince Rainier of Monaco and the beautiful American film star, Grace Kelly. It would be quite possible for Richard to have asked to cover the story: it suited his style and he liked going to Monte Carlo's casino anyway. He'd reached a point where he could almost pick and choose his assignments.

The marriage took place on 19 April, 1956, and to my great delight I was chosen to accompany Richard for the wedding and the celebration programmes before the day. Although we had worked together frequently, this was the first time we went abroad together. We flew to Monte Carlo and needed every hour of the five days we spent there to do our 'homework', as it was difficult to get information.

Our best informants were members of the Cathedral church, who were equipped with printed handouts for the press written in several languages. These described the service, the music and the sermon, and included a list of people expected to arrive as guests: Hollywood stars like Frank Sinatra, Ava Gardner and Bing Crosby, and other famous names such as Somerset Maugham and the Aga Khan. There was even a description of the wedding dress. Unfortunately my copy of the handout was in Swedish. It had been given to me by a well-meaning chorister who had decided that this must be my nationality as I had very fair hair.

The worst of it all was that we never saw the bride, except on television: White tickets edged with gold were issued for our seats at the service, but Richard was appalled to find that these seats were not in the Cathedral, overcrowded as it was with Hollywood stars. We were located in Monte Carlo's famous Aquarium, near the Cathedral, and sat on two chairs working to a television monitor. The Aquarium was full of fish tanks, and the fish swam round and round, opening their mouths as they passed us (there was one enormous eel I didn't care for). Only Richard could have sounded so professional and calm in such circumstances. But the London office was very complimentary to us both in a message sent down the line afterwards.

It was such a hectic week that it was liable to affect character, as I discovered on an evening before the wedding. I was billed in the *Radio Times* to describe a programme of folk music sung by enchanting groups of local school-children in pretty peasant dress. I had watched a rehearsal earlier in the afternoon out of doors, and was looking forward to doing the programme on my own. When I entered the theatre box allocated to me I found it already fully occupied by Richard Dimbleby. I pointed out that I was billed for the programme but, looking very firm, he said: 'I think it will be much better for me to do this. Yes, I'm sure I'd better do it'. In every sense there was nothing more for me to say. I was literally speechless and astonished at his unbounded confidence.

As it turned out, his rearrangement did not work out quite as he expected. Prince Rainier and his bride were nearly half an hour late arriving at the theatre. Soon I was aware of panic signals in my direction for help to fill in the gaps. This was just a little too much. He ploughed on, but as a Dimbleby broadcast it was as near as he'd get to a fiasco.

I kept thinking of the row I'd get into when I returned home – and made sure that I immediately told the head of Outside Broadcasts how it happened. The episode certainly revealed the tremendous esteem in which Dimbleby was held by the hierarchy of the BBC: 'Oh, Audrey, you must realise that Dimbleby generally knows best.'

Of course we made it up. We had to – he was that kind of person. On the evening of the wedding he invited me out to dinner at the lovely restaurant that Churchill often went to at Roquebrune. The place was packed with what seemed like one enormous party – and so it was. One could recognise the Kelly family face. The head waiter, anxiously looking for a table, turned to Richard. *'Monsieur, vous venez joindre la famille Kelly?'* Most of them had spotted us as strangers, and they gave us a wonderful welcome with champagne!

CHAPTER FIFTEEN

Delightful Ostentations

The very all of all is . . . that the King would have me present the Princess, sweet chuck, with some delightful ostentation, or show, or pageant, or antic, or firework.

William Shakespeare, *Love's Labour's Lost,* Act 5 Scene 1

From the point of view of broadcasters and other followers of the Queen's travels, three-day State visits to friendly foreign powers are more like a party than is any Royal tour.

No doubt the Foreign Office would disagree with this ingenuous comparison between State visits and Royal tours, emphasising that some of the greatest diplomatic coups and treaties have been achieved when the proceedings were cloaked and enveloped with elegant entertainments of all kinds. For those of us on the fringe, a Commonwealth tour is like going to see a distant relative – a worthy aunt or cousin with whom family matters must be discussed and settled – and the Queen's programme is littered with industrial development plans, hospital visits, the opening of colleges, schools and scientific laboratories, to say nothing of the State Openings of Parliament and other major events that are generally the focal point of a tour. A State visit, on the other hand, is for us almost all fun and entertainment.

Gala performances of opera and ballet are a tradition (as they are when Heads of State come to see the Queen in Britain). In Europe the entertainment, on occasion, is some interesting and little-known work. In Denmark we watched *The Dancing School* by Bournonville, an early nineteenth-century choreographer whose work in the French style is said to have survived in a purer form in Copenhagen than anywhere else.

In Norway, a seat in the dress circle of the Oslo State Theatre is always kept empty as the ghost of Henrik Ibsen is reputed sometimes to occupy it. It was left empty when the Queen went to see a performance of *Peer Gynt*, but there was no sign of Ibsen. I know this for a fact, as I was put to sit next to him.

I can think of a long string of performances remembered with much pleasure: *Der Rosenkavalier* in Munich, Verdi's *Falstaff* in Rome, the Portugese ballet of the love story of Prince Pedro and Inez, based on fact, in Lisbon. The operetta *Die Fledermaus* was much enjoyed in Vienna, although many Viennese opera lovers complained that a greater and more important masterpiece should have been 'put before the Queen.'

With their heritage of the past, the European capital cities rely extensively on great works of art and architecture in welcoming and entertaining Heads of State. The French in particular go to great lengths to achieve special aesthetic effects. On the first State visit to France in 1956 they decided that the regular Arrivals Lounge at the airport was too mundane for a Royal visitor (anyway, it complicated the normal traffic arrangements), so a temporary staircase was built outside the airport building reaching

The author (*Camera Press Limited*)

up to a first-floor reception room. The window was turned into an entrance and inside a famous equestrian work of art was strategically placed on a big easel so that the Queen's first glimpse on entering a building in France would be of something to do with horses. They had to pass the equivalent of an Act of Parliament to be allowed to take the beautiful work out of the Jeu de Paume Museum. It was labelled with a new brass nameplate reading '*Promenade à L'Anglaise*' by Henri de Toulouse Lautrec, and depicted a young woman riding side-saddle – it could have been in Rotten Row. The Queen and the Duke, accompanied by President Coty, mounted the stairs to be greeted by the Mayor of Paris who quickly ushered them in for a long line of municipal presentations, but forgot the picture! There was no opportunity to pause before it later. The designer in charge was in tears after this gaffe, and who could blame him?

Some time afterwards I was anxious to get a reproduction of the work, as I needed it for one of the lectures on art that I occasionally give at the Victoria and Albert Museum. It took me years to find it, searching through catalogues for 'Promenade à l'Anglaise': I wasn't to know that to make it more appropriate for the Queen, the designer had changed the name! Toulouse Lautrec had called it 'L'Amazone' and so it was listed at the Jeu de Paume. Ceremonial detail can be a delicate commodity.

Most European countries have the same feelings on the choice of subjects for works of art for the Royal State Apartments. It is nearly always horses for the Queen and yachts and ballerinas for the Duke. Organisers of State visits are always very proud of the private apartments arranged for the Royal guests and are glad to show them off to the press, whether they are in a palace, a private mansion or an hotel.

As for the European treasures brought out for the occasion, I should add that some object is invariably unearthed from a store-room that was once the gift of Queen Victoria to her opposite number ruling at the time. I have seen Indian ivory boxes to put things in by the score, huge bulbous vases, and dinner gongs supported by tusks of an elephant. The historical significance appears to outweigh all artistic considerations. Queen Victoria's gifts can be picked out instantly.

Although a State visit is certainly 'a party' for those without immediate responsibility for the detailed arrangements, I have often been certain that diplomatic implications between one country and another can create situations which make members of the Royal Household wary and watchful of protocol and etiquette in faraway places. It is a question of distinguishing between different codes of manners and a blatant attempt to pull rank. The latter was probably often true during the Queen's controversial tour of Ghana.

Loudspeakers on a route for a Royal procession would blare out the message 'Osagyfo is coming – Osagyfo is coming.' This was offensive in two ways. A translation of the word is Messiah, a title that some Ghanaians had given in their adulation to Nkrumah. It was an occasional afterthought when the loudspeaker voice sometimes added: 'Osagyfo is coming; he is bringing with him the Queen.' This was banned by the Queen's press secretary.

In Africa and elsewhere the delightful ostentation of a firework display is considered a fitting conclusion to a day of special celebration. The craze for fireworks is parallel to the fashion for them in England 200 years ago. They are noisier in Africa than anywhere else: people like it that way, and there is no Noise Abatement Society to complain about it afterwards. But for many journalists on a State visit or Royal tour a display of pyrotechnics is liable to become the last repetitive straw in a long day. Adjectives are then running low, and seem no longer meaningful, to this writer anyway, and so the display gets scant coverage all round.

Not so in Ghana. President Nkrumah spared no expense for the best possible conditions for a lavish display when the Royal party were in Accra. Mr Thomas Bennett, then managing director of the oldest private pyrotechnic firm in Britain, was in charge. For many years this firm had a representative travelling with us whenever a display was to be organised. Although their handiwork creates something pretty, decorative, entertaining and exciting, all the 'firework men' I've met seem to be reserved characters, gloomy, worrying that rain will damage the explosives or that they are under-insured. It must be an extremely dangerous job, especially with foreign labour. They seem to be 'loners', and are often seen having an early meal in an empty hotel dining room, morosely waiting to be served. Mr Bennett was the exception – probably because the conditions were perfect. The huge open space of Black Star Square was available for the crowds; Nkrumah had built a permanent concrete platform as a firing site; technicians were given a covered working space for storing the explosives; and as the square was adjacent to the beach, the sea provided a superb background and 'fallout area' for the wilting fireworks – which were also reflected in the calm water.

However, it was not the perfect conditions that brought the entire press corps to Black Star Square that night. It was further rumours of threats on Nkrumah's life. A firework display would seem to provide an ideal cloak for misdeeds of that kind and Mr Bennett recalled two instances of this happening in his own time, in Russia in 1912 and in Bolivia in 1948. With hindsight it can be said that the Queen was Nkrumah's greatest protection.

The Royal and Presidential parties sat in a specially designed box, protected by bullet glass and illuminated with shaded lights making it look like a tropical fish tank. I mingled with the crowds along the beach, a portable tape recorder strapped round my middle and at the ready – a doomwatch patrol indeed. The Queen sat beside Nkrumah looking astonishingly calm and relaxed. The President was voluble and flamboyant as usual.

There can be an element of fear in a firework display, and this is sometimes encouraged by pyrotechnic experts. Intentionally the noise was terrific, and the titles of the set pieces added to the drama: 'A Swarm of Hissing Cobras', 'The Chase of Fiery Serpents', 'Flaring Aigrettes with Echoing Reports'. It was said afterwards to be one of the most spectacular displays ever fired in the continent of Africa. I felt deeply thankful when it stopped. Advance publicity had made it known that it would be a programme of half an hour, costing the government of Ghana £30,000. £1000 a minute was impressive and in keeping with the panache of Kwame Nkrumah.

There are some State visits that unroll with an orderly predictability that can even be considered a little dull. However, during the visit to Portugal in 1957 there was a special quality in the air. The whole atmosphere was lively, spirited and spontaneous. I believe the Queen felt it and was part of it too. There was a series of unexpected incidents, as when the Queen and Prince Philip spent a day in Oporto (home of Sandeman's port) and the car provided to drive them round was very closed-in, with small windows. Suddenly Prince Philip spotted an old green open charabanc being used by the press. So that the crowds could see the Royal visitors better, it was commandeered for the rest of the drive. The bewildered, hilarious photographers rode in the Royal car!

Then the BBC engineer supposed to be with me for the programme at the Royal Opera House in Lisbon unfortunately mislaid his passes and theatre ticket. His nickname is Jacko, a most resourceful man. For the Lisbon police he produced, of all things, a season ticket to Epsom. The effect was miraculous; he was not only admitted to the theatre but ushered up to the then empty Royal Box. From my position in the auditorium I saw the embarrassed figure of Jacko and could not believe my eyes. Then he disappeared.

President Craveira Lopes, who was already in the anteroom of the box, saw Jacko, asked him who he was and offered him a glass of champagne. The Queen's arrival was but minutes away so, straightening his orders and decorations, the President hurried to the foyer with Jacko in pursuit. He happened to be carrying a battery operated baffle light, used sometimes for television. The Royal arrival was almost immediate. As the Queen walked along the corridor where Jacko had flattened himself against the wall, she smiled and said: 'Good evening, Mr Jackson, shouldn't you be shining that light on me?'

My own personal odd incident happened on the last day of the visit. A Portuguese broadcasting friend asked me to take a present to London for a surgeon to whom he was deeply grateful after successful surgery in the dangerous procedure of removing one lung. The surgeon was Sir Clement Price Thomas, who had operated on the late King. I did not ask what the gift would be but, when undressing for bed with an early start next morning, I heard a curious creaking noise. Then I noticed a large basket on the floor containing four very large and very live black lobsters padding about inside. I was appalled. The kitchens were closed so, for me, the only thing to do was to tip the night porter to tip the chef to cook them at first light. This was done, but I fear Clem thought I was a bit unadventurous.

An innate liveliness and style seemed to envelop all we did in Portugal, ranging from seeing dozens of patchwork and embroidered bedspreads charmingly hanging from windows in the poorer quarters instead of the flags that people could not afford to buy, to becoming familiar with the rich ornamentation and slender columns in the pure Manueline style of architecture and learning that a transitory event such as a luncheon can be made into a work of art. This was the most beautifully planned and engaging luncheon party I have ever encountered, held for the Queen in the refectory of the Cistercian monastery of Alcobaca. It was an event with fascinating literary associations.

It must have been tempting for the university authorities to suggest to Buckingham Palace that the meal prepared by the Cistercian monks 'for the Author of *Vathek*, William Beckford (1759–1844)' should be reproduced for the Royal visit. Beckford had scandalised London by his ambidextrous affairs and was cold-shouldered by the English colony in Portugal for the same reason. When he first visited Lisbon, attended by twenty servants, he was perhaps best described as handsome, bored, idle and rich. Evidently his reputation had not reached the ears of the Three Grand Priors of the Cistercian Order at Alcobaca who welcomed and entertained him lavishly in the Refectory in the late eighteenth century. Beckford, in his book written years later, *Recollections of an Excursion to the Monasteries of Alcobaca and Batalhia*, described some 'extras' served at the meal:

> The Banquet itself consisted not only of the most excellent and usual fare, but rareties and delicacies of past seasons and distant countries – exquisite sausages, potted lampreys, strange messes from the Brazils and others stranger still from China, edible birdsnests and shark's fins (dressed after the latest mood of Macao by a Chinese lay brother). Confectionery and fruits were out of the question here. They awaited us in an adjoining and sumptuous apartment to which we retired from the effluvia of viands and sauces.

Her Majesty the Queen and the Duke of Edinburgh leaving the Sao Carlos National Theatre, Lisbon, February 1957 (*Barratt's*)

Tactfully, this vast list of delicacies was curtailed by someone in Buckingham Palace down to a delicious luncheon to suit the more modest tastes in food of the Queen and her husband. From nine courses it went down to three. The menu was delicious – hot lobster Peniche, roast veal with petit pois Algarve and endive, and chestnut parfait with hot chocolate sauce, served with fine wines, coffee and liqueurs and all cooked in the same kitchen that Beckford had rather coarsely described as 'the kitchen of Gluttony'.

The most remarkable thing about the whole affair was what was done to make the refectory into the most beautiful setting for the occasion. I find that many ancient buildings, such as Guildhall, Westminster Hall, and The Binnenhof in the Hague, are too uncompromisingly themselves to enhance a party. Heavy stone pillars and Gothic arches seem to be a reproach to the ephemeral essence of an enjoyable social gathering. The kind of room that can adapt itself to an occasion is what is needed; and this is just what happened to the refectory of Alcobaca.

Every single object in that room was a work of art. The arrangement took months to assemble and as far as I could determine the whole organisation was in the hands of one cultured and elegant woman, who was supervising every little detail on the morning of the lunch. This was no caterers' plate and cutlery affair. Priceless porcelain and glass were borrowed from some of the surrounding mansions of the district. There were no complete sets of services – some were too old and rare for that – but colours and periods were studied and a superb selection was set out on a damask tablecloth of gold, stitched with real gold thread and made specially by the textile industry of Alcobaca. There were places for 50 guests. It was as if the organisers had been given the keys of, say, the Victoria and Albert Museum, and been permitted to borrow whatever they liked.

Every possible Anglo-Portuguese connection was emphasised. The cover of the menu bore the arms of King John I and Queen Philippa of Lancaster, the daughter of John of Gaunt. A small coffee cup and saucer, presented by an old lady, had the coat of arms of King Charles II on one side and the arms of his bride, Catherine of Braganza, on the other. This was recognised as such a treasure that they advertised in the press all over Portugal to make it a pair. They succeeded, and the owner of the second cup and saucer generously made them a gift in honour of the occasion. This was such an unlikely triumph that it was decided to have a small boy, dressed in scarlet livery, to stand behind the Royal chairs with a silver gilt salver to serve coffee in these two antique cups and saucers.

Just before luncheon I was invited into the famous kitchen where a band of chefs were putting the finishing touches of garnishing to the delicious dishes. I do not think that the medieval ovens were used, but I know that there were difficult conditions in several ways – particularly in keeping the food hot, as could be seen from the use of small electric fires on the serving tables. 'The brisk rivulet of the clearest water', as described by Beckford, was still running through the kitchen into the refectory where, in medieval and eighteenth-century times, guests could select their choice of every sort and size of the finest river-fish. I am glad to say there were no fish that day, and the water was crystal clear.

About ten minutes before luncheon was served an unexpected routine took place. A barber with a cut-throat razor and towels rapidly shaved the dark blue jowls of the sweating waiters in the crowded kitchen. Each man in rotation sat down close to the lobsters waiting to be carried in. This manoeuvre went so quickly and smoothly that I expect it had centuries of experience behind it.

Later that day, before returning to Lisbon, I returned to the refectory to thank everyone concerned for allowing us to watch all the preparations in that historic place. I expected to find everything cleared away and the refectory back to its grey stone day-to-day existence. On the contrary, the tables had been re-laid and it looked as if another luncheon was about to begin at any moment. The refectory was to be opened to the public for 24 hours. We drove out of town against a stream of incoming traffic, including farm carts packed with family parties, cyclists, chauffeur-driven limousines and people on foot, all making their way to see how Alcobaca had entertained the Queen of England.

CHAPTER SIXTEEN

The Abbey Workshop

. . . where the enmities of a thousand years lie buried

Macaulay

Richard Dimbleby would sometimes jokingly refer to Westminster Abbey as his 'workshop' – with some reason, as the number of State occasions and services of commemoration broadcast from there greatly increased during the fifties and sixties. There were several reasons for this, including perhaps the development and growing popularity of television and sound outside broadcasts, but essentially it was because a new Abbey tradition was, as many people fancied, becoming firmly established – that of Royal weddings. As we all know, the Abbey has been the setting for Coronations since 1066, but until Princess Patricia of Connaught (grand-daughter of Queen Victoria) married Commander the Hon. Alexander Ramsay in 1918, there had not been a Royal wedding in the Abbey since King Richard of Bordeaux married Anne of Bohemia in 1382. As a general rule, for centuries Royal marriages took place in the private chapels of palaces or castles, wherever the sovereign was in residence.

After Dimbleby's supreme broadcast at the Coronation, he was inevitably the first choice for television commentaries on Royal weddings and many other Abbey occasions, until his untimely death in December 1965. I have always regarded it a special privilege to broadcast from Westminster Abbey and feel I could almost say it was my 'workshop' too. I know of no place where ceremonial happens with such an 'effortless inevitability', as if any other way would be unthinkable. Processions invariably move at the right pace. There is an element of simplicity in spite of the grandeur of the surroundings. Although Henry III started rebuilding Westminster at the East End in 1245, and the Abbey as we know it was not finished until 1506, the original style of Gothic architecture was kept throughout the Nave and so processions stream up to the Choir and on to the High Altar and there is no need for an onlooker to adjust to a different architectural setting. This is true of several English cathedrals including Durham, but, for some reason I cannot analyse, the effect is particularly noticeable at Westminster. I remember discussing all this with a friend of mine who was Dean's Verger at the time, a great character, whom everyone called Algy. (His full name is Mr Algernon Greaves MVO, now retired.) As Dean's Verger, carrying an eighteenth-century silver-tipped rod, he led many of the most important processions with precision and impeccable timing. He did not always agree with my views and would say: 'It's not a question of fast or slow but *how* you walk and how you *think* when in a church procession.' This gave me further insight into the meaning of ceremonial.

Having been involved as a broadcaster for sound radio in no fewer than eight Royal marriages since the war (four of them in the Abbey, one in York Minster, the most recent in 1981 in St Paul's, and two in Europe), I could not, even at this distance of time, pronounce one or another as the prettiest, or the most elegant. A Royal wedding is always brilliantly special, and as most people when on the subject of Royalty quote Walter Bagehot, I suppose I must add: 'and as such it rivets mankind'. Frankly the thing I remember most about Royal weddings is how easily and naturally members of the Royal Family can drop into informality like everyone else. I have seen it so often at the wedding rehearsals, generally held a day or so before the wedding day. While waiting for the Archbishop of Canterbury to begin the rehearsal for Princess Margaret's wedding, the Queen Mother, already seated, suddenly crossed the wide Sacrarum to talk to the bridegroom's mother, Lady Rosse. They met in the centre and for at least ten minutes the two future mothers-in-law chatted amiably together in the middle of Westminster Abbey.

At the rehearsal for Princess Alexandra's wedding in April 1963, the Queen impulsively left her chair to help Princess Marina organise the spacing out of the four small bridesmaids and two kilted pages. Princess Anne was the chief bridesmaid, looking very tall and slim – and very grown-up, with her long fair hair swept up and worn coiled round her head for the first time. She walked alone at the end of the bridal procession, revealing a most attractive ability to keep still at all the right moments, an attribute she has to this day. It was hard to believe then that she was only twelve and a half years old. In all, Princess Alexandra had seven attendants in the retinue. Was it, I wonder, this occasion that prompted Princess Anne to turn down ideas of 'yards and yards of uncontrollable children' for her own wedding in 1973, settling for the two most perfect bridal attendants I have ever seen at any wedding? They took their responsibilities so capably and unselfconsciously, and all with the most innocent and charming dignity imaginable. I am sure they are well remembered: Lady Sarah Armstrong-Jones and Prince Edward, both then eleven years old.

When chosen for some special occasion in the Abbey, the broadcaster's first reaction is : 'Where will the commentary point be?' There was no thought for the modern media when most cathedrals were built, and a variety of positions must therefore be found and designated as 'possibles'; – I believe I have tried them all!

For Princess Margaret's wedding I was installed in an adapted builder's cradle, approached from the Triforium and jutting out over the heads of the congregation 70 feet below in the Nave. A bird's-eye view if ever there was one – if and when one had the courage to look down. The BBC outside broadcast engineer in charge sympathised with my purely psychological fear of heights and lent me a harness which I wore at the rehearsal, feeling like a child in a pram. But the harness was therapeutic for I found I was able to abandon it just before the broadcast next day, and to do so gave me more confidence.

At the end of the ceremony, I discovered that I could even see over the top of the altar screen into St Edward's Chapel. I must have been the only member of the congregation to see part of the signing of the registers, and the bride and bridegroom being congratulated by each other's in-laws. In those few minutes a formal Royal occasion became a pleasant family affair.

There were further adaptations to the builder's contraption for the wedding of Princess Alexandra. The sides were filled in and a top put on to isolate me from the organ pipes in the Triforium, which were deafening at times. It was better, but I am glad I was never asked to be there again.

The organ loft is a perfect location for any broadcast, not too high and with a view both ways, looking down to the West door and up to the High Altar. With the kind permission of the organist and choirmaster I have often worked from there at Royal Maundy services, and at memorial services too. However, when State Trumpeters are involved, there simply isn't room for us all and very naturally they have preference. The organ loft is an ideal situation for them, and for the reverberation of sound throughout the Abbey. The trumpeters look splendid standing in line on a wide ledge across the organ loft as they sound a fanfare for a Royal arrival.

The BBC made excellent arrangements for Princess Anne's wedding in 1973. Both sound and television were side by side in commentary boxes in the Triforium immediately above the High Altar. Again it was a distant panoramic scene before us, but immediately below was a close view of almost the whole of the Sacrarium, with the bride's and bridegroom's families sitting facing each other as by tradition. The bright lights for television at this focal point enhanced the glittering display of silver-gilt Abbey Restoration plate set out on the altar and around the Sacrarium. Incidentally, for the first time ever, a security man asked me if he might stand behind my chair, chosen as the best place to view the overall scene. This was a sign of the times, as also were the police dogs sent scouring through the Abbey for fear of explosives at a very early hour on the wedding morning.

I have mixed feelings for one other place from where I have frequently broadcast. Under the organ loft there is a deeply recessed doorway leading to a narrow slip room, affectionately known to broadcasters as the 'boot cupboard'. I have never seen any boots there but I have come across a few cassocks, socks and surplices. In its favour, it is at ground level and blissfully near the scene of action. Yet it can be slightly embarrassing to be at such close quarters to a procession as it passes by. People on the spot can hear what you are saying: it seems paradoxical to mind this, remembering the vast outside audience of listeners or viewers, but to describe what someone is wearing is like making impudent personal remarks when you know that the Royal personage is likely to hear it.

Once, however, I was more than glad to broadcast from such a 'close-up' viewpoint. It was a sad occasion but it was also unique. On 1 April, 1965, a large and distinguished congregation assembled at Westminster Abbey to remember and pay tribute to the late Princess Royal, who had died on 28 March. The memorial service was synchronised to take place at the same hour as the funeral service in Yorkshire at Harewood Parish Church. This was to be attended by the Queen and the Duke and close members of the family. The reason for this synchronisation was that the Duke of Windsor and his Duchess were in London at the time. It was barely four weeks after his serious operation for a detachment of the retina at the London Clinic. To his chagrin he was strongly advised by his surgeon not to travel to Yorkshire. A certain gossip column implied that there were other reasons, but there was no foundation in this whatever. I happen to be able to confirm this with more authority than usual as two years later I was to develop a detachment myself, and it was at least three months before I was allowed to lead anything like a normal life. Many of the Duke's close friends were at Westminster. I spotted the Duke of Beaufort, Lord Louis Mountbatten, Lady Churchill, Lady Sefton and Lady Monckton, widowed only three months before by the death of the Duke's great friend and adviser, Walter Monckton. There were inevitable gaps: it was 29 years since the Abdication. His best man and 'most loyal friend', Fruity Metcalfe, died of cancer in 1957. The Duke had attended his memorial service at the Chapel Royal, St James's Palace. I noticed on that day that there was still a youthfulness in his

Princess Anne and Captain Mark Phillips on the Balcony of Buckingham Palace, 20 December, 1973 (*Hulton Picture Library*)

mannerisms – the settling of his tie, for example – but that his drawn features looked as if he wished no one could see him.

Before the congregation arrived at the Abbey I went to confirm where the Windsors would be sitting. They were to be but a few feet away from the 'boot cupboard'. The Sovereign's stall was reserved for them, and the place-cards read: HRH THE DUKE OF WINDSOR, HER GRACE THE DUCHESS OF WINDSOR. Knowing his bone of contention about the Royal title, I felt sad.

This was the first time that the Duchess was to accompany the Duke at a public engagement in London. The arrangement was that the Duke and Duchess should drive first to the Deanery and then walk into the Abbey by the West Cloister door – the Duke with the Dean, Dr Eric Abbott, and the Duchess escorted by the Archdeacon of Westminster, Canon Carpenter (who has now succeeded Dr Abbott as Dean). When it came to it, the Duke would have none of it. They would walk three abreast with the Archdeacon accompanying the Duke's private secretary, John Utter.

The congregation stood as they entered, a soft organ voluntary was playing and the three of them were talking as they passed me and went through the open gates of the Choir screen to the elaborately carved stalls. The Duke, wearing dark spectacles, did not look around much at the Abbey, which must have held many memories for him of his sister the Princess. Restlessly he sat thumbing through a prayer book and the Order paper; he took an interest in the two place-cards, and the Duchess's hand stretched out several times to restrain him from fiddling with them. To quote from my diary written up a few days later:

> . . . When the service began, it became a dialogue of hands. The Duchess found the places in the hymn books for him, pointing to the exact page with a black-gloved hand, holding a pair of marcasite lorgnettes. Her hands made gentle helpful gestures which he clearly took for granted as a child might do.
>
> I had a narrow shave in my brief description of the Duchess's clothes. I thought she wore a small fur hat, but luckily didn't say so. As they were leaving and she was close to me, I saw that her hair was backcombed into a sort of pad effect across her forehead.
>
> The Duke had firmly picked up the white name-cards, putting them carefully away in a breast pocket. With the Abbey bells ringing half-muffled, and led this time by the Dean's verger, they walked together back to the Deanery where they were to meet and talk to the rest of the clergy. I was told afterwards that the Duke introduced the Duchess to several clerics with 'this is my wife – and my devoted nurse.' She looked very elegant and well preserved.

Recently, when working in the Muniment room of the Abbey, I came on the Duke's letter of thanks, sent to the Dean, 'for the beautiful memorial service for my dear sister'.

Clearly, the Duke and Duchess approved of all the arrangements and the service, which included a prayer specially written for the Princess Royal by Dr Abbott himself. The final paragraph of the Duke's letter reveals a touching humility from the man who briefly was our King:

> It was a sad occasion but your sympathetic reception of us at the Deanery and your accompanying us to our seats was, we can assure you, greatly appreciated.

> Yours very sincerely

> (*signed*) Edward, Duke of Windsor

The author (*B.B.C. copyright*)

It has been said that Westminster Abbey is too famous for its own good and that too many people come to see it for the wrong reasons. I do not agree with the first statement, and find the second offensive for it is very difficult to substantiate. However, watching the thousands of tourists, some bewildered and dazed, being escorted smartly round the Abbey (with the Changing of the Guard, the British Museum and perhaps Hampton Court to be included in the same commercial coach tour) one does see the Abbey in a certain secular danger. At the height of the summer season 9000 to 10,000 people pass through its doors each day — that is about 3,000,000 visitors a year.

The staff are vigilant and experienced in dealing with the public: they can spot cigarette smoke from the length of the Nave, and ice cream is generally dealt with outside the doors. I have never seen the situation anything but very much in hand.

One of the most impressive gestures to preserve the sanctity of the Abbey, in between the services, is that every day on every hour a chaplain climbs into one of the pulpits, calls for silence, welcomes the visitors and says a very short prayer. The effect is instantaneous; though many may not understand our language, people from all over the world stop in their tracks, attentive and aware. When the Abbey celebrated its nine hundredth anniversary in 1965 it was proclaimed that it stood for the unity of mankind, and the theme was 'One People'. The two-minute prayer is generally of topical interest, simple and direct. One time I heard the chaplain say: 'let us pray for those who do not have enough to eat' and, watching the faces of all colours upturned towards the pulpit at this heart-stopping sentence, I felt that, however briefly, the noble aim of 'One People' can be said to be achieved 'on the hour' in Westminster Abbey.

CHAPTER SEVENTEEN

The Maundy

The Office of the Royal Maundy is believed to be one of the oldest services in the Church of England. A similar service is celebrated regularly in Christian churches in many lands. The ceremony of washing the feet of the recipients was discontinued in our British Royal Maundy in about 1730, but the service is still a commemoration of the compassion, grace and humility of Jesus Christ the night before the Crucifixion.

For over 300 years the service of the Royal Maundy was held in London on the Thursday before Easter. For nearly 100 years of this time the service belonged to the Abbey. It was the Queen's first official engagement on her accession to the throne in 1952. Easter was early that year and there was no time to mint new coins, so the pure silver Maundy pennies still bore upon them an effigy of the King's head, instead of her own. Wearing deep mourning, the young Queen, who as a child had once seen the Lord High Almoner make the distribution, went faultlessly through the ceremony, and with a special gentleness towards each of the elderly recipients. That year 26 men and 26 women received Maundy pennies, as many as the years of the Sovereign's life, together with small gifts of money instead of the clothing and provisions that used to be given in kind.

One of the first changes of the reign concerned the Abbey and the Royal Maundy. The Queen decided that people all over Britain should, if possible, be able to participate in the ancient service and that the recipients should not all be Londoners. In alternate years, therefore, the Maundy service has 'gone on tour'. It has been held in other years at the following places:

1953	St Paul's	1972	York
1955	Southwark	1974	Salisbury
1957	St Albans	1975	Peterborough
1959	Windsor	1976	Hereford
1961	Rochester	1978	Carlisle
1963	Chelmsford	1979	Winchester
1965	Canterbury	1980	Worcester
1967	Durham	1981	St David's
1969	Selby	1982	Exeter
1971	Tewkesbury	1984	Southwell

As can be seen, the phrase 'alternate years' cannot be taken literally. There are many requests from clergy all over the country for their diocese to be considered appropriate for a Royal Maundy service, and if these can be backed up by some important anniversary at the cathedral or church itself they are likely to be successful.

However faithful one may be towards Westminster Abbey and its Gothic splendours, it is always enjoyable to go travelling with the Royal Maundy, meeting and possibly staying in the same hotel with all those who, in one way or another, are involved with the arrangements: not only members of the Royal Almonry Office from Buckingham Palace and the Lord High Almoner and the Sub Almoner, but also the florist and herbalist who make the nosegays overnight and the four Wandsmen who volunteer to look after the recipients during the service. In the Queen's reign it has become a small fellowship of people who care deeply for the service and are glad to meet each other every year though they may never see each other in between. It is also a splendid way to tour round the great cathedrals of Britain!

Different styles of architecture and stonework create interesting effects on the two long and imposing processions that open the ceremony. The clergy and choirs escort the Queen and the Duke of Edinburgh to their places. Both carry the traditional nosegays of spring flowers and sweet herbs, once considered to be protection against the plague. Following them comes the Royal Almonry Procession, up to now rarely seen outside London, bringing the Queen's gifts set out on the heavy silver gilt Maundy dish that is part of the regalia, with at least three other alms dishes carried on the heads of the Yeomen Dish Carriers of the Queen's Bodyguard of the Yeomen of the Guard, all wearing their scarlet Tudor dress. The architectural settings for the Maundy have now included Norman or Romanesque, Gothic, Early English, Perpendicular, and some additions of Victorian Gothic revival. To give a personal choice, I felt that the perfectly proportioned rounded arches and pillars of Durham Cathedral gave the pageantry of the processions an especial beauty.

In the provinces the arrival of the Queen puts a whole town or city *en fête*. There are exuberant crowds everywhere and extensive coverage in the local press with huge photographs of the Queen and of the recipients chosen from all over the diocese. In the welter of newsprint on what is a unique event for the district, slight errors are understandable. I felt sympathy for the duty editor of a local paper in Selby, Yorkshire, in 1969. In a column devoted to BBC programmes for the day, the entry read: 'Radio 4. 10.40 Audrey Russell. The Queen distributes the Royal Family at Selby Abbey.'

The ceremony of the distribution is a graceful but intricate one. This ritual was devised by Mr Lawrence Tanner, one of the Abbey's most distinguished historians, when King George V revived the custom of the distribution of the Alms by the Sovereign in 1932. For over 200 years before that the Lord High Almoner (who is always a Bishop) officiated regularly. Lawrence Tanner, then Secretary of the Royal Almonry, was most anxious to strengthen the Royal connection with the service again and it was through him that the Royal Almonry Office was moved to Buckingham Palace. His careful consideration of all the details showed that he left nothing to chance. With his lighthearted, typically Victorian sense of humour he wrote in his autobiography: 'I remember once, if anyone chanced to come unexpectedly into the Archbishop of Canterbury's study (who was Lord High Almoner at the time), they would have been astonished to find the Archbishop, the Sub Almoner and me apparently engaged in some strange intricate dance, rather like the Mock Turtle and the Walrus in *Alice*. We were working out exactly how the purses on the alms dishes could be passed from hand to hand to the King without awkwardness — it is a small ceremonial formula carried out with style and dignity to this very day.'

The Queen has 'kept her Maundy' 29 times since her accession. On the four occasions when she was unable to attend, the distribution was made once, in 1954, by the Lord High Almoner, the Right Rev. Gresford Jones, twice by the Queen Mother, in 1960 and 1970, and once by the Princess Royal, in 1963. All these services were at Westminster Abbey. Watching the two Royal ladies was to appreciate how much

Mr. William Irons holding up his Royal Maundy money, 1953 (*Hulton Picture Library*)

temperament, as well as faith and Christian ethics, is involved in being the central figure of this service. The Princess carried it out gravely, with great sincerity and, true to her personality, with much reserve.

The second time the Queen Mother took part, her charm and obvious interest in the old people caused something of a sensation amongst those of us concerned with the music and the timing of the broadcast. At least two of the recipients chosen were known personally to Queen Elizabeth: a retired district nurse, living near Buckingham Palace, who had once attended the Royal children when they had measles, and a retired naval man who had served on the same ship as the Duke of York at the Battle of Jutland. Of course the Queen Mother spoke to both of them – and by doing so, she decided to have a word (much more than a word!) with everyone as she walked along the long lines of 88 men and women recipients.

The joint choirs ran out of anthems, which are sung during the ceremony. My old friend and colleague, the producer John Haslam, who for many years has been with me on major outside broadcasts, pleaded with the organist not to run out of Organ Voluntary, in case I ran out of words. He telephoned the BBC to inform of a possible overrun.

The old people were enchanted with their Queen Mum and at the second distribution several decided to take the initiative to carry on the conversations. I distinctly heard one old man continue: 'Now the rheumatism has gone to the other side'. Queen Elizabeth continued to nod her head and smile and be sympathetic and kind.

Minor mishaps during the distributions are few and far between. I can remember only two of them. Once the long purse strings of two red and white purses became inextricably mixed. Like lightning Mr Peter Wright, now Secretary of the Royal Almonry who indicates each recipient to the Queen, produced a pair of scissors and, to the barely concealed amusement of the Queen, rapidly cut the purses free. The other slight hitch happened when, out of town, one of the old gentlemen moved his chair out of the line of recipients and was nearly passed by. Again Peter Wright spotted it almost instantly and the Queen, smiling broadly, waited as the old man shuffled forward to receive his gifts.

One of the most notable of recent Maundy services in the Abbey was in 1977, the year of the Silver Jubilee. For everyone who had been present in 1952 there was a strong sense of occasion, and everything went perfectly. The service was an echo of that first year with most of the same hymns, psalms and anthems. The Queen was as calm and gentle as always, and as watchful of the old people as if this was still a first occasion for her.

'The devouring hand of time' was hardly noticeable. Two extra anthems were sung as the two distributions took longer: the number of recipients was now 51 old men and 51 old ladies.

I went to a funeral in the Abbey two days before Christmas in 1979. Dear Lawrence Tanner, the Maundy Secretary, had died at the age of 90 after a lifetime spent giving his devotion, service and scholarship to Westminster School and the Abbey. His father had been housemaster at Westminster and the family lived in 2 Little Dean's Yard, forming part of the community that revolves around school and church. Lawrence was christened in the Abbey's magnificent Henry VII Chapel. Later, at the age of four, he astonished his nurse by saying that he meant to be buried there too.

This indeed was what was happening. As it was Christmas, more crowds than ever were coming to services and carol concerts, as well as to see a near life-size Christmas crib in the Nave. It was planned for the funeral to be held after the Abbey was closed to the public, in the evening. Somehow I felt fearful of a funeral at night – for me there is a macabre quality in descriptions of seventeenth-century Royal funerals held at midnight.

From the moment I entered the chapel I knew I was wrong. The atmosphere was quite unlike the stark reality of daylight, for even sunshine can be cruel at such rites. This was the most bearable funeral I have ever attended.

The slender coffin draped with a cream-coloured pall, exquisitely embroidered with the Abbey's arms, stood in front of Torrigiano's great tomb of Henry VII and his Queen. The subdued lighting of the chapel created strong shadows in the fan tracery of the ceiling, yet it still answered to Washington Irving's famous and often quoted eulogy: 'The stone seems, by the cunning of the chisel, to have been robbed of its weight and density – suspended aloft as if by magic and the fretted roof achieved with the wonderful minuteness and airy security of a cobweb.'

Through one of the plain glass windows, the night sky blended with the scene. Probably it was the sense of fulfilment in Lawrence's life that was so affecting and reassuring. He did what he wanted in life, and was loved and appreciated for it. He was a perfectionist in all things. As was said wisely by one of the present masters of the school: 'He loved Westminster, and his love of the place enabled him to love life with intensity.'

The service was a cheerful one and included the processional hymn so often heard at the Royal Maundy Service to which, as Secretary, Lawrence had contributed so much. The funeral was private and the congregation small. I realised that the evening darkness softened the finality: it was as if we were just saying a gentle goodnight to Lawrence Tanner.

CHAPTER EIGHTEEN

From Where I'm Standing . . .

The live outside broadcast commentary on sound radio or television is acknowledged to be one of the most exciting kinds of broadcasting in the business. Ad-libbing in the present tense, watching the scene rather than reading from a script, needs an immense amount of preparation beforehand: memorising names, studying the procedure of a ceremony, finding associated material that could be of interest if there is a delay. When abroad it is often essential to study photographs of famous people you may never have seen and to learn the correct pronunciation of foreign names (obtainable from the BBC's pronunciation unit). I have found sometimes that with a difficult language 'short-cut study' can be double-edged. Before the Queen paid her State visit to Portugal in November 1957, I spent lunchtime each day for a fortnight with a man in the Portuguese Tourist Office phonetically learning to pronounce the names and titles of people, buildings to be visited, even street names that might come into a broadcast. I am fairly good at accents and the result of this word by word tuition was so useful that it was assumed that I could speak the language. Any question I asked in English brought forth a flood of Portuguese that left me no wiser.

On one occasion it also left me very wet. While waiting to describe a State drive by the Queen and the President of Portugal on their way to a banquet, I was directed by an official (in Portuguese) to sit in the basin of a well-known fountain. I thought he was reassuring me that the water was definitely turned off. It was a wonderful view, above the enormous crowd. As the Royal and Presidential car came into sight, I suddenly felt fine sprays of water on my head. I was eventually drenched.

Obviously, with the title of 'outside broadcaster', we work far away from studios and nearly always out of doors, without the luxury of a microphone that can flatter the human voice. Furthermore, we are all at the mercy of events – anything can happen, and very often does.

On Commonwealth tours it is likely to be the weather that unexpectedly causes problems. On the Queen's first visit to Sri Lanka (then Ceylon), the Royal party attended an evening reception for over 800 guests in the garden of Queen's House. It lasted exactly twenty minutes. A few flashes of lightning, a deep roll of thunder, the Queen and the Duke rushed for shelter in an ivy-clad summerhouse. I watched the heavy rain filling hundreds of champagne glasses at once on a long buffet table. There was no provision for the whole party to move indoors: Queen's House is not large. No announcement of any kind was made, but the staff rushed round with umbrellas; the guests' chauffeurs (as if well used to it) ran to the car parks and in a matter of minutes there was a long single file procession of cars to take their owners home. The Queen and the Duke were provided with two brilliantly coloured golf umbrellas and walked across a sopping lawn to the house.

I believe I have experienced almost all the extremes of weather now. Certainly I can never forget a fierce, cold wind at the air-force base in Uplands, Canada, where the Queen's plane was being diverted owing to bad weather. Scaffolding had been erected for the cameramen, up the side of a hangar. They were already installed and I realised the only free space left was three narrow planks above the hangar roof which were devoid of shelter. A young man from the Canadian Broadcasting Corporation kindly lent me a parka suit which made me look as if I'd come from the North Pole. I was very thankful for it, especially as he had thoughtfully put a small flask of brandy in a pocket.

In contrast, I look back with pleasure at the ceremonial opening of the great hydro-electric scheme at Kariba, Central Africa, in May 1960. The ceremony was being performed by the Queen Mother during her third visit to the then Federation (now Zimbabwe, Zambia and Malawi). Certainly it must have been the most important project, before Independence was achieved, in raising the standards of living and of work for both Africans and Europeans through the supply of electricity for industry. The major components included an underground power station, a huge transmission system and a mighty dam across the Zambesi River. This time the broadcasters' problem was a mercilous hot sun.

Andrew Gardner (now working for Thames Television in London) shared the broadcast with me, and we were both desperately in need of protection. We had been allotted a dais built alongside a huge covered stand for at least 700 guests, with a central platform from where the Queen Mother would make her speech. The temperature was in the mid-nineties, but we had no canopy to give shade. Preparations for a Royal visit are always extensive (especially in the wilds of Kariba!) but often the arrangements for broadcasters are left to the last and probably unfinished. The universal hazard is wet paint. The panorama before us was a breathtakingly beautiful lake created by the flooded waters of the Zambesi, extending over 2000 miles across the bush. The surface of the lake flickered and shimmered with the multicoloured wings of millions of insects and, though the lake was deep, the foliage of tall trees was to be seen in places greenly sprouting up through the water. During the speech by the Chairman of the Power Board, I was beginning to wonder how long I could stand the heat of the sun ('stand' was the operative word, as our two chairs were covered with wet paint). Then there was a slight commotion in the Royal Box. Andrew said in a low voice: 'Hold on . . . Help is on the way.' A slim beige parasol was being passed hand to hand from the Royal Box in our direction. We gratefully bowed and smiled our thanks and took it in turn to hold the parasol over each other's head during the broadcast.

When the moment for the opening ceremony came I remember thinking how miraculous it was that everything involved in making this immense electrical and civil engineering feat work could be compressed into a single sentence, printed beneath a switch in front of the Queen Mother's chair: TO START THE MECHANISM TURN HANDLE CLOCKWISE.

At the end of the broadcast I found a young man beside me waiting for the return of the parasol. I did not like to probe too deeply exactly where it came from, but wondered if it did belong to the Queen Mother. 'Well,' he said, 'yes indeed, the whole *idea* was hers.'

* * *

In Britain we are inclined to think that our kind of ceremonial is the best in the world. I am often guilty of such prejudice myself, at least, I am certain that no country carries out a ceremonial function better and with greater style and discipline than we do. I have seen and admired many full dress occasions all over the world, but many uniforms do remind me of Peter Ustinov playing a much epauletted and bemedalled colonel. I fear this may be irrational insularity for, come to think of it, the splendid black bearskin cap of the British Guardsmen's Review Order, which I greatly admire, is a bizarre kind of headgear if looked at objectively. To put it in reverse: do foreign tourists watching Trooping the Colour find the Guardsmen's bearskin strange and even hilarious? I have always been too busy to ask anyone on the spot. Within the regiments it is revered and respected. There are several versions of its historic origin in the British Army. The most usual explanation stems from the romantic idea that, having routed the Grenadiers of Napoleon's Imperial Guard, Wellington's First Guards were given their present name of Grenadier Guards and allowed to adopt the French head-dress, presumably as a kind of battle honour. To this day, it is worn by all Foot guards on ceremonial occasions.

The bearskin has an almost perpetual news value. People write to the newspapers when reporters call it a busby. The late Duke of Windsor discovered that it gave him a certain anonymity and used to say he liked wearing it as people couldn't see him so well. From time to time, to be provocative, journalists like asking questions about the manufacture of the bearskin cap: Surely they are now made of nylon? If not, why not? And how many bears are needed for one cap? I once had to put this question to Whitehall myself and received this patient and informative reply:

Headquarters London District,
Horse Guards,
Whitehall SW1A 2AX.   March 3rd, 1977
Dear Miss Russell,

Reference: Bearskin caps

Although I gave you a rough estimate on the telephone, as being one bear, one cap, people's interest always seems to lead them to wanting further information, so I enclose the following details which I hope will be of interest and of use to you.

One Guardsman, Other Rank is one bear one cap. It is built on a cane frame and the height is 9″ from brow to the top of the cane.

Officer's bearskin caps average three pieces of selected pelts. These could be from as many as three bears. Each of the three pieces must match and be thick and silky. The principle is as in a fur coat. The fur must be long enough to conceal the join. The cane frame for the Officer's cap is heavier and thicker and the height from brow to top is 13″.

The bears are Canadian, never Russian. The skin is taken from the back of the bear. Evidently, because bears sit down, the actual bottom of the back skin gets worn and that is why you might need to use as many as three pelts for one cap.

I hope this information will be of use to you.

Working on State occasions gives me the great good fortune of being surrounded, drenched even, with music of the highest quality of performance, both at rehearsals and 'on the day'. It happens at the many gala performances held for the Queen in the opera houses of Europe and elsewhere, as well as in great ceremonies of Church and State at home.

One particular aspect of music can be of special importance, especially to commentators. It is the relatively modern custom for a fanfare for trumpets to be composed by some eminent composer in honour of the principal Royal personage taking part in a formal ritual. Many of these works have become famous and can often be heard, such as the Fanfare for the Coronation of King George VI by Ernest Bullock and the one by Bax for Princess Elizabeth's wedding. The most glorious fanfare I ever heard, and I believe it to be the most stirring composition of its kind in this century, is the Antiphonal Fanfare by the late Sir Arthur Bliss, played almost at the end of the ceremony of the Investiture of the Prince of Wales at Caernarvon on 1 July, 1969. This was to hear a Master of the Queen's Music doing his job very well.

The word 'fanfare' derives from the Spanish *fanfarrio* ('a noisy arrogance') but today it has little to do with the military belligerence it once expressed. There are many anecdotes of its uses in war. In the reign of Elizabeth I an army commander, Sir Roger Williams, on a campaign in the Low Countries, deliberately took his trumpeters right up to the enemy's lines and by 'impudent trumpet fanfares' taunted the French to leave their strong position and come out to fight.

Today an opening flourish of trumpets sets a seal of stylishness on the event and is a robust military compliment to the person concerned. For a broadcaster, a fanfare can steady the nerves, give a feeling of 'now we are under way' and, what is even more useful and practical, provide a short 'breather' of between 30 and 45 seconds when it is sometimes possible to observe what the Queen and other members of the Royal Family are wearing — and also to decide how best to describe the clothes. Dressmakers' details are not always released until after the wearers have left their home. This is useful for fashion journalists, but the information does not always filter through to someone already on the air. Besides, being so detailed they rarely make good broadcasting. What is needed is an attractive *impression* of style and colour and accessories, for it is unlikely that there will be time to go into such minute accounts as 'the traditional princess line is emphasised with graduated pin tucks, the Elizabethan sleeves (over finely pleated white silk chiffon under-sleeves) are delicately edged with pearls and mirror jewels . . .'

On the subject of Royal wardrobes, the attitudes of the Buckingham Palace press office, the dressmakers and the public have changed considerably since my first Royal ceremony at the wedding of Princess Elizabeth. Royal clothes have been rationalised. At least they are no longer a state secret! Sometimes the Palace press office will even permit designs and small patterns of fabric to be distributed (as on the night before Princess Anne's wedding) to those journalists who specialise in fashion.

Of course, everyone must enjoy seeing the Queen on television and is fascinated to hear of the colour of her coat and hat on sound radio. But even the public now accepts that fashion plays a minor role in a solemn ceremony. It was not always so. When I arrived at York Minster in 1961 for the wedding of the Duke of Kent (this was to be a broadcast lasting an hour and a half in which I was the sole commentator for sound), a clergyman greeted me condescendingly with: 'Ah, Miss Russell, I suppose you've come to describe the *hats.*'

I am surprised that there aren't more women commentators. I was the first woman reporter in the BBC Home-newsroom in 1945 and I am glad to say this opened up the job for a great many of us. Commentating seems to be different. I was not the first woman commentator but I think I can claim to be the first one to be regularly employed on most Royal tours, State visits to friendly foreign powers and State occasions at home over a period of nearly 30 years.

The reason cannot be male chauvinist prejudice these days nor that women have little aptitude for this kind of work. The talent among women broadcasters today is very high. I sometimes fear that many women don't think they are going to like it, once they have had an audition, or a try-out to be a commentator. Admittedly it can be a troublesome job, with unpredictably long and unsocial hours. There is a lot of hanging about waiting for things to happen. I find men rather like this: they are more 'matey' than women.

Someone aiming to be more than a token woman, making a brief appearance in a programme almost entirely handled by men, must become specialised in some subject of interest to *them*: not just fashion, but state ceremony, politics, art, architecture or sociology – the list can be much longer than this. I sometimes wonder if women with these good qualifications are the type willing to put up up with the need to climb ladders that bend in the middle and scaffolding leading to some dusty narrow ledge 70 feet up with no rail in front. The extremes of weather, especially in the tropics, can play havoc with the female voice. I dislike the ladders but am grateful for an unexceptional all-weather voice that, touch wood, seldom gives trouble.

All commentaries are something of a challenge: this is part of the fascination. Some unexpected surprise (probably unimportant in itself) sets one free from the careful notes written by midnight oil. I relax, think on my feet, and the broadcast generally becomes airborne. It depends on imagination.

Once a large dismounted party of Lifeguards of the Household Cavalry in full dress were lined up on the staircase which leads to the Royal Box at Covent Garden. This was similar to the procedure at the House of Lords for the opening of Parliament. This time they were waiting for the arrival of the Queen and the Duke of Edinburgh and their guests, General de Gaulle and Madame de Gaulle, on a State visit in April 1960. As the Royal and Presidential party walked up the stairs I noticed that the Guardsmen coming to attention were reflected over and over again in the huge gold-framed mirrors on the staircase walls and the first landing. Never have I seen a Guard of Honour of such magnitude; with the festoons of garlands and delicate flower arrangements which were part of specially designed decorations by the late Cecil Beaton, the effect was magical. I found myself calling them 'the Looking Glass Guardsmen' and dared to predict that the General might find himself acknowledging the salute of an officer's reflection. I didn't think he did, but the listeners liked it, judging from telephone calls afterwards.

The most serious challenges come when one is least prepared. After the broadcast from Westminster Abbey at Princess Margaret's wedding, I was asked to go down in the afternoon to the Port of London to complete the picture by seeing the bride and bridegroom sail off on the Royal Yacht *Britannia* to the West Indies on their honeymoon. It was tempting to accept, although I was leaving next day to cover Queen Elizabeth the Queen Mother's visit to Rhodesia. I needed time to pack, but above all there was no time to do any 'homework' on the departure at Tower Pier.

I was persuaded that it was a simple matter of eight to ten minutes only on the air, breaking into a light music programme and also to be recorded for Canada. After the Abbey service I lunched with Byng Whittaker, a well-known Canadian broadcaster, who asked to come with me 'just for the fun of it'. The commentary position was on Tower Pier itself, facing the bascules of Tower Bridge, soon to be raised majestically for the Royal Yacht. Huge crowds lined the streets as far as one could see. Trinity Square was crammed with people, as was the slope down to Tower Wharf. There was a small open space reserved for the Princess and the future Lord Snowdon to board the Royal Barge. *Britannia* dressed overall lay at anchor in the Pool.

Little did I think it would be 47 minutes of broadcasting before we would see the open-topped Rolls Royce come to a standstill at the landing stage. Suddenly a message from Broadcasting House came through the headphones : 'Canadian radio has got Royal Wedding fever – would like you to start now, they'll take it live. Light programme will follow. Shall we say in fifteen seconds from . . . NOW .'

It was easy at the beginning, the crowds, the Royal Yacht, the Royal Barge, the blue skies and the seagulls. An (illegal) helicopter full of tourists circled overhead and later on the noise it made gave me an excuse to stop talking for a few seconds each time it passed over. It was fortunate to be situated in such an historic part of London. I took the Tower of London down stone by stone and built it up again – racking my brains as I did so to recall some of its horrific history. Was it Anne Boleyn or Katharine Howard who asked to see the block the day before her execution? I found myself going back to seagulls many times. Byng Whittaker gave me wonderful support, pointing to anything of the remotest interest. Then we spotted the Port of London Authority yacht with the Chairman, Lord Simon, and his guests on board. The engineers paid out yards of cable and I walked to the end of the pier to look down on the upper deck of the *St Katherine*. This was quite amusing. I recognised some of the guests who were at the Abbey in the morning. It was still very much a top hat and tails affair. Afternoon tea was being served and silver caterers' plate glinted in the sun. I described plates of very thin slices of bread and butter being handed round as well as criss-cross slices of fruit cake which nobody touched. Byng then steered me back to be ready for the belated Royal arrival. The ebbing tide was then causing much anxiety to *Britannia's* captain – but as we know, when they did arrive all was well, Princess Margaret in a charming sunshine-yellow coat and dress by Victor Steibel, and the bridegroom in a light grey suit. They were quickly ferried on board and *Britannia* slipped anchor just in time to catch the tide.

Almost simultaneously, I saw a crew member of the *St Katherine* coming up the pier steps carrying a tray. On it was a silver teapot, some very thin bread and butter, and fruit cake. 'With Lord Simon's compliments,' he said, and saluted. I like to claim that this must be the first time a listener has served tea to a broadcaster while on the air.

Three evenings later in Salisbury, Rhodesia, at a Government House reception, I was summoned to 'please come and talk to Her Majesty about the wedding'. I felt the ladies in waiting had run dry on the subject by then.

Queen Elizabeth was standing in an alcove in the drawing room. Her Majesty asked me about the Abbey broadcast and hoped I could see at least some details from that great height. (This was the occasion when I was situated in a converted builder's cradle level with the Triforium some 70 feet up.) She hoped Princess Margaret's bridesmaids kept in line properly all the time? This could not be seen from the Sacrarium. We agreed that the wedding dress was superb, especially the way the train fell gracefully in folds as they walked up the steps towards the altar.

I knew already, of course, that the delay at Tower Pier was caused by immense crowds stopping the Royal car several times in the narrow streets of the City. Queen Elizabeth volunteered to me that she had very much wished to go herself to see them off, but was advised strongly against it because of the excessive traffic. She had turned on the television picture only and listened to me on sound radio. This was most gratifying, but I prayed that Dimbleby would never hear of it.

I know well that etiquette forbids a literal account of a conversation with Royalty, but this was a conversation with a loving mother. 'Did anything else happen at Tower Pier?' Luckily, I remembered that as the bride and groom stepped from the car, they paused on the quayside to shake off the quantities of rose petals showered on them by friends and relatives as they left the Palace. As they were being ferried quickly to the Royal Yacht, there was a sudden rush by some of the crowd to retrieve the petals as souvenirs. Queen Elizabeth smiled and went on : 'I think Londoners love my daughter . . . Of course, I am so sorry for the poor policemen. The crowds pressed them hard against the car — the paintwork is covered with round scratches made by their brass buttons. My car is having to be serviced!'

This chapter aims to give an impression of working in a specialised type of communication. From the questions I am asked, it seems that few people have much idea what it is like. 'How lucky to have a front row seat at all these wonderful occasions.' It's not always a front seat. 'Does the Queen ever speak to you?' Yes. 'What do you wear?' Very often a boiler suit would do, but you have to get to the commentary point and the approach is generally by a main entrance, so I reckon I try to look like an imitation lady in waiting, quietly but neatly dressed.

A well-known woman journalist once asked if she could sit in my commentary box to watch a live broadcast going out to the world. We were in Ottawa at the time and I was to describe the arrival of the Queen and the Duke of Edinburgh at the Peace Tower entrance of Parliament House. This was the first occasion in Canada that a Parliamentary session was televised. There is a subtle difference between appearing before an audience, which I enjoy, and being carefully watched by someone with a notebook: the intense concentration needed for commentating can easily be diverted. However, she was quiet and tactful and I almost forgot her presence — but the impression I must have created was astonishing to me. In her article I was described as 'a lonely, self-absorbed figure talking to herself'.

CHAPTER NINETEEN

On the Fringe of the Arts

I've been on the phoney
to Annigoni
But now that I've seen
His things of the Queen
I'm not keen . . .

Much as I enjoy great musical performances on State occasions, I admit that in my spare time I am more likely to wander into an art gallery or read a book about art and artists or even start a painting myself than to buy a ticket for a concert. The visual arts come first with me and I have had marvellous opportunities of visiting art galleries all over the world.

In London there are so many options, with special exhibitions supplementing the permanent collections of the major galleries, that I can hardly keep pace with them, to say nothing of the many small commercial galleries centred in and around Bond Street in the West End.

One of the most rewarding for me of these is the Redfern Gallery, Cork Street, that now has the distinction of being the oldest of its kind specialising in the work of contemporary artists. It was acquired in 1923 by a remarkable young New Zealander named Rex Nan Kivell. He concentrated almost entirely on experimental work, encouraging young and unknown artists by showing their work alternately with and sometimes alongside that of the very famous. His flair and judgement were acute. For a student exhibition in the twenties, he had the perception to include the work of two very youthful sculptors – their unknown names were Barbara Hepworth and Henry Moore.

I first went to the Redfern in 1942 as it was one of the few commercial West End galleries that managed to keep open in the last war. At a time when most people were sending precious possessions out of London for safety, Rex was defiantly showing a number of original French masters. I remember seeing a Vuillard, a Matisse and a Soutine, the last of which is now in the Tate Gallery. It was rare to see original works of such calibre at that time.

It was several years before I discovered that Rex had an even greater interest that was for ever kept separate from his expertise on modern art. As a New Zealander he was accumulating a vast collection of eighteenth- and nineteenth-century pictures and *objets d'art*, trifles and curiosities – some of great value, all associated with the early history of Australia, New Zealand and the Pacific islands. His range was prodigious. It is claimed he found the first drawing by a white man of a kangaroo. He spotted and acquired Thomas Lawrence's painting of Lord Hobart, lost for years in Tasmania. He traced the priceless navigating instruments used by Captain Cook. For years there had been rumours of the whereabouts of these instruments. Rex tracked them down to a private house in Hampshire. He had the charm, diplomacy and patience of the true collector.

A bishop's widow in Edinburgh refused to part with a portrait of her New Zealand grandfather (also a bishop) because a mark would be left behind on the wall if Rex bought the work. Of course, he gallantly offered to redecorate the room ... and eventually returned in triumph to London with the bishop under his arm.

Before I went on the Queen's Coronation tour of Australia and New Zealand, Rex advised me to visit as many small local museums as I could. In this way I saw many fascinating drawings and watercolours done by early settlers and missionaries who have left charming amateur first impressions of the new world into which they had ventured. One felt this is what it was really like. In particular, I remember a collection of faded photographs in the museum at Dunedin. They were pictures of some of the first married couples from Scotland to emigrate to New Zealand – dour and serious, husband and wife already resembling each other in their expressions of determination to overcome the hardships, loneliness and dangers of those early days. Rex's collection was a mammoth one to be assembled in the lifetime of one man. Eventually he made it possible for the National Library of Australia at Canberra to acquire it. It then contained over 15,000 exhibits and he kept augmenting it almost to the end of his life. In so doing he gave to the Antipodes an historic and cultural identity that was unrecognised before.

Rex died in 1977, less than a year after he had been knighted by HM the Queen. His loyal staff at the Redfern who understood his ways have carried on his policies of exhibiting modern masters as well as the unknowns. He was a dear friend and unexpectedly we were brought closer together when by chance we met at Buckingham Palace when the Queen knighted him at an Investiture. It was unforgettable to see him bravely walk towards the Queen without his sticks – he was crippled for most of his life. It was a great day for both of us, for I was honoured with an MVO of the Royal Victorian Order. It was tragic that time was so short for Rex. Less than a year later I gave a memorial address for him at St Paul's Cathedral.

It is still one of the pleasures of the week to wander in and see the Redfern's current exhibition. Sometimes the artists' names are new to me, sometimes I do not understand what they are getting at, but the work is imaginative, startling and full of vitality – either abstract or figurative in an idiosyncratic way. There is a communication of ideas in this searching to find new meanings to life. Of course, there are also one-man shows by countless leading artists of the day, including Ben Nicholson, Victor Passmore, Bryan Kneale and Patrick Procktor.

In 1962 I was edging my way into BBC television programmes on art. I managed a few interviews with artists at the Redfern and persuaded the editor of 'Town and Around' to film the impressive collection of Graham Sutherland's working drawings for the Coventry Tapestry. Happily, this led to a series of programmes including the opening of the Queen's Gallery and a sequence of programmes on the first ten exhibitions held there. I believe this gallery to be one of the most important additions to the art world of London in the twentieth century. In 1961 the Queen and the Duke decided to build a small art gallery on the site of the old conservatory that was converted into a private chapel for Queen Victoria in 1843 but destroyed 97 years later by German bombs. Only the four walls were left standing. It was a bold innovation to decide that the building should again include a private chapel as well as an art gallery open to the public showing, in rotation, some of the great treasures belonging to the Queen.

The gallery is relatively small and intimate, cleverly designed so that the visitor can view the exhibits from a first-floor balcony, as well as at ground level. The private chapel is screened off from the public (I have never been allowed to see it.) When a large number of the family attend a Sunday service, the partition wall screen can be rolled back and chapel and gallery are incorporated into one interior.

The historic Royal collection has never been so easily available to the public nor so splendidly displayed. By comparison I remember a mammoth, overwhelming and exhausting exhibition of over 500 of the King's pictures (the year was 1946) held at the Royal Academy, Burlington House. This was recognised as a tremendous event and a rare privilege and a first-time opportunity for all art lovers. It was indeed – but the creation of the Queen's Gallery goes more than one better than that. In the regular series of exhibitions, each of about a year's duration, the focus is narrowed down to the details of a single great master or period. As an introduction, the first exhibition was a selection made from all parts of the collection – pictures, furniture, china, silver, miniatures, jewellery and drawings – illustrating within a narrow compass the great riches of the Queen's collection. Over 200,000 people came to see it.

I was to interview the Surveyor of the Queen's Pictures. He was a Professor of the History of Art who, having served in France and later at the War Office in the Second World War, then became Surveyor of the Pictures of King George VI. I had read his brilliant introduction in the catalogue of the huge Royal Academy show in 1946 and felt nervous at confronting such a distinguished scholar on the important occasion of the opening of the Queen's Gallery. I need not have worried. He did most of the talking.

The interview was conducted from the balcony as we surveyed the expanse of pictures below. He was a fluent speaker, with the eloquence that goes with love for and deep knowledge of a subject. When I asked a question, he replied without hesitation. One felt as if he knew something about every brush-stroke on every canvas. He was never at a loss for a detail and knew an anecdote about, or the provenance of, every picture we looked at. Why, for example, Van Dyck painted King Charles I's head in three positions for the sculptor Bernini to carve a marble bust of the King, which some said was destroyed by the fire at the Palace of Whitehall. But the Surveyor's opinion was that it was stolen – it would be almost impossible to burn a large block of white marble, and it had never been seen since. As we stood before the famous Zoffany of Queen Charlotte and her two children in fancy dress at a dressing table, I couldn't resist trying to put him at a loss by asking whose pretty, tiny face was reflected in the looking glass in the far, far distance of the picture. 'Oh,' he said immediately, 'that's a governess or nurse waiting to take the children away.' He made a very good broadcast.

Recently, when looking back at the catalogue, I was astonished to find that I had spent that morning in Buckingham Palace with the late, notorious Anthony Blunt.

For the rest of the sixties and into the seventies I had the privilege of broadcasting on television annually at successive ravishing displays that included masterpieces of some of the greatest painters of Europe.

The exhibition, 'George IV and the Arts of France', will always be associated for me with a foolish gaffe that I made at a rehearsal. For several minutes I feared it might bar me from the Queen's Gallery for good. I noticed the brass latch on one of the showcases seemed to be ajar. Instinctively I put up my hand to close it, but it did the reverse and swung open setting off a loud burglar alarm. I was transfixed where I stood, for in a matter of minutes I could hear police sirens converging on the Palace. The then Deputy Surveyor of the Queen's Pictures, now Sir Oliver Miller, rushed across to me and, looking serious but not unkind, said in a quiet voice: 'Say absolutely nothing . . . Say *nothing*. I'll say it's me.' In this way I was absolved and will never forget the generous gesture.

Integrated into the showing of great works of art, the Queen's Gallery often reveals intriguing little facets of a Royal lifestyle (through its attractive catalogues) – for example, in the collection of portraits of Royal children shown in 1963, which ranged from the boy King Edward VI (artist unknown) to a work in coloured chalks of our own Prince Andrew at three years old. It demonstrated how valiantly and successfully a great many artists, including Van Dyck, Liotard, Landseer and Winterhalter, triumphantly overcame the notoriously difficult commission of painting a young child.

Not many of the world's children are likely to have to sit for a portrait and it must be accepted that the strain on the sitter probably equals that of the artist, and that this tedious burden is part of the regular duty of being a Royal child. This was recognised by some in Victorian times. Princess Beatrice at the age of four rebelled against a miniaturist, crying: 'I do not like Paint Bodies.' Lady Lyttelton, governess to the Royal children, was endearingly sympathetic to Queen Victoria's eldest daughter, the Princess Royal, when she wrote in 1842, 'Oh dear, I wish there were no portraits being done of the Princess Royal and that all her fattest and biggest and most forbidding looking relatives ... did not always come to see her at once and make her naughty and her governess cross. Poor little body. She is always expected to be good, civil and sensible.' At that time the Princess Royal was only two years old.

The earliest inventories date from the time of Henry VIII, but other Tudors as well as the Plantagenets and Lancastrians owned collections of their own, though their quality and condition are now uncertain. The earliest English King of whom a portrait of any significance survives is Henry V. This oil painting was shown at the attractive Silver Jubilee Exhibition of 1977.

The works of art are selected from the various palaces in which they are permanently kept and include a large number from apartments not usually accessible to the public. As a result the Queen and Duke often have to forgo the pleasure of waking up each morning to enjoy looking at some favourite masterpiece, considered essential for a current exhibition. This can mean an absence of about a year and sometimes the Queen prefers a blank space to an unfamiliar replacement on the wall.

Her Majesty's interest in the preparations for exhibitions and hanging of the pictures is great. There have been several occasions when the word came to me that the Queen had left her study and was coming across the lawn for her own private view and probable discussion with the Surveyor of her pictures and works of art. Filming stops at these times, and we make ourselves scarce.

Over the centuries, the Royal patrons' choice of subject invariably included a portrait, either as a commission or in acceptance of a gift from another Head of State. This is not always so now. The development of portraiture is represented only by the giants of the art in the past: Gainsborough, Lawrence, Rubens, Rembrandt, Van Dyck and others. It saddens me to think of the low standard of Royal portraiture today. One begins to think that the camera has won. To take an example: the exhibition of paintings and photographs at the National Portrait Gallery in honour of the eightieth birthday of Queen Elizabeth was a sad story of what has happened to Royal portraiture in the twentieth century. With a few exceptions, the collection was unworthy of the positive and charming personality of the Royal sitter. Sir Gerald Kelly probably came out best on the whole; his paintings are honest illustrations of the symbols of Royalty: the pearls, the Garter ribbon and Star and the tiara; and the humanity of the subject is retained.

The Queen Mother's hands are painted firmly clasped in front of her – depicted as they really are, sturdy, strong, interesting hands. By contrast, the work of a once fashionable artist of the early twenties gives Her Majesty slim fingers that could do as an advertisement for nail varnish.

To acquire a portrait, the usual procedure is that the Royal Society of Portrait Painters is approached for advice and help. The Society issues a list of its members – painters and others who as members are bound to exhibit at the Society's exhibitions. No one, however internationally famous, is included in the list unless they fulfil the Society's conditions for membership. Many of today's most eminent artists do not belong and inevitably the number of artists of the right quality is greatly reduced. Clearly there will always be a demand in our heavily populated country for the 'please everyone' kind of picture, but with a list of painters limited to the members and exhibitors of a single academic society, it follows that the results are often a long way from the high standards to be expected for Royal commissions.

Perhaps the greatest difficulty in achieving a successful Royal portrait is a psychological one, and this applies to artists of great repute as well as to the middle-rank professional. Young contemporary painters hold that a rapport must be established between artist and sitter. Bryan Organ, who painted an engaging picture of Princess Margaret for the Treasurer and Masters of the Bench of Lincoln's Inn, has described portrait painting as a 'joint venture between artists and sitter'. Another well-known artist, David Hockney, makes sure the rapport is there by accepting commissions only from friends he knows well.

The sense of responsibility for a sensitive artist must be heavy, knowing he is about to face the Sovereign, whose image in this age is already known all over the world. He feels expected to produce a masterpiece. The Queen is acknowledged to be aware of all such problems and is known to show very patient consideration, even with a full programme. If the artist finds he needs more sittings than planned they will always be 'fitted in somehow'. The Queen has sat for approximately 65 portraits, painted between 1952 and 1976. There was no time for sittings at all in the Jubilee Year of 1977, and the number of requests for sittings has been less in the last seven years, as so many works have been completed and proudly shown in regimental messes and the like.

Two portraits commissioned by the Queen Mother, and now in the Portrait Gallery, reveal the delicate subtlety of the 'joint venture' that can sometimes disturb the most talented and experienced. The first was Augustus John's portrait of the Queen Mother full-face, sitting in a gilded chair: not a very happy success. The caption for the work stating that John was 'nervous and overawed' seems incredible remembering how understanding and approachable Queen Elizabeth can be. The second work has a rather mysterious background: under a brilliant study for a portrait by Graham Sutherland the caption states, without comment: 'The project for this picture was not taken further.' It is already a work of art. What happened? Who withdrew? Did Sutherland withdraw? Perhaps for the same feelings as John? The more is the pity, but there it is.

When one recalls the magnificence of the works of art that adorn the Queen's Gallery, it is humiliating to know that art experts 100 years hence will be hard put to find any work of real aesthetic quality in twentieth-century portraits of the present Royal Family. I expect there will continue to be a demand for the kind of work that is generally turned out, but can we not improve on this? Could we not have a small committee of advisers on contemporary art? This could work under the auspices of one of the many important art organisations in this country, and in this way would have the power (and some of the finance) to 'designate' the artist for a Queen's Gallery portrait.

It was very thrilling to discover that the National Portrait Gallery had approached Bryan Organ to paint the first portrait of Prince Charles to hang in the Gallery. The idea first came about in September 1979. Artist and sitter met in November of the same year and agreed to abandon the age-old and traditional formal sittings. Bryan Organ worked out the designs in an outdoor setting and these were shown to the Prince. The finished work was acquired by the Gallery in June 1980. The preparatory work was carried out in probably the nearest to the ideal conditions that contemporary artists have been pleading for. Much of the work was done at Windsor, but Bryan also accompanied Prince Charles on a number of official engagements; he took photographs, made dozens of working drawings in his studio and showed them all to his subject, discussing every problem in some detail, all in an effort to create the vital rapport between them. Professor Lawrence Gowing, Slade Professor of Fine Art and Head of the Slade, heaped praise on the picture at the unveiling ceremony. He wittily described the work as 'peeling the corn off the public image of the Prince'; adding that 'the artist has avoided the Hail-Fellow-Well-Met aspect of the daily contacts'.

When the Royal engagement was announced, it was obvious that Bryan's work was by no means finished. A companion picture was essential. The Prince's portrait was joined by a charming, if lightweight, likeness of his future wife. Bryan achieved it in a matter of weeks, not months. It is a very clever, pretty work and it is inexplicable that it should have been vandalised in its first weeks on show — happily it was restored almost immediately by the Gallery experts, and the outrage almost forgotten.

The Prince's portrait is a most searching study, and in my opinion the best and most interesting Royal portrait of the century. Bryan has said that there was a 'really excellent working relationship', adding: 'But I must have a lot of time and then when I am ready to finalise things, I hope to quietly distil the essence of the human being without ever forgetting that I am painting a portrait of someone whose standing and position are unique.'

CHAPTER TWENTY

Full Circle

Thoughts of his own death
Like the distant roll of thunder
At a picnic.

W. H. Auden, 'City without Walls'

Most of my years spent in radio and television have been on a contract basis, rather than as a member of the established pensionable staff. This is an experience that plays havoc with one's attitude to retirement. The idea does not exist. For a time it feels like a charmed life. Frequently one is invited to the official retirement parties of one's contemporaries, but thankfully it does not happen to you. These affairs are fairly sedate, a quick tea or drinks party and sometimes a luncheon in the Council Chamber of Broadcasting House, according to rank. As a rule, a head of department or a controller graces the proceedings with a speech, to which the retiring member of staff must reply, probably feeling more retiring than at any time in his or her career. Then follows the presentation of an autograph album filled with signatures and good wishes from colleagues and friends – and with it a cheque that I always fancy is modest or handsome according to the energies of the secretary given the job of seeing to it that a money box is widely circulated around the appropriate departments.

The atmosphere of these affairs varies enormously: sometimes it is merely a punctuation in a career, at others there is the finality of a very full stop.

It is changes in programme policies and in management that can gradually affect the life of a contract broadcaster. I am now a freelance operator and therefore am much more at arm's length from the BBC. However, having worked on so many occasions that are now part of history, I seem to have acquired a sort of anniversary value – some may already call it a 'fossil value'. The editors of several BBC television magazine programmes and the Canadian Broadcasting Corporation, as well as the French 'Antenne Deux' television network in Paris, are likely to call me up when the anniversary of some important event occurs. The Paris engagements involve about a day and a half's work but the company generously includes a few extra days, sometimes a week, in a first class hotel, all expenses paid, as part of the contract fee. This bonus has something to do with its financial links with a chain of French hotels.

The programmes are broadcast in French and are mostly about British Royalty. Subjects have included Queen Victoria, Queen Elizabeth II and on more than one occasion the invalid Duchess of Windsor, still surviving in a lonely mansion in the Bois de Boulogne. I very much enjoy these assignments, observing the new techniques and the new kind of professionalism of young producers at home and abroad. The approach to broadcasting is slicker and more cut and dried than it was in those hectic, though tentative, war years. Facing a microphone in those days was still rather an unusual experience for some of us. I think we worried more about our work — for example, spending longer than necessary on a simple editing job.

I am often interviewed these days by someone who wasn't born when the event I am asked to talk about took place. I suspect that they are pretty vague about a career that began in 1942, and I've had some absurd questions. No one has yet asked me if I ever *met* Florence Nightingale, but it could still come.

Throughout my career I have had wonderful assistance from the BBC's back-up services. For me, the most important is the Reference Library, now situated on the ground floor of the old Langham Hotel with a branch library at the TV Centre. I would not have survived in the BBC without its help. Without offence, it can be described as a great rag-bag of books. It is a true broadcasting library, stocked with short, concise information on almost any subject imaginable. At the same time the library has access to most of the great libraries in London so, when a subject is being studied in depth, it will obtain all the volumes you could possibly need. The BBC's reputation for accuracy is due in great part to the BBC librarians, who do so much for the broadcasters. The other day I needed to know the date when the shelling stopped in Dover. I telephoned and had the answer in minutes.

Another 'back-up' service to be marvelled at is the mammoth Catering Department with a London staff of 550 people. They cope with every aspect of providing food and drink at all hours of the day and night. There are separate departments for radio, television, and the External Services at Bush House. It's a 24-hour service, seven days a week, ranging from the modest coffee trolleys wheeled along the office corridors every morning to the *cordon bleu* luncheon served in the Council Chamber for Her Majesty the Queen on the occasion of the fiftieth anniversary of the BBC in 1972.

The Hospitality Chefs look after the needs of the Board of Governors and guests of the Director General, and the BBC restaurants in London (there are no canteens these days) regularly serve 6000 meals a day to staff. That is but a fraction of the undertaking, which is run so efficiently that it is very much taken for granted. It looks after several outside events too. Every year BBC staff have a full-scale catering service at Wimbledon!

However, there was a narrow shave in 1972 when the Queen came to lunch. On that day London taxi drivers were involved in an industrial dispute, protesting with a procession of empty cabs in the West End. The Queen's car was delayed by nearly 25 minutes and the Chef de Cuisine had already started cooking. It was a desperate situation. The Head of Catering went to a studio where he monitored the slow progress of the Royal car, giving calm instructions to the kitchens: 'Take the fillet steak out . . . in . . . out . . . in.' Things were even more critical for the dessert, an orange sorbet frozen rock hard. 'Put the sorbet near the cooker.' Would it ever melt in time? The Queen decided on arrival to shorten her tour of the library so that luncheon could be served on time. In the confusion no one told the kitchen — but even then, professionalism triumphed. The steaks were not too rare and the sorbet was delicious.

I think it was the French philosopher Blaise Pascal who wrote: 'The last thing one discovers when writing a book is what to put *first* . . .' From the start I chose to tell my story chronologically as far as possible, but I find at this stage that it's more difficult to know what to put *last*! There is so much to remember.

The seventies and the eighties have produced a fascinating succession of anniversary celebrations. I played a broadcasting part in all of them with much pleasure for they

The author (*B.B.C. copyright*)

were singularly happy events. They involved ceremonial at its best, matching the importance and character of the events, and the inevitable informal 'extras' provided a perfect foil. I will always treasure the details.

The twenty-fifth anniversary of the wedding of the Queen and Prince Philip took place on 20 November, 1972. It was the nearest thing to a very personal, private affair that could be achieved by such a public figure as the Sovereign. The remarkable fact was that the Queen or the Duke or both were personally acquainted with almost everyone present, and Westminster Abbey was packed with a congregation of just over 2000 specially invited guests. Representatives of all the many organisations with which the Queen and the Duke were associated as Patron, President, Colonel in Chief or Chairman were present. They also remembered individuals with whom they had been in contact over the years, friends such as a retired chaplain from Sandringham and a sergeant-major of the Grenadier Guards.

All the bridesmaids were able to be present, sitting with husbands and children. All were daughters of peers, and their husbands seemed to represent a social history of the previous 25 years – among them a West country farmer, a business tycoon, a publisher, an MP and Junior Minister, and the famous interior decorator David Hicks who married Lady Pamela Mountbatten. Only one bridesmaid had been widowed.

The Queen's invitation to couples married on the same day and year to share the Thanksgiving Service at Westminster Abbey was a wonderful notion. Over 100 accepted and with thoughts revived of their own wedding day were happy and proud to be sharing the service with the Queen. They came from all over the country, from Cumberland, Scunthorpe, Stockport, Northern Ireland, Wales, the Home Counties and London, and they had specially reserved seats in the North and South Transepts. There was so much to recall about the years in between. It was remembered that 1947 was still a year of austerity: there were many restrictions, including clothes rationing, which affected the Royal Wedding too. Everyone knew that King George VI had decreed that there should be no concessions for clothes coupons to augment the Princess's trousseau. This encouraged members of the public generously to send some of their own as a gift, for 'good luck'.

There had even been suggestions, in keeping with Britain's austerity, that the Princess and her bridegroom should have a quiet wedding in St George's Chapel, Windsor! Public opinion was emphatically against such harsh economies. After further discussions, ideas changed and the nation seized the chance of celebrating to forget the drabness of the times.

The Silver Wedding Anniversary was a friendly, warm occasion. Many guests found that they were meeting friends and acquaintances they had not seen for 25 years. A luncheon was held at Guildhall after the Service and the Royal Family drove to the City in a procession of open carriages. Everyone was enchanted with the Queen's speech – especially when it revealed that she was well aware that a phrase used frequently had become an affectionate joke to her subjects. She rose to her feet, smiling, and began: 'I am sure that on this day you will concede that I should begin with the words, "My husband and I . . .".'

Less than five years later, on 7 June, 1977, London celebrated an even greater event of world importance, the Silver Jubilee of the Queen's reign. Mr Hardy Amies had made the usual arrangements for his press office to distribute sketches of one of the new models Her Majesty was expected to wear on this important occasion. To his surprise and *delight*, as the Queen stepped from the carriage he saw the ensemble that he had designed for the Olympic Games in Montreal the year before! Officially, it was described as 'a dress and coat of pure silk soft pink crêpe with a hat to match'.

There is a widespread belief that the Queen never wears anything twice, but nothing could be further from the reality. Her Majesty wears clothes she loves over and over again. I remember being told once by another designer that he'd just been sent a nine-year-old dress with instructions 'to shorten the hem'!

On Jubilee Day the inevitable 'hat to match' was very original and pretty. It had a neat 'dome' crown in the same fabric as the coat and was trimmed (in person by the milliner, Mr Freddie Fox) with tiny bell flowers on stalks or *rouleaux* of silk. There were no fewer than 25 little blossoms that danced every time the Queen turned her head. 'By the way,' said Mr Fox to me, 'that ensemble isn't *soft* pink — it's a strong bright tone. In fact, it's *shocking pink*!' We could all appreciate that and so could the vast crowd waiting outside St Paul's after the service for the Queen and the Duke to make their most extensive walkabout of the reign — all the way from the steps of the Cathedral to Guildhall for the Lord Mayor's luncheon. The fifteen-minute walk took at least half an hour.

For the first time the BBC was permitted to follow the Queen quite closely as she walked, stopping every few yards to have a word with the eager clamouring people on both sides of the street who were clapping, cheering, shouting, struggling to give flowers and sometimes trying to shake hands. Her Majesty did most of the talking: 'Where do you live?' 'How long have you been standing?' 'Are these your children?' The Queen spotted Brian Johnston. 'I didn't know you were here, I'll have to think of some new questions.' The Duke, who is inclined to lag behind on these occasions, caught up. Brian said: 'How are you doing, Sir?' A pause: 'In this noise I can't hear myself think.'

Luncheon at Guildhall must have been welcome after that. The atmosphere continued to be happy and relaxed. All the very important Commonwealth guests at the service were taken on a short coach tour during the walkabout before being set down at Guildhall. It was a contingent of Heads of Government. Nearly every Commonwealth country was represented, with eight Presidents, including the impressive figures of Archibishop Makarios and the Sultan of Brunei. There were also Prime Ministers, Governors General, Commissioners, Lord Lieutenants and trade union chiefs.

The Birthday of the Year in 1980 was on 4 August, when HM the Queen Mother celebrated her eightieth birthday. This was no 'single day' celebration. It was an occasion remembered throughout the whole of the year. It became essential to spread the birthday engagements over the months as so many people wanted to show their affection and admiration. Queen Elizabeth must have spent one of her busiest years, acknowledging gifts (she wrote masses of letters herself) as well as making public appearances.

It could be said that, as soon as summer came, Clarence House was regularly filled with gifts of flowers, chiefly roses, with greetings cards, letters, telegrams and presents mounting day by day, particularly after the Service of Thanksgiving in St Paul's Cathedral on 15 July.

There was originality and generosity in many of the gifts sent by those who knew how welcome they would be. It gave Queen Elizabeth special pleasure to receive 4000 free tickets for the London Zoo in Regent's Park. This handsome gift was carefully distributed to over 25 children's and young people's charities. There were many functions on more conventional lines. Congratulations on an eightieth birthday were read out in the House of Commons and the House of Lords. A dinner was given at 10

Downing Street by the Prime Minister, Mrs Thatcher, with the entire Cabinet present to welcome the birthday guest. A galaxy of stars entertained her at the London Palladium, and another event in which the public could share was a tribute from the River Thames with a display of 10,000 balloons, boat races of all kinds and a super firework display as the finale.

There were other engagements, including semi-private visits to Glamis in Angus and to St Paul's, Waldenbury, where she lived as a girl. Visits to the races were squeezed in and, as the first Honorary Life Member of the Press Club, London, Queen Elizabeth attended a reception given in her honour in early December 1980. She showed no signs of fatigue and was in wonderful spirits, and the visit produced one of the most unusual photographs ever taken of her. With cue in hand Her Majesty is stylishly taking pot luck in a game of snooker.

On 4 August, the staff at Clarence House reckoned that the greetings cards, telegrams and birthday letters had reached just over 30,000 in number. The day was spent relatively quietly, waiting for what must have been one of the greatest Royal Galas ever seen at the Royal Opera House, Covent Garden.

The Royal family, including the Queen and the Duke of Edinburgh, drove to Clarence House to escort Queen Elizabeth to the Royal Box for a special ballet performance. Princess Margaret had organised the programme for her mother. Supper was served at Covent Garden before the curtain rose on *Rhapsody*, the ballet specially composed by Frederick Ashton for the occasion. Although it was described by one critic as a 'glittering fast-moving eye-catching firework display which feasts the eye rather than lingers in the heart', the applause was thunderous.

Afterwards there was a cake, and the Royal party joined the cast, stage management, stage staff, janitors, tea ladies – all hands on stage – for the final, very informal episode of The Birthday. Once the cake was cut and the candles blown out, the Royal party gradually left the scene backstage in twos and threes. They left quietly, disappearing without fuss, leaving the stage (literally!) to the Queen Mother on her own. The Prince of Wales waited to escort his Grandmother home to Clarence House. Watching the Royal Family together reminded me of some wise words of the Archbishop of Canterbury at the service in St Paul's, a fortnight before: 'Royalty puts a human face on the operations of government and provides images with which people of a nation can identify and which they can love.'

On a cold day in February 1981, I was telephoned at an early hour and asked to come to the BBC Newsroom studio to be interviewed by Sir Robin Day. It was taken for granted that I knew why and I felt it was more tactful not to ask. The voice said: 'We're sending a car – it should be with you in half an hour.' By then I was pretty certain it was the announcement of the engagement of the Prince of Wales.

Lady Diana Frances Spencer, daughter of Earl Spencer of Althorp, near Northamptonshire, was being introduced to Britain (via the media) on the lawns of Buckingham Palace. Together the young couple went through the routine photographs, arm in arm, walking, standing, and with a close-up of the diamond and sapphire engagement ring. They smiled, they were serious, sometimes wary, perhaps on the lookout for a difficult question, and both showed remarkable good humour on what must have been a happy if awesome day. The background of her distinguished family must have helped on that nervous morning.

Lady Diana was born in her parents' country house near Sandringham on 1 July, 1961 (receiving a whiff of Court life at a very early age!). Later she was brought up at

The Prince of Wales and Princess Diana, 29th July 1981 (*Hulton Picture Library*)

her father's stately home, Althorp, famous for its collection of great works of art. This was an assurance that the future Princess of Wales would never be overwhelmed by the grandeur of palaces, nor by the exigencies of life lived very much in public, and at Court.

In a way, Lady Diana's background is similar to that of the Queen Mother. Both are the daughters of Earls. Both have Royal blood in their veins, and have Royal associations. The Princess's father was Equerry to King George VI for a number of years. He was invited to stay on as Equerry to the Queen when she came to the throne and I remember him in attendance during the Queen's round-the-world Commonwealth tour. At the end of the tour, it was not long before he married his first wife, the Hon. Frances Roche, now Mrs Shand Kidd, who was to be the Princess of Wales' mother.

The Prince of Wales' wedding was fixed for 29 July and the greatest surprise in all the arrangements was the choice of St Paul's Cathedral for the ceremony. It was certainly felt strongly that a twentieth-century tradition for Royal Weddings to be held at Westminster Abbey was building up nicely. The Dean and Chapter and others whose life work is in the Abbey were much too sophisticated (and Christian) to show their disappointment at the change. I suppose we will never know the real reason for it, except that the Prince was heard to say: 'St Paul's is the Church in which I want to be married.'

The contribution made by the BBC in giving free facilities to Commonwealth and foreign broadcasters was extensive. Very little was made of this tremendous undertaking yet it certainly contributed to the size of audiences all over the world, said to be in the region of 750 million viewers. 108 television services from 72 countries transmitted the BBC's pictures of the wedding, together with the commentary in English. At least 30 countries sent over their own broadcasters, among them one from Japan who broadcast in his own language over a copy of silent film.

The most ambitious programmes were mounted live by the Canadians. They brought their own camera team and commentators to describe the scenes for sound and vision from points along the route. I was honoured to be invited by the Canadian Broadcasting Corporation as a commentator to describe the marriage service in St Paul's Cathedral. Of course, I was thrilled as it was to be my eighth Royal Wedding broadcast.

The setting of St Paul's was superb, with its spacious classical architecture by Wren. It was able to meet the heavy demands of television – even the famous extravagances of that wedding dress managed to live up nobly to the scene. Everything that day seemed geared to the beauty of the bride. She set the standard for it all.

It was interesting for me to work with a team of four experienced Canadian broadcasters, who had done their homework and were taking part in their first Royal ceremonial occasion with style. There was one tiny lapse for one of them. He was watching the scene from the Victoria Memorial outside Buckingham Palace. He expected to see the bride and groom appear on the balcony. There was a slight delay and he was running out of steam. He got very excited when the big Palace window opened: 'The bride's coming out . . . She's coming out . . . She's coming . . . She's still got her dress on . . .'

Time seems to go faster for the Princess of Wales than for the rest of us. All in one year she had her twenty-first birthday, her first wedding anniversary, and a son. With her strong personal magnetism, she has endeared herself to the British people: you only have to look at the faces of children surrounding her on a walkabout, intent and in wonder at the slim, beautiful lady who understands them so well.

The craft of commentating can be absorbing, the nearest thing, sometimes, to trying to write a poem – without a pen! Outside broadcasts are a special challenge and responsibility. They depend on the intense concentration of the speaker, who endeavours to bring the whole event into the mind's eye of the listener. The atmosphere, the sentiment, the beauty, the solemnity must be sympathetically evoked. It is generally worth it.

I hope I never know when I have done my last broadcast. Inevitably remembrance will be poignant when such things are out of reach.

Index

Index of Places on Royal Tours and State Visits